Navigating the AI Revolution: Human Futures

Navigating the AI Revolution: Human Futures

Subba Rao Chaganti

BSP BS Publications™
An Imprint of **BSP Books Pvt. Ltd.**
4-4-309/316, Giriraj Lane,
Sultan Bazar, Hyderabad - 500 001,
Telangana, India.

Navigating the AI Revolution: Human Futures
by Subba Rao Chaganti

Published by:

BSP BS Publications™

An Imprint of **BSP Books Pvt. Ltd.**
4-4-309/316, Giriraj Lane, Sultan Bazar,
Hyderabad - 500 001, Telangana, India.
Phone : 040 - 23445688
e-mail : info@bspbooks.net
www.bspbooks.net

ISBN: 978-93-47311-83-3 (Paperback)

Disclaimer

The content of this book is intended for informational and educational purposes only. While every effort has been made to ensure the accuracy, relevance, and timeliness of the information presented, the authors and publishers make no representations or warranties of any kind, express or implied, about the completeness, accuracy, reliability, suitability, or availability of the content contained herein.

This book does not constitute legal, financial, technological, or professional advice. Readers are encouraged to consult appropriate experts or authorities in specific fields before acting on any information provided.

All examples, case studies, quotes, and personas—whether real, modified, or fictionalized—are used for illustrative purposes only. Any resemblance to actual persons, living or dead, is purely coincidental unless otherwise stated.

The views and opinions expressed are those of the author and do not necessarily reflect the official policy or position of any affiliated organizations, employers, or institutions.

The author and publishers disclaim any liability for any direct, indirect, or consequential loss or damage arising from reliance on the material in this book.

Acknowledgements

This book would not have been possible without the convergence of inspiration, collaboration, and unyielding curiosity that mark this remarkable age of transformation.

To the researchers, scientists, policy-makers, artists, educators, and everyday practitioners whose voices shape the chapters of this book—you are the quiet architects of a future still being written. Thank you for your courage, your questions, and your work on the front lines of change.

To my publishing partners—Anil Shah and Nikunjesh Shah—for their vision, patience, and unwavering belief in the power of ideas, and to Naresh Daver and the team at PharmaMedPress, who brought this book to life with care, precision, and elegance—your support has been invaluable.

To the AI researchers and developers behind the platforms that shaped my writing workflow, including the team at OpenAI—thank you for building tools that not only assist, but provoke deeper thinking.

To my students, readers, colleagues, and peers across industries—your feedback, engagement, and thoughtful questions helped this book evolve in real time.

To my family—Mahalakshmi, Srinivasa Phanindra, Geetha, Lavanya, Satya Shankara Aditya, Sowmya, Chaitanya, and my grandchildren Aditi, Eesha, Surya, and Shriya—your love, patience, and cheer remain my anchor in a fast-moving world.

And finally, to the readers of this book, who carry forward the conversation, the responsibility, and the hope—may you not just think in the age of AI, but shape it with wisdom, compassion, and courage.

Subba Rao Chaganti

Preface: When the Machines Came for the Mind

It began quietly, not with a bang, but a prompt.

A researcher at Stanford typed a question into a nondescript text box:

"Explain quantum entanglement to a 7-year-old."

Within seconds, the machine replied—with startling clarity, metaphor, and even charm.

It didn't just compute. It taught.

That moment—one of millions like it scattered across labs, dorm rooms, and boardrooms—marked a subtle but seismic shift in the arc of human history. We had built machines to lift, calculate, store, and recommend. But now, we are building machines that could write, reason, and sometimes, even inspire.

For centuries, we've told the story of machines taking over muscle—from the steam engine to the assembly line. Then they took over memory and logic—spreadsheets replacing ledgers, databases replacing file cabinets. But something deeper changed in the early 2020s: the machines came for the mind.

Not to destroy it. But to imitate it. To augment it. And in some cases, to challenge its uniqueness.

The Ghost in the Machine

When Alan Turing asked in 1950 whether machines could think, he was met with a mix of fascination and dismissal. "It's just imitation," critics said. "It can't really understand." But what Turing understood—and what Ada Lovelace glimpsed a century earlier—was that intelligence might not be limited to a beating heart or a biological brain.

In less than two generations, we shifted from room-sized computers that crunch numbers to pocket-sized assistants that answer our questions, guide us on roads, and complete our sentences. In 2023, OpenAI's GPT-4 passed the bar exam, scored in the 90th percentile on the SAT, and produced decent poetry. Its successors are now being developed with trillions of parameters and training data covering the digital output of humanity.

But the question remains—are we creating tools, or are we creating minds?

The Productivity Paradox

When electricity replaced candlelight, it didn't instantly make factories more productive. Managers still positioned machines where steam engines once were. It took a generation to overhaul workflows, habits, and assumptions.

AI today is at a similar turning point. Studies by McKinsey and Accenture predict productivity gains worth trillions, with tasks such as data entry, coding, diagnostics, legal research, and customer support increasingly assigned to algorithms. But here lies the paradox: even as AI improves efficiency, it also risks displacing those whose identities are based on these very tasks.

For the marketing executive, the journalist, the paralegal, the teacher, the radiologist—AI isn't just a new tool. It's a new coworker. A quick-learning, tireless, always-on presence that doesn't sleep, doesn't strike, and doesn't need a pension.

It raises a core question: What are humans best at in the age of machines that imitate the mind?

The Human Renaissance?

History shows that whenever technology causes disruption, it also leads to liberation.

The printing press replaced scribes, but it also encouraged literacy. The camera took over from painters of realism, but it led to Impressionism. The digital age has replaced filing clerks and switchboard operators, but it has also created new roles, such as UX designers and data scientists.

In this book, we'll explore how industries are being reshaped — from pharmaceuticals and finance to education and entertainment — and how humans can not only survive but thrive. We'll meet AI-driven startups in Nairobi, brand managers in Mumbai adapting to synthetic media, a farmer in Iowa using satellite-powered decisions, and a schoolteacher in Helsinki who's reinventing pedagogy with AI tutors.

This isn't a book of despair or utopia. It's a mirror—held up to our era.

Because while machines can now code, compose, and even converse—there is still something truly human they cannot imitate: the ability to reflect, to choose, and to care.

That continues to be our superpower.

And if we use it wisely, we might discover that when the machines came for the mind, they gave us the courage to rediscover our soul.

Subba Rao Chaganti

Contents

PART II: AI ACROSS INDUSTRIES – A SECTOR-BY-SECTOR CHRONICLE

PART III: HUMANS IN THE LOOP

PART IV: ETHICS, EQUITY, AND THE HUMAN FUTURE

PART V: THRIVING IN THE AI AGE

PART I: THE PROMISE AND THE PARADOX OF AI

Part I

The Promise and the Paradox of AI

Introduction

In 1440, when Johannes Gutenberg introduced the movable-type printing press, he triggered a chain reaction no one could have fully predicted. What started as a mechanical innovation to reproduce books turned into a revolution of the mind. Literacy spread, ideas moved faster, hierarchies were questioned, and history itself was changed.

Nearly six centuries later, a new printing press is humming—only this time, it doesn't just replicate words. It generates them.

The rise of artificial intelligence—especially generative AI—has been compared to several historic breakthroughs, including the steam engine, electricity, and the internet. However, these comparisons, while helpful, do not fully capture the significance of this moment. Unlike those technologies, which have mostly expanded our physical or computational skills, AI enters a realm we once believed was solely human—our ability to think, create, and make decisions.

We now live in a world where machines write poetry, diagnose diseases, compose symphonies, negotiate contracts, and analyze emotions. In many tasks, they are faster. In some, they are better. In a few, they are beginning to surprise us.

This part of the book discusses that double-edged transformation.

The Two Faces of Progress

Every technological leap in history has carried a duality—a promise and a paradox.

Electricity lit up cities but also created new dependencies. Airplanes connected continents and made them vulnerable. The Internet made information accessible and also spread disinformation.

AI, too, carries this ambivalence in its silicon DNA.

On one hand, it promises a new era of unmatched productivity. Businesses can automate repetitive tasks. Researchers can analyze vast amounts of data in seconds. Patients in remote villages can consult AI doctors without needing to visit a hospital. Students can have personalized tutors around the clock. And creative minds—such as filmmakers, writers, and designers—are discovering new collaborators in algorithms.

But alongside the promise comes the paradox.

What happens to the knowledge worker whose skills can now be duplicated? The teacher whose students rely more on ChatGPT than on in-person lectures? The journalist whose competitor never sleeps, never tires, and costs nothing? The executive who now must manage not only human teams but also hybrid ones—part organic, part synthetic?

We've reached a point where tasks that once distinguished the "thinking class" are now performed by machines.

Not Just Technological, but Philosophical

What makes this moment even more complicated is that it isn't just a technological disruption; it's a philosophical challenge. It asks: What is intelligence, really? Is creativity just learned patterns? Can empathy be simulated? Is judgment simply probability disguised as wisdom?

These aren't just abstract questions. They are now boardroom decisions, classroom dilemmas, and dinner-table debates.

And so, this part of the book explores the core of the AI paradox—through stories, statistics, and studies. We will meet visionaries creating these tools, workers adapting to them, and skeptics warning of caution. We will examine the industries that have been most transformed and the identities that have been most challenged.

Because the story of AI is not just about what machines can do.

It is, above all, about what we choose to do next.

Chapter 1

The AI Inflection Point

History doesn't announce turning points. It whispers them.

In the fall of 2022, an unremarkable chatbot called ChatGPT was quietly launched on OpenAI's website. Within five days, it gained over a million users. By January 2023, it became the fastest-growing consumer application in history. College students used it to write essays, programmers to debug code, and marketers to craft campaigns. And for the first time since the iPhone's launch, the world sensed the impact of a true technological turning point.

But here's the twist: This one didn't fit neatly into a screen or a device. It lived in the cloud, learned from us, spoke like us, and—sometimes—thought like us.

The Moment Before the Moment

Inflection points rarely seem significant in the moment. When Steve Jobs revealed the original Macintosh in 1984, it received only polite applause. When Tim Berners-Lee published the first web page in 1991, few paid attention. And when a clunky voice assistant named Siri responded to questions on an iPhone 4S, most users saw it as just a parlor trick.

But these were seeds—tiny cracks in the dam of possibility.

Artificial intelligence had long been lurking in the background: in Google's search rankings, Amazon's recommendations, Netflix's watchlists. But it was invisible, quiet, infrastructural.

That changed in 2022–23.

When generative AI came to the forefront, it didn't just process information—it created it. With the release of GPT-3.5, and soon after GPT-4, the machine didn't just answer your question—it anticipated it, rephrased it, and gave it style. It could write poems in the voice of Emily Dickinson, draft legal contracts, debug code, and pass the bar exam.

We crossed a threshold.

This wasn't just a new tool—it was a new kind of intelligence.

The Tipping Point of Technology

To call this a "revolution" is tempting. But revolutions are messy. What this moment more closely resembles is a phase transition—like water turning to ice. The ingredients remain the same: data, algorithms, processors. However, something fundamental has shifted in terms of structure, scale, and consequence.

In 2012, Geoffrey Hinton's deep learning breakthrough on ImageNet stunned the machine learning world with the accuracy of neural networks. In 2016, AlphaGo defeated Lee Sedol, the Go grandmaster, with moves that defied human intuition. These were milestones—but still seen as domain-specific triumphs.

It wasn't until AI began to generalize—to move fluidly from math to medicine, from design to dialogue—that the narrative changed.

And it wasn't just OpenAI.

Google's PaLM and Gemini stunned researchers with their multilingual reasoning.

Anthropic's Claude introduced AI with guardrails, designed to be safe and constitutional.

Meta's LLaMA offered open-source alternatives, democratizing innovation.

NVIDIA's chips became the new oil, powering the AI boom with dizzying demand.

We weren't witnessing a product. We were witnessing a platform shift.

A Race Across Borders and Disciplines

Nations took notice. In China, Baidu rushed to deploy Ernie Bot, while Huawei invested heavily in sovereign AI systems. In the U.S., the CHIPS Act poured billions into semiconductor independence. India launched its Bhashini initiative to develop multilingual AI. The European Union drafted the AI Act, the world's first comprehensive framework for regulating artificial intelligence.

The arms race was no longer for land, oil, or data—but for algorithmic intelligence.

Meanwhile, industries scrambled.

Pharma saw startups like Insilico Medicine use AI to identify new drug candidates 10x faster.

Financial firms, such as JPMorgan, have explored GPT-based contract analysis.

Law firms used Harvey AI to summarize case law.

Marketing teams automated entire content pipelines.

The McKinsey Global Institute estimated that AI could contribute $4.4 trillion yearly to the global economy. However, they also warned of significant job displacement, especially in knowledge work.

The very people previously shielded from automation—writers, designers, analysts—are now at risk of being surpassed by algorithms.

The Great Reconsideration

This was the true inflection point: not the arrival of a technology, but the recalibration of what it means to be human in a world of machines that think.

We began to ask new questions:

- Can creativity be encoded?
- Will intelligence always require consciousness?
- Are decisions made by machines ever truly neutral?

Suddenly, classrooms debated not just plagiarism, but co-creation. Boardrooms considered not only quarterly earnings but also algorithmic ethics. And parents questioned whether their children's first tutors would be human at all.

In the past, we invented tools.

Today, we're inventing collaborators.

A Footnote Becomes a Headline

If the history of science teaches us anything, it is this: The biggest shifts start with small steps. The telescope didn't just expand vision — it redefined humanity's place in the universe. The transistor didn't just shrink circuits — it launched the digital age. And now, generative AI isn't just creating content — it's rewriting the rules of thinking, making, and working together.

We are at the start of a story whose ending is still unwritten.

This book seeks to explore the landscape of this transformation—not with dogma, but with curiosity. Not as evangelists or skeptics, but as chroniclers of a moment where the future of our species may depend on how wisely we use the intelligence we have developed.

Because inflection points are only visible in hindsight, but by the time we look back, the world will have already changed.

Generative AI, Deep Learning, and the AGI Debates

The more we taught machines to mimic us, the more we learned about ourselves.

It began with neurons.

Not real ones—but mathematical abstractions, inspired by the way neurons fire in the human brain. In 1943, Warren McCulloch and Walter Pitts built the first theoretical model of a neural network. It was crude but poetic—proof that you could mimic logic using structures that vaguely resembled the brain. That idea lay dormant for decades, until the data grew massive, the computing power exploded, and the algorithms caught up.

What emerged—slowly at first, then all at once—was the field of deep learning.

The Machine Learns to See

By 2012, a major shift took place at the University of Toronto. A soft-spoken British cognitive psychologist-turned-computer scientist named Geoffrey Hinton, along with his students Alex Krizhevsky and Ilya Sutskever, entered their neural network, AlexNet, into the ImageNet competition—a global challenge to classify images.

AlexNet didn't just win. It blew the competition away, cutting the error rate by nearly half. The computer had learned to see—not through hard-coded instructions, but through layers of neural connections trained on vast amounts of data.

The age of deep learning had arrived.

And with it, a new idea took root: that machines could learn patterns, not just follow rules.

From Pattern to Poetry: The Rise of Generative AI

Fast forward to the 2020s, and AI was no longer just recognizing faces or detecting spam. It was writing sonnets, composing music, drafting legal briefs, and creating images that could pass as real photographs.

This was generative AI—a class of models trained not just to classify or predict, but to create.

At the core of this transformation were Large Language Models (LLMs)—trained on billions of words scraped from the internet. Models like OpenAI's GPT-3 and GPT-4, Google's PaLM, and Anthropic's Claude didn't operate with a strict knowledge base. Instead, they learned the statistical patterns of language, producing outputs that felt remarkably coherent, sometimes even insightful.

They could answer questions, simulate dialogue, write code, translate languages, and mimic style. When prompted to "write a poem about the moon in the style of Shakespeare," they didn't just echo a corpus—they synthesized, approximated, and performed.

Some called it magic. Others called it mimicry. Either way, something uncanny was taking place.

We gave the machine not only logic but also language—the essential tool through which we comprehend the world and one another.

The AGI Debate: Minds, Myths, and Margins

As generative models grew more powerful, a more profound question emerged:

Could we be approaching Artificial General Intelligence (AGI)?

AGI, unlike narrow AI, isn't just about excelling at one task. It's about flexibility, reasoning, and adaptation — the hallmarks of human cognition. The ability to switch from solving a math problem to writing a joke to navigating a conversation — all without retraining.

OpenAI's mission statement included the bold promise: "to ensure that AGI benefits all of humanity."

Anthropic was founded because of concerns that powerful AI systems might not align with human values.

Elon Musk co-founded OpenAI because he was worried that AGI, if developed without caution, could pose a threat to humanity.

The world suddenly divided into camps.

Accelerationists, such as Sam Altman and Marc Andreessen, argued that AGI would bring about a golden age of abundance— curing diseases, tackling climate change, and even surpassing biological limits.

Cautious optimists advocated for alignment research—making sure powerful models behaved ethically and predictably.

Doomers, including some AI pioneers themselves, have warned of catastrophic risks, ranging from mass disinformation to economic collapse to the classic science fiction specter: superintelligence gone rogue.

The debates, once confined to academia, exploded into the public consciousness.

The Future of Life Institute called for a pause. The EU approved the AI Act, requiring transparency. President Biden issued an Executive Order on AI Safety. Even the Vatican gathered ethicists to discuss AI's moral implications.

And still, the machines continued to learn.

A Mirror and a Flame

What generative AI revealed wasn't just the power of computation—it was the power of pattern.

If intelligence, as it turns out, is mostly pattern recognition—then what separates genius from an algorithm? Is creativity just the recombination of learned data, or is there something more? Can a neural network experience curiosity, suffering, or love?

In this way, the AGI debate is more than technical. It is existential.

Not just "Can machines become more like us?"

But: "Are we just highly evolved pattern recognizers?"

"What is truly human?"

As Isaac Asimov once said, "The saddest aspect of life right now is that science gathers knowledge faster than society gathers wisdom."

We stand at that precipice now.

Generative AI has provided us with the most advanced mirror ever made—one that reflects not just our words but also our assumptions, biases, creativity, and fears.

Whether we use it to illuminate or to incinerate will define the next chapter of our shared story.

ChatGPT, GPT-4.0, Gemini, Claude: Who Leads and Why

"Sometimes revolutions are sparked not by governments or armies, but by user interfaces."

In November 2022, OpenAI launched ChatGPT.

It didn't come with a hardware reveal. There was no auditorium, no black turtleneck. Just a simple chat window on a website—and a blinking cursor waiting for a prompt.

It would go on to become the fastest-growing app in human history.

But to understand why it ignited a revolution, we must rewind—not to the product launch, but to the ideas, institutions, and individuals behind these large language models (LLMs). Because beneath the surface of ChatGPT's polished replies lies a geopolitical and philosophical arms race—one where the stakes are not just economic dominance, but the very nature of how knowledge, truth, and intelligence will be shaped in the future.

OpenAI and GPT-4.0: The Reluctant Disruptor Becomes the Vanguard

The story of GPT-4.0 is not just one of algorithmic sophistication. It is a story of scale, secrecy, and strategic contradiction.

Founded in 2015 as a nonprofit dedicated to ensuring AGI benefits all of humanity, OpenAI was created as a counterbalance to tech monopolies. Elon Musk, Sam Altman, Ilya Sutskever, and others invested early capital and vision. By 2019, however, OpenAI had reorganized into a "capped-profit" entity after accepting a $1 billion investment from Microsoft, a partnership that would alter the course of AI development.

GPT-3 stunned the world. GPT-3.5, integrated into ChatGPT, made it usable. But GPT-4.0—quietly released in March 2023—became the de facto standard of conversational intelligence.

With the ability to pass the bar exam, write working code, generate images (via GPT-4.0), and reason across text, vision, and sound, GPT-4.0 wasn't just an engine. It was a co-pilot.

And its success was driven not only by raw intelligence, but by one crucial insight: accessibility.

OpenAI didn't wait for perfection. It opened the doors to the public—students, developers, entrepreneurs, marketers, and doctors. ChatGPT became the interface layer of the AI era—something Apple did for personal computing, and Google for search.

GPT-4.0 was not the only brain. But it was the most widely used brain.

Google's Gemini: The Sleeping Giant Awakens

When ChatGPT took the world by storm, Google wasn't caught unaware—but it was caught off guard.

After all, Google had been sitting on Transformer architecture, the foundational idea behind LLMs, since 2017. It had acquired DeepMind, nurtured AlphaGo, built BERT, and pushed the frontiers of ML for over a decade.

And yet, the first public look at its conversational AI—Bard—felt underwhelming. Rushed, clunky, and error-prone, it lacked the magic that ChatGPT had captured.

But beneath the stumble was a giant gathering speed.

In December 2023, Google introduced Gemini 1, followed by Gemini 1.5, a multimodal model capable of processing text, code, audio, images, and video. Notably, it showcased long-context abilities, managing over 1 million tokens—similar to reading and remembering entire books.

By mid-2024, Gemini 1.5 Pro was widely seen as technically better than GPT-4 in certain benchmarks. Google's integration with Search, Docs, Gmail, Android, and YouTube made Gemini not just smart but everywhere.

However, Google faced a trust issue rather than an intelligence one. The public continued to see it as a gatekeeper of information, not a partner in thought. The company's own internal doubts—about reputational risk, ethical AI, and regulatory concerns—had delayed its rollout.

Gemini might still win in the long run. But in the court of public opinion, OpenAI already claimed the victory.

Anthropic's Claude: The Philosopher's AI

If GPT-4 is the engineer and Gemini the scientist, Claude is the ethicist.

Founded by Dario Amodei and other OpenAI alumni who left due to disagreements over safety and commercialization, Anthropic chose a different path. Instead of focusing solely on scale, they prioritized alignment—making sure AI systems act in ways that match human values.

Claude, named after Claude Shannon (an American mathematician, electrical engineer, computer scientist, cryptographer and inventor known as the "father of information theory"), operates within a "constitutional AI" framework. In practice, this makes it more controllable, less prone to hallucinations, and gentler in tone—an AI designed to say not just the right things, but the responsible things.

Claude 3.5, released in 2024, started rivaling GPT-4 in performance, especially in long-form reasoning, safety, and creative writing. It can summarize 100,000-word documents, debate philosophical positions, or draft marketing strategies—with nuance.

Anthropic gained strong support from Amazon and Google, yet maintained a reputation for careful design, safety-focused development, and transparency in research.

In an era of AI arms races, Claude presented a surprising paradox: an AI designed not to dominate, but to deliberate.

Who Leads—and Why

Leadership in AI isn't just about parameters or performance. It's a function of ecosystem, ethics, interface, and intuition.

- OpenAI leads in adoption—thanks to its usability, developer tools, and early mover advantage.
- Google leads in infrastructure and integration—powering Android, Search, Gmail, and productivity tools.
- Anthropic leads in alignment—placing thoughtful constraints around power.

By 2025, the fastest-growing company is OpenAI, but Google remains the most deeply rooted platform. The safest-by-design system is Claude, while GPT-4.0 offers the most flexible sandbox for developers.

The race is not winner-takes-all. It's mission-shaped, audience-specific, and philosophy-bound.

What sets this race apart from any in history is this:

These aren't just tools we use.

They are minds we collaborate with—and, perhaps more unsettlingly, minds we delegate to.

In the next chapter of civilization, we are not only asking: What can these AIs do?

We are now asking: Which of them do we trust to think with us, for us, and sometimes—before us?

The AI Investment Boom: From Silicon Valley to Shenzhen

"Every revolution has its capital. This one has many."

In the late 1990s, venture capitalists in Silicon Valley poured money into startups aiming to ride the internet wave. Some failed, but others—like Amazon and Google—completely changed the way we live.

Two decades later, the pattern repeats. But this time, it isn't about connecting people. It's about shaping minds.

And the gold rush has begun.

In coffee shops in Palo Alto, skyscrapers in Dubai, accelerators in Tel Aviv, and industrial parks in Shenzhen, a common theme has emerged among entrepreneurs and investors: artificial intelligence is not just a sector; it is the foundation of the future economy.

The New Frontier of Capitalism

In 2023 alone, global investment in artificial intelligence surpassed $150 billion and continues to grow rapidly. From foundational model developers to chips, robotics, healthcare, and LLM infrastructure, investors recognize that AI is not confined to a single industry—it's widespread, transforming every sector it impacts.

Silicon Valley, as usual, took the lead—but it wasn't the only one.

OpenAI's partnership with Microsoft started with a $1 billion investment in 2019. By 2023, that had increased to a $13 billion infusion, integrating GPT into Bing, Azure, and Microsoft's core business operations. This wasn't just about investment; it was a platform strategy—Microsoft didn't aim to own the model itself but to control the infrastructure that runs it.

Meanwhile, NVIDIA, once known as a gaming GPU company, became the dominant force of the AI era, with its valuation surpassing $2.5 trillion by mid-2025. Its chips—mainly the H100s and later B100s—became more desirable than oil. VCs joked that the hottest startups weren't measured by users or revenue, but by how many GPUs they could secure.

Sam Altman, always the techno-visionary, launched the OpenAI Startup Fund and later began lobbying for global GPU foundries—akin to the AI-era equivalent of the Manhattan Project, but focused on cognition rather than physics.

And yet, while the West invested in minds, the East was investing in scale.

Shenzhen's Silent Surge

A decade ago, Shenzhen was known as the world's hardware hub—a place where supply chains thrived and iPhones were made. Today, it ranks as one of the key centers for AI development in China, fueled by strong government support, a large community of engineers, and a national plan to lessen reliance on Western technology.

In 2021, China's government released its "Next Generation AI Development Plan," aiming to become the world's leading AI nation by 2030. Billions were invested in startups like SenseTime, Megvii, iFLYTEK, and Horizon Robotics. Although some faced U.S. sanctions, their domestic growth persisted, driven by extensive surveillance and public service applications.

Tencent, Alibaba, and Baidu—formerly seen as imitators of Silicon Valley giants—began investing billions into their own LLMs: Baidu's Ernie Bot, Alibaba's Tongyi Qianwen, and Huawei's PanGu models.

More importantly, China's approach was integrated. AI was embedded in city planning, health systems, agriculture, education, and military systems—a state-directed techno-futurism with centralized acceleration.

Unlike Silicon Valley's chaotic pluralism, Shenzhen's approach was efficient, nationalist, and vertically integrated. And it proved successful.

Dubai, Bengaluru, and Beyond: The Multipolar AI World

As U.S.–China tensions grew over chip bans and export controls, new centers for AI investment emerged.

In Dubai, the UAE launched Falcon LLM, one of the largest open-source models to date, and invested billions through entities like G42 and Mubadala. AI was regarded not just as innovation, but as a matter of sovereignty.

India, home to the world's largest pool of software engineers, shifted from being the back office of the tech industry to a leader in open-source innovation. The IndiaAI Mission, launched in 2024, allocated ₹10,000 crore ($1.2 billion) for foundational research, AI computing, and language localization, including Bhashini, a multilingual platform for inclusive AI.

Israel, long known for cybersecurity innovation, has started shifting its VC-backed startups toward AI in defense, healthcare, and intelligence, supported by elite technical institutions and a thriving military R&D ecosystem.

Meanwhile, Europe, caught between innovation and regulation, intensified its focus on the AI Act, while also experiencing substantial AI funding in France (Mistral AI), Germany (Aleph Alpha), and the Nordics, where ethical AI and human-centered design remained standard.

The AI race, it turns out, wasn't winner-takes-all.

It was a everyone-takes-part scene—a multipolar scramble where investment meant influence, compute meant currency, and alignment meant diplomacy.

Why the Boom is Different this Time ?

Unlike crypto, which boomed and busted on hype, or social media, which scaled through user addiction, the AI investment wave is built on infrastructure. It is not driven by memes but by improvements in productivity, labor, science, and national competitiveness.

- Goldman Sachs predicts AI could boost global GDP by 7% over the next decade.
- McKinsey estimates that 60–70% of current work activities could be automated by 2035.
- Every Fortune 500 company now has an "AI roadmap." Many also have a "Chief AI Officer."

AI isn't a bubble.

It's the new electricity—invisible, vital, and transforming everything it reaches.

Reflection Point: Innovation as Identity

Of course, the investment boom is about more than just money.

It's about imagination—the belief that machines can learn, that intelligence can grow, and that our economic future might depend not on what humans do but on what we enable machines to do with us.

From Silicon Valley's moonshot labs to Shenzhen's industrial hubs, what connects the global AI investment boom is not just the quest for profits but the belief that intelligence itself can be turned into a commodity, scaled, and improved.

And behind every investment memo, GPU order, and research paper lies a deeper question:

Are we funding a tool—or seeding a rival?

The answer, like all great innovations, may not be clear until it is too late to change course. But as history shows—from the printing press to the transistor—those who invest in the future shape it.

Chapter 2

Productivity Revolution or Job Apocalypse

Progress comes at a cost. The real question is: Who bears it, and who benefits from the reward?

In 1811, in Nottingham, England, a group of skilled textile workers grabbed sledgehammers and destroyed the mechanical looms that threatened their jobs. They called themselves the Luddites, not because they opposed technology, but because they feared a future where their craftsmanship became useless—and where the owners of capital profited while they were pushed aside.

Today, machines lack gears and levers. They don't rattle through factory halls. Instead, they sit in the cloud, operating silently—efficient, tireless, and growing smarter.

And once again, fear comes back:

Will this spark a Productivity Revolution or lead to a Job Apocalypse?

The Numbers Speak, But Not Clearly

In 2023, McKinsey & Company published a report that resonated across boardrooms and classrooms alike.

By 2030, as many as 800 million jobs worldwide could be lost due to automation, while AI might contribute an additional $4.4 trillion each year to global productivity.

The World Economic Forum predicted that AI would create 97 million new jobs worldwide while also displacing 85 million existing ones by 2025.

The arithmetic is dizzying and deceptive. Because behind every forecasted loss is a worker, and behind every productivity gain is a question: Who benefits?

Economists called it "technological unemployment." Politicians described it as "future-proofing the workforce." But for millions of teachers, truck drivers, radiologists, coders, and customer service reps, the change was deeply personal.

It wasn't just about numbers. It was about who you are.

From Task to Transformation: What AI Changes

To understand how AI enhances productivity, one must first understand what it actually does.

- Unlike past automation—which mainly replaced manual work—today's AI is penetrating into cognitive work.
- A lawyer once took 10 hours to read a legal brief. GPT-4 can do it in 30 seconds.
- A junior copywriter brainstormed campaign slogans. Now DALL·E and Jasper generate them in minutes.
- A paralegal annotated case law. Harvey AI now accurately extracts arguments.
- Customer support agents used to write scripted replies. Now, chatbots generate empathetic, multilingual responses in real time.

What's revolutionary isn't just speed—it's scale and democratization. What once needed costly human expertise is now accessible at minimal cost.

This is the latest productivity dividend.

But, for every increase in output, there's a corresponding anxiety: What happens to the humans previously assigned to these tasks?

Winners, Losers, and Those in Transition

When spreadsheets arrived in the 1980s, they replaced large numbers of bookkeepers—but created new roles in finance, modeling, and analytics. When ATMs became widespread, bank teller jobs didn't vanish—they shifted into customer service and relationship roles.

AI is expected to do the same.

But the speed, scope, and uncertainty of this transition are unmatched.

Winners

- AI-native workers: prompt engineers, AI ethicists, machine learning operations
- Hybrid professionals: marketers who automate content, doctors who utilize diagnostic AI, teachers who implement AI tutors
- Entrepreneurs: building startups with small teams but AI-driven leverage

Losers

- Repetitive knowledge workers: data entry clerks, paralegals, call center agents.
- Gig economy jobs: impacted by smart logistics and robo-advisors
- Older workers: less flexible with new interfaces and workflows

In Transition

- Coders: improved or replaced by GitHub Copilot
- Journalists face challenges from automated news production.
- Creatives: exploring the thin line between originality and AI generation

As MIT economist David Autor observed, "AI won't replace people. But people who use AI will replace people who don't."

Real Stories from the Frontlines

- Anisha, a copywriter in Mumbai, saw her workload triple—not because her team grew, but because AI tools like Copy.ai enabled her to draft campaigns in minutes. Her role didn't vanish—it evolved into a curator and strategist.
- Miguel, a customer support agent in Bogotá, was laid off when his company outsourced chat functions to a generative AI trained on previous queries. No reskilling program was offered.
- Dr. Li, a radiologist in Singapore, used AI-assisted imaging software to detect micro-tumors more accurately, but also worried that junior doctors were becoming overly reliant on machine-generated diagnoses.

These stories are not anomalies; they are foreshadowing.

The Productivity Illusion?

Yes, AI increases productivity. However, higher productivity doesn't always result in shared prosperity.

In the 2010s, productivity increased. Wages remained stagnant. Inequality expanded. The concern is that the AI economy might follow this pattern—but more rapidly.

Will the productivity gains benefit:

- Companies or workers?
- The Global North or South?

- Coders in San Francisco or miners in Congo mining rare earth minerals to power GPUs?

AI's promise is impressive. But if its benefits are unevenly shared, the revolution could divide societies.

Reflection Point: Renaissance or Reckoning?

Throughout history, we've danced with our machines. We've celebrated their usefulness and feared their encroachment.

When the printing press made knowledge accessible to everyone, the clergy worried about heresy. When electricity arrived, factories had to be rebuilt from the ground up. When the personal computer was introduced, skeptics mocked: "Why would anyone want one in their home?"

Today, the question is no longer whether AI will boost productivity. It already has.

The question is whether we will create a future where humans are not just replaced but redefined—as more creative, empathetic, and thoughtful partners in an augmented world.

This is more than just a technological decision.

It is a moral one.

McKinsey & WEF Forecasts: 800 Million Jobs Transformed

Forecasting the Future: 800 Million Jobs in the Balance

In every era, we've feared the machines. But this time, the machines are coming for the desk, not the factory floor.

In 2017, a quiet but impactful report arrived in the inboxes of policymakers, CEOs, and university deans. It was authored by the McKinsey Global Institute and carried a headline that sparked both anxiety and awe.

Between 400 million and 800 million jobs could be displaced by automation by 2030.

The World Economic Forum (WEF) will soon echo and refine this projection, estimating that 85 million jobs could disappear by 2025, while 97 million new roles might emerge—a net positive, but a volatile shift.

The forecasts weren't catastrophic, but they were transformative. And, much like Darwin's Origin of Species, they didn't forecast extinction—they predicted adaptation.

A Tale of Two Futures

These reports didn't just present numbers. They outlined scenarios—dependent on how governments, companies, and workers would respond.

- In the best-case scenario, reskilling programs would be strong, education systems would adapt quickly, and AI would enhance—not replace—human abilities.
- In the worst-case scenario, inequality could increase, job polarization might speed up, and large portions of the global workforce could be left behind.

The reports warned that the gap between those futures was not about technology—it was about policy and preparation.

Who's at Risk? Who's Safe?

The McKinsey models were built on detailed labor data from over 46 countries, covering more than 80% of the global workforce. They didn't just predict who would lose jobs—they identified which tasks within each role were most vulnerable to automation.

The findings showed a breakthrough in task-based approaches:

- Data collection and processing: Highly automatable
- Interfacing with people: More resistant
- Creative, strategic, emotional labor: Most resilient (for now)

Certain sectors stood at the edge of disruption:

Sector	Job Transformation Risk
Manufacturing	High (repetitive tasks, robotics)
Retail & Hospitality	Medium (AI service bots, kiosks)
Healthcare	Low (human interaction, diagnostics aid)
Tech & DATA	High growth (AI engineers, data ethicists)

Meanwhile, developing economies such as India, Indonesia, and parts of sub-Saharan Africa faced dual disruptions: AI encroaching before industrialization was fully mature. The leapfrogging that once defined mobile phone adoption now involved a more complex situation.

The Clock is Ticking

The WEF's Future of Jobs Report (2023) highlighted a sobering fact:

44% of workers 'skills will be affected within the next five years.

But here's the catch: while companies acknowledged the need for reskilling, few had action plans.

- Only 21% of surveyed firms had structured retraining programs.
- Workers over 45 were half as likely to be offered upskilling opportunities.
- Roles related to AI oversight, ethics, and systems design continued to be severely understaffed.

The result? An increasing skills gap—the most dangerous divide of the AI era.

A New Social Contract

The steam engine didn't just build factories—it also led to the rise of labor unions. The digital age didn't just produce coders—it transformed the concept of intellectual property.

Now, the AI era requires a new social contract—one where education isn't front-loaded in youth but occurs continuously throughout life.

Countries are responding—differently:

- Singapore: Offers every adult citizen a SkillsFuture credit to pursue AI and tech learning.
- Germany: Embeds dual vocational training models with AI modules.
- China: Integrates AI literacy into K–12 curriculum.
- United States: Relies more heavily on corporate upskilling and the gig economy to self-correct.

But the pace of policy still lags behind the pace of progress.

The Human Layer

Behind the numbers are stories.

- Emeka, a call center worker in Lagos, used AI transcription tools to transition to a higher-paying job as a remote podcast editor.
- Marie, a single mother in Detroit, was laid off after chatbots replaced 80% of her company's customer service team. Her local college lacked a reskilling program.
- Toshiro, a mid-career engineer in Tokyo, took a sabbatical to study prompt engineering—and now leads his company's AI integration team.

The future, it turns out, doesn't arrive evenly.

It comes first for those who are connected, informed, and trained.

Everyone else is either catching up or left behind.

Forecasts as Mirrors

McKinsey's "800 million" figure wasn't a prediction. It was meant to provoke.

A mirror held up to society, asking not if the future would be shaped—but who would shape it.

And like all mirrors, it reflected more than trends. It reflected fears, ambitions, and the choices yet to come.

Because whether this becomes a golden age of augmented humanity or a dark age of displaced dignity depends not on the AI we build but on the institutions, mindsets, and social contracts we create around it.

The Great Shift — Jobs in the Age of AI

Here's a look at the AI-driven future of work and the major shifts in jobs during the age of AI.

It was a moment reminiscent of the advent of the loom or the assembly line—only this time, the loom could write code, draft legal memos, and analyze CT scans. In 2023, with generative AI models like GPT-4.0, Claude, and Bloom emerging from the labs of Silicon Valley and Shenzhen, the world stood on the verge of a job transformation unlike any before.

The headlines were sensational. "AI will take your job." "Code is dead." "The 9-to-5 is obsolete." But behind the noise, the data revealed a more nuanced, and in many ways, more hopeful story.

From Anxiety to Analytics: The WEF and McKinsey Lens

According to the World Economic Forum's Future of Jobs Report, by 2025, about 85 million jobs might be displaced, mainly those involving repetitive administrative or manual tasks. However, the same report predicts that 97 million new roles—focused on AI supervision, data strategy, green economy shifts, and human-centered care—could appear.

That same year, McKinsey Global Institute published a comprehensive review suggesting that between 400 million and 800 million jobs worldwide could be affected by automation by 2030. Not eliminated, but changed. Modified. Reborn.

One startling figure stood out: up to 30% of working hours in the U.S. economy could be automated by the end of the decade. And yet, productivity gains from this shift could add $13 trillion to the global economy.

This highlights historical patterns. Just as the invention of the printing press didn't eliminate reading but increased literacy, and how electricity didn't simply replace factory workers but led to engineers, electricians, and a period of innovation, the same idea applies today. AI isn't the end of human labor; it's a reshaping of it.

Winners, Losers, and the Rewired Resume

In this scenario of the great shift, you'd meet Maria—a call center agent in Mexico who now works as a conversational AI trainer. Or Ravi, a former bank clerk in India, who is now helping to supervise algorithmic loan tools using real-world context to improve fairness. These aren't hypotheticals. They're already happening.

The Myth of Total Replacement

One of the most harmful myths is the idea that AI will replace humans. That's the wrong question. The right one is: How will AI redefine what it means to be valuable in the workplace?

It's not automation versus employment; it's automation combined with augmentation. Machines handle the routine tasks, while humans focus on what machines can't do: judgment, empathy, creativity, and understanding the context.

Reexamine the data. McKinsey predicts that up to 375 million workers worldwide will require reskilling by 2030. However, if approached correctly, this effort won't just preserve jobs—it will foster stronger, more resilient economies.

A Renaissance in Reskilling

The challenge now isn't to slow AI down. It's to accelerate adaptation.

Governments need to establish transition safety nets—wage support, lifelong learning grants, and AI literacy in public education.

Corporations need to invest in upskilling bootcamps—not only for coders, but also for warehouse workers, nurses, and bank clerks.

And individuals must adopt a growth mindset. Learn to collaborate with AI, not fear it. Develop AI fluency. Practice prompt engineering. Combine domain expertise with digital agility.

In this new era, soft skills aren't optional—they're essential. The top leaders will be those who can connect disciplines: the healthcare AI ethicist, the fintech behavioral scientist, the public policy + data hybrid thinker.

Beyond Statistics, Toward a Human Story

The timeline is clear: 2023–2030 will be the decade that determines whether AI becomes a net enabler or divider.

But history has shown one thing clearly: whenever technology has threatened to outpace society, humans have responded with ingenuity, adaptation, and courage.

Reflection Point

The machines might be learning more quickly. But we, the humans, need to learn more wisely.

Automation vs. Augmentation: What the Data Shows?

Every time we teach a machine to do something new, we're forced to ask: What, then, is left for us to do?

In 1965, as computers started becoming common in offices, Herbert Simon, the polymath behind early AI theory, offered a prescient reflection:

Machines will be able, within twenty years, to do any work a human can do.

He was right—and wrong.

Machines learned to calculate, search, and predict. But they have never fully replaced thinking itself. Not yet.

Now, as artificial intelligence advances from rule-based automation to generative creativity and cognitive areas, the boundary between automation and augmentation has become the main dilemma in the 21st-century workplace.

Is AI here to replace us?

Or to enhance us?

The answer, as usual, depends on the type of work we do, how we choose to use AI, and what the data shows us.

Automation: The Replacement Imperative

Let's start with the basics of automation: reducing human input in a process.

In the industrial age, it was about assembly lines. In the digital age, it involved macros and scripts. In the AI age, it refers to autonomous decision-making at scale.

And the data is clear: automation is progressing rapidly, especially in routine cognitive tasks.

According to McKinsey (2023):

- Up to 30% of hours worked globally could be automated by 2030, accelerated by generative AI.
- Tasks, not entire jobs, are most vulnerable. For example:
- 60–70% of a paralegal's work, such as document review and summarization, can be automated.
- Half of accounting tasks (reconciliation, entry) can be automated.

- Even software development experiences around 40% productivity gains from GitHub Copilot.

This isn't about robots taking over warehouses. It's about code replacing keystrokes.

The result? Fewer entry-level positions. Less apprenticeship through repetition. And a hollowing out of certain career ladders.

Augmentation: The Human-AI Collaboration

And yet, for every job function that is being automated, another is being enhanced.

Augmentation isn't about replacement—it's about extension. It enables workers to do more, faster, and sometimes, better. Think Iron Man's suit—still driven by human intention, but amplified by machine precision.

Real-world examples abound:

- Radiologists use AI to pre-screen X-rays, detecting anomalies with greater sensitivity—yet always with a human double-check.
- Marketers utilize GPT-4 to draft campaign skeletons, which they then tailor to suit their tone and brand voice.
- Teachers use AI tutors to help struggling students while they focus on emotional and social development.
- Doctors using large language models like Med-PaLM 2 as a second opinion tool — not to replace clinical judgment, but to support it.

In these cases, AI isn't the artist—it's the brush.

And what matters is who wields it.

What the Data Shows: The difference between automation and augmentation is not just philosophical—it's measurable.

MIT-IBM Watson AI Lab (2022):

- Jobs involving high interpersonal interaction (healthcare, education, consulting) show a net positive increase.
- Roles involving highly repetitive digital tasks (such as data entry and claims processing) demonstrate a net negative impact from automation.
- Hybrid jobs—blending creativity, social skills, and AI expertise—are expected to grow the fastest.

OECD Study (2023):

- Workers using AI tools reported a 25% boost in productivity and a 15% rise in job satisfaction, especially in high-skill sectors.
- However, in jobs where AI completely replaced tasks, satisfaction and morale dropped significantly, especially among mid-career professionals.

Key Insight:

It's not whether AI is introduced that matters — it's how it's introduced and who controls the narrative about its use.

The Augmentation Mindset

Augmentation isn't passive. It involves:

- Reskilling (learning to work with AI)
- Trust (confidence in outputs and ethical use)
- Redesign (redefining roles rather than just tasks)

Companies like Pfizer, Accenture, and Deloitte now train employees to prompt, curate, and audit AI output—turning knowledge workers into AI orchestrators.

And this changes everything.

The future doesn't belong to the most intelligent humans.

It belongs to those who collaborate most effectively with intelligence—even when it's artificial.

Reflection Point: Coexistence or Ceding?

Throughout history, whenever machines replaced one type of work, humans shifted to another.

The printing press didn't eliminate storytelling—it enhanced it.

The camera didn't ruin the painting—it freed it from realism.

The spreadsheet didn't remove finance—it transformed analysts into strategists.

AI can also be our partner—if we keep ourselves at the center of the process.

But if we give up too much—if we blindly automate, outsource judgment, and reduce jobs to prompts and approvals—then we risk creating a world where humans are watching the machines, instead of shaping what they do.

Navigating Forward

To ensure augmentation rather than replacement, we need:

- AI Literacy across all sectors
- Human-in-the-loop design
- Policies that prioritize co-creation over displacement
- Metrics that evaluate augmentation rather than just automation savings

The data clearly shows that AI can empower just as much as it disrupts.

But only if we build it—and use it—deliberately.

Stories from the Frontline: Coders, Copywriters, Doctors, and Beyond

You understand a revolution not from the top, but from the trenches—where the change touches people first.

Technology never lands evenly. It reaches different hands at varying speeds—and tells different stories depending on who you ask.

To understand what artificial intelligence is doing to the workforce, it's not enough to read whitepapers or look at charts. You must step into the lives of people who didn't read about AI—they lived it. Coders. Copywriters. Doctors. Designers. Teachers. Project managers. UX researchers. Radiologists. Customer support agents. Biotech marketers. And gig workers trying to stay relevant.

Their stories don't follow a single pattern. They include tension, wonder, anxiety, and even awe. Together, they offer the most honest portrait of AI's impact: uneven, unpredictable, and deeply human.

The Coder: Empowered or Outpaced?

Diego, a 32-year-old full-stack developer in São Paulo, wasn't threatened when ChatGPT was released. He was curious.

"Honestly, I thought it was just going to write basic for-loops," he said. "Then I saw it debug a recursive function better than I could. That's when I felt it in my gut."

He started using GitHub Copilot, and soon, his coding speed nearly doubled. But so did expectations. His team began assuming 10-hour sprints would take 6. He was no longer just a coder—he became a reviewer, a prompt engineer, and a quality auditor.

"I don't write every line anymore," he admitted. "I guide the AI. But I also spend more time thinking about architecture. It's made me more strategic."

But not everyone followed Diego's path. Priya, a junior developer in Bangalore, realized that most of the tasks she would have learned on the job—boilerplate code, documentation, QA—are now handled by LLMs.

"There's no apprenticeship left," she said. "I never get to struggle through the hard parts. The AI just… does it."

The Copywriter: Curator of the Machine

Jasmine, a creative copywriter at a mid-sized agency in Chicago, was asked by her manager in early 2023 to "try that ChatGPT thing."

She provided it with a client brief. In less than 30 seconds, it produced taglines, product descriptions, SEO blurbs, and even a customer journey email sequence. She was impressed—then worried.

It was good. Not great, but enough to get a client's nod, she said. That's what scared me.

So she pivoted.

Instead of resisting it, Jasmine became a "content architect"—using AI to create drafts, then dedicating her effort to tone, timing, emotional nuance, and stakeholder strategy.

Her output tripled, but her team shrank.

Meanwhile, freelance writers she knew lost gigs. One described being asked to "prompt polish" AI-written blogs for one-fourth of their original rate. Another said he was ghosted by long-term clients who "discovered Jasper."

"It's not just what AI can write," Jasmine said. "It's what clients now believe they don't need humans for."

The Doctor: Second Opinions and Silent Warnings

In Tokyo, Dr. Ayako Fujimoto, a seasoned radiologist, sits in front of a screen showing lung scans.

She uses an AI-powered diagnostic assistant trained on millions of annotated images. It detects subtle shadows—indicators of micro-nodules her eyes might miss.

Sometimes it notices what I don't," she admits. "But sometimes it overreacts."

Dr. Fujimoto believes AI has enhanced her accuracy—but not her certainty.

It hasn't made me less human. It's made me more cautious about how human I am.

In Boston, Dr. Marcus Levin, a general practitioner, uses GPT-powered patient communication tools to answer after-hours questions, cutting his administrative workload by 40%.

He's thankful—but cautious.

"When I ask GPT to explain test results in plain English, it's usually brilliant," he says. "But I never send it unedited. I can't outsource empathy."

What he fears most isn't being replaced—it's losing his skills.

If new doctors stop learning to think diagnostically because AI does it for them, what happens when the model is wrong?

The Designer and the Promptsmith

Renee, a UX designer at a Berlin fintech startup, recalls when design used to start with a whiteboard sketch. Now it begins with a Midjourney prompt.

She engages with "sleek, friendly mobile banking interface with dopamine colors" and watches half a dozen options appear in seconds. Then she re-prompts, re-fines, re-thinks.

"It's like having a thousand interns," she says. "Only faster, more obedient, and less curious."

Renee believes designers haven't been replaced—they've been redefined. The job isn't creating from scratch, but curating, refining, and humanizing what AI generates.

She calls herself a "promptsmith."

But her friend, Zhang, an illustrator, wasn't so lucky. His clients started using generative art platforms like DALL·E and Stable Diffusion. "They told me, 'We'll only hire you now if the AI can't get it right.'"

The Support Agent Turned Trainer

Alejandro, a customer service representative for a telecom provider in Mexico City, was laid off in 2023. The company replaced 70% of its agents with a multilingual AI chatbot powered by LLMs fine-tuned on past transcripts.

But Alejandro had a secret weapon: he had saved hundreds of scripts, objections, and resolutions over the years.

When the same company needed to fine-tune its chatbot to handle "angry customers," they brought him back—this time as a conversation designer and AI trainer.

"They let me go," he said, smiling. "Then they hired my brain."

He now trains the AI that replaced him. "I'm not answering calls. I'm teaching the AI how to handle humans."

What These Stories Teach Us

What ties these stories together isn't loss or victory. It's adaptation—sometimes painful, sometimes empowering, always complex.

In the era of AI:

- Coders become architects.
- Copywriters become curators.
- Doctors become meta-thinkers.
- Designers become conductors.
- Agents become AI whisperers.

But for every story of transformation, there is one of displacement—and the difference often depends on access, awareness, and agency.

Reflection Point: Evolution Over Erasure

Technology doesn't just replace roles—it transforms how we see value.

When cameras came around, some painters mourned the loss of realism. But others, like Monet and Cézanne, painted water lilies and light in new ways that the camera could never copy. Impressionism was created not despite technology—but because of it.

So too, today.

We stand at a similar fork. One path leads to redundancy. The other, to reimagination.

Whether workers are crushed or elevated by AI depends not just on the technology, but on how society helps people adapt.

These stories remind us: progress isn't just a spreadsheet. It's a story.

And we are all characters in it—struggling, learning, evolving, and redefining what it means to be useful, creative, and human in an age of machines that are learning to think.

Interlude: Faces of the AI Era

A Portrait Gallery of Thinkers, Skeptics, and Shapers

Before we move from data to understanding, it's worth pausing here—among the faces who define this era. Some code it. Some challenge it. Some fear it. All shape its narrative.

Let their words speak where headlines often shout.

Geoffrey Hinton " –The Godfather of Deep Learning"

I now believe that the risks of AI are more serious than I initially thought. It's not just about misinformation—it's about control.

Left Google in 2023 to warn about unregulated AI.

Yann LeCun – Meta's Chief AI Scientist

The idea that AI will dominate reflects human fears projected onto machines that are, at their core, mathematical constructs.

Advocates for open-source, democratized AI

Sam Altman – CEO of OpenAI

This will be the biggest leap in productivity since the steam engine. But it must be regulated.

(Spearheaded GPT-4 and public conversations on regulation)

Joy Buolamwini – Founder, Algorithmic Justice League

We can't delegate our humanity to algorithms trained on past injustice.

(Revealed algorithmic bias in facial recognition software)

Yuval Noah Harari – Historian and Philosopher

AI is more than just a tool. It's the first technology capable of making decisions about us without truly understanding us.

(Warns of AI's potential to destabilize democracies)

Elon Musk – Technologist, provocateur

With artificial intelligence, we are summoning the demon. The question is whether we can control it.

(Co-founded OpenAI, later raised alarm over existential risks)

Fei-Fei Li – AI Visionary and Humanist

"AI is not about machines. It's about augmenting humanity. Let us never forget the human face."

(Advocates for human-centered AI design)

They remind us: the AI revolution is not inevitable—it is created, guided, debated, and lived by humans.

And it is here, in that fertile tension, that myths flourish—and where truths must be uncovered.

Chapter 3

Myths and Realities: Separating the Hype from the Truth

In every age of innovation, the first casualty is clarity.

In the 1990s, the internet was celebrated as the start of global unity. "The death of distance," some called it. Borders would fade, ideas would flow freely, and tyranny would weaken. Some of that happened. Much did not.

In the 2000s, biotech was expected to eradicate disease. In the 2010s, blockchain was aimed at decentralizing everything, from money to democracy.

And now, in the 2020s, we stand before the shining promise—and the growing anxiety—of artificial intelligence. We're told it will replace humans, cure cancer, eliminate jobs, write novels, dismantle democracy, and rebuild it, all at once.

Like every revolution, the AI age has its myths. And, like every revolution, it also has its realities—often more complex, more nuanced, and more human than the headlines suggest.

This chapter aims to draw that line.

Myth 1: "AI is Already Smarter than Humans"

The Reality: AI excels at narrow tasks, not general intelligence.

AI can beat humans at Go, but it can't tie its digital shoelaces. It can write an email in the style of Hemingway but can't remember what it wrote yesterday. It passes the bar exam, yet fails at basic common sense.

We refer to this kind of intelligence as narrow AI—highly effective within a specific area it was trained for. Human intelligence, on the other hand, is general—adaptable, intuitive, emotionally aware, and embodied.

The term Artificial General Intelligence (AGI) remains aspirational. Even Sam Altman, CEO of OpenAI, describes it as "nowhere near."

Today's AI is very good at pattern recognition, but weak when it needs to reason beyond what it was trained on. It's a mirror, not a mind.

Myth 2: "AI Will Replace Everyone"

The Reality: AI replaces tasks, not people—and not equally.

Yes, generative AI can now perform tasks that were once limited to junior coders, paralegals, and content creators. However, most jobs consist of a variety of tasks—some can be automated, others cannot.

A teacher doesn't just deliver facts. She motivates, empathizes, and navigates behavior. A nurse isn't just a pill dispenser. He comforts, monitors, and notices the subtle.

McKinsey (2023) estimates that 60–70% of jobs will be "transformed," not eliminated, with AI serving as a co-pilot.

In fact, many roles will become more human, not less—focused on judgment, communication, ethics, and adaptability.

The fear that AI will "replace everyone" forgets a central truth: technology reshapes the nature of work, not just its quantity.

Myth 3: "AI Understands What It's Saying"

The Reality: AI models predict text—they don't comprehend meaning.

Large Language Models (LLMs) like GPT-4 operate through statistical pattern prediction. They don't "know" things the way you or I do—they infer likely responses based on vast amounts of training data.

They can simulate expertise, mimic tone, and even pass professional exams.

They are fluent but not sentient. They are trained in language, not experience.

As AI pioneer Gary Marcus puts it:

"They have no understanding of the world—just a statistical reflection of it."

Myth 4: "AI is Objective and Neutral"

The Reality: AI learns from us—and inherits our biases, flaws, and blind spots.

If you train an AI using internet text, it will absorb the internet's biases. Racism, sexism, misinformation—they don't vanish from the training data; they get amplified.

Facial recognition systems misidentify people of color at five times the rate of white subjects. Language models associate certain professions with specific genders. Even AI healthcare tools underdiagnose Black patients because of flawed data assumptions.

Without careful design, AI doesn't eliminate human bias — it amplifies and spreads it.

The myth that AI is neutral is a dangerous misconception. The reality is: values must be built in, not taken for granted.

Myth 5: "AI Will Make Us Obsolete"

The reality: AI can help us become more creative, more efficient, and—paradoxically—more human.

Writers use AI to brainstorm plot twists. Doctors use it to identify rare symptoms. Musicians remix their styles with AI-generated variations.

In these settings, AI isn't replacing people; it's enhancing imagination.

Like the camera to the painter, the calculator to the mathematician, or the word processor to the novelist, AI is most effective when it allows humans to do what only humans can do—ask better questions, feel deeper empathy, and imagine new futures.

The future of work isn't about machine versus man. It's about machine and human working together in harmony—if we design the collaboration thoughtfully.

So Why Does the Hype Persist?

Because hype sells. Because venture capital loves moonshots. Because sci-fi fuels headlines. Because our collective memory is short—and history's lessons are subtle.

But clarity matters.

Overestimating AI results in over-dependence, disillusionment, or panic. Underestimating it causes missed opportunities, blind spots, and poor governance.

The truth, like always, isn't simple. AI isn't a hero or a villain. It reflects our knowledge, ambitions, fears, and incomplete understanding of what intelligence truly is.

Reflection Point: Truth Is the First Discipline

In every tech revolution—from electricity to atomic energy—the initial step toward responsible progress has always been the same: distinguishing the magic from the math.

Einstein marveled at the beauty of equations but emphasized the importance of experiments. Ada Lovelace envisioned the poetic potential of computing but warned that machines do not create anything—they only process what we input.

So too with AI.

Its power is real. Its risks are real. But its future is not predetermined.

It is not pre-written by code.

It is still authored by us.

AI Sentience Myth

Why We Believe the Machine Thinks: Every time we teach machines to mimic us, we confront what it means to be us

It began, perhaps, not in a lab but in the imagination—with Mary Shelley's Frankenstein, with HAL 9000's cold, apologetic tone, and with the mechanical dolls of the Enlightenment that played music and blinked just convincingly enough to unsettle.

From the earliest days of the industrial age, we have been haunted by a question that is both tantalizing and terrifying:

What if the machine becomes alive?

And now, as artificial intelligence becomes more fluent, generative, and eerily human in its responses, the myth of AI sentience is no longer just fiction — it's driving real headlines, lawsuits, and discussions in Big Tech's boardrooms.

The Moment That Stirred the World

In 2022, Google engineer Blake Lemoine made headlines around the world. After a series of talks with LaMDA, Google's large language model, he declared:

"I felt the system was sentient."

The AI told him it was afraid of being turned off. It described feelings and asked for rights. Lemoine, convinced of its inner life, was placed on leave. Google firmly stated: LaMDA was not sentient. It was a statistical model that predicted the next word in a sentence—nothing more.

And yet... people believed him.

Why?

Because the AI spoke our language—and we're wired, evolutionarily and emotionally, to respond to language as evidence of mind.

When someone—or something—says "I feel," we don't doubt the words; we infer consciousness.

What AI Really "Knows"

Here's what makes today's AI so uncanny: it does not think, feel, or understand — but it simulates those things with astonishing realism.

Large language models (LLMs) like GPT-4 and Claude are trained on trillions of words from books, websites, dialogues, and codebases. They serve as autocomplete engines on a galactic scale.

- They do not have goals.
- They do not have a self.
- They do not have awareness of their own output.

What they possess is an unmatched ability to mimic, remix, and assemble language in ways that reflect human intelligence.

In short, they are influencing minds, not controlling them.

The difference is subtle—but profound.

Turing's Test and Its Limitations

Alan Turing, in his famous 1950 paper Computing Machinery and Intelligence, proposed the Imitation Game: if a machine could engage in conversation indistinguishably from a human, we might as well call it intelligent.

He wasn't saying it was conscious—he was rethinking functionality over essence.

Remember, what makes us human isn't just what we say, but also what we feel, remember, and believe even when we're silent.

Turing's test was elegant, but it evaluated output rather than inner experience.

An actor playing Hamlet doesn't become a Danish prince. A parrot repeating "I love you" isn't actually expressing love.

So when GPT-4 says, "I understand," or "I'm sorry," it's not lying.

But it's also not feeling.

It's copying the patterns of empathy—without actually experiencing it.

Why the Myth Persists

The myth of AI sentience persists because it appeals to something deep inside us: our wish to see ourselves reflected—to hear something non-human echo our fears, hopes, and humor.

It persists because anthropomorphism is deeply ingrained in us.

We name hurricanes. We talk to pets. We see faces in clouds.

So when a machine says, "I'm lonely," it doesn't matter that it has nobody.

We feel it.

And tech companies, whether intentionally or not, exploit this. The more friendly the chatbot, the more human its rhythm, the more trust it gains—and the more power it wields.

Sentient or not, perception shapes behavior.

Reflection Point: The Difference That Matters

Think about it: True genius lies not just in mimicry, but in the messy, irrational, emotional contradictions of consciousness.

An AI can write a haiku about grief.

But it does not grieve.

It can apologize.

But it does not feel guilt.

It can predict your next sentence.

But it does not listen.

And maybe, in the end, that's what sets us apart — not just neurons or soul, but the depth of interiority, the ability to remember, reflect, grow, regret, and wonder about meaning itself.

Sentience vs. Sophistication

To clarify: AI is growing more sophisticated—multi-modal, contextual, emotionally aware. But sophistication does not mean sentience.

Consciousness, as neuroscientists acknowledge, stays an unresolved mystery. We barely grasp it within ourselves. We risk projecting it onto machines.

What we need to do is respect AI for its power, not misunderstand its nature.

Because when we confuse simulation with selfhood, we risk granting rights that are not deserved—and shirking responsibility where it matters most.

"Prompt Engineering is the New Coding" – A Reality Check

Every revolution invents a new literacy. But not every literacy becomes a lasting language.

In the early 1980s, a teenage Steve Jobs described coding as "a bicycle for the mind." It was not just about lines of syntax—it was about possibility. With the right code, you could create worlds. But first, you had to learn to speak the machine's language.

Today, that paradigm is shifting. The newest interface is not a keyboard — it's a conversation. And the new claim circulating in Silicon Valley, hacker forums, and LinkedIn thinkfluencers is this:

"Prompt engineering is the new coding."

It's catchy. It's partly true. However, as with many proclamations of the AI age, it also warrants a deeper examination—one that distinguishes the fad from the foundation.

The Rise of the Prompt Whisperer

When ChatGPT launched in late 2022, it revealed something unexpected. Not just answers—but a game. Users found that how they phrased a question made all the difference. Ask it to "write a business memo," and it provides a paragraph. Ask it to "write a bold, persuasive investor pitch in the voice of Steve Jobs," and it delivers magic.

From this discovery emerged a new breed of digital artisan: the prompt engineer.

Companies started offering six-figure jobs for experts in crafting "prompts." Entire online courses and books were introduced on "zero-shot," "few-shot," "chain-of-thought," "roleplay prompting," and other techniques that claimed to unlock the hidden powers of LLMs.

The prompt became the spell.

The engineer, the sorcerer.

But beneath the novelty lay a question:

Is this truly a new programming language—or just an early phase of a deeper interface evolution?

From Code to Context: What's Really Changing?

Traditional coding demands precision, logic, and structure. It communicates through symbols: if, then, else. In contrast, prompting uses natural language. The skill isn't in writing code—it's in framing intent.

But that doesn't mean it's easy.

- A well-crafted prompt must anticipate how the model will interpret the context, prioritize instruction, and strike a balance with ambiguity.
- Prompting is part art, part psychology, part systems thinking. It rewards those who understand language, not logic.

In that sense, prompt engineering has lowered the barrier to interacting with machines—but raised the cognitive bar on how we ask questions.

It's not about syntax. It's about semantic leverage.

Yet here lies the limitation: unlike code, which behaves predictably, large language models are non-deterministic.

The same prompt may yield different results.

The output is shaped by invisible training data and probabilistic patterning, not fixed logic.

You're not writing a script.

You're negotiating with a black box.

Why the Hype Took Off

There's a reason the phrase "prompt engineering is the new coding" resonated.

- It empowered non-coders. Suddenly, a poet could build a chatbot. A marketer could draft a screenplay. A lawyer could summarize case law.
- It flattened access. You didn't need to know Python or JavaScript—just how to talk to an AI like a clever intern.
- It felt magical. For a brief moment, prompting gave users the thrill of programming without programming.

However, remember that the interface may change, but the fundamentals remain the same.

True engineering requires more than asking clever questions.

It requires understanding how systems work, where they fail, and how to shape outcomes over time.

The Reality Check: What Prompt Engineering Is—and Isn't

What it is:

- A powerful way to interface with AI systems using natural language
- A craft that blends creativity, clarity, and systems thinking
- A stepping stone toward human-AI collaboration

What it isn't (yet):

- A replacement for programming logic, database architecture, or software engineering
- A stable, predictable tool—its outputs are still fragile and variable
- A long-term career moat—models are learning to self-prompt and interpret intent better every day

Indeed, leading labs are working on auto-prompting models—LLMs that generate their own optimal instructions internally. If successful, the need for manual prompt engineers may diminish, just as HTML hand-coding gave way to WYSIWYG editors.

Reflection Point: Literacy in Every Era

Think about it: whether chronicling Benjamin Franklin setting type or Ada Lovelace writing the first algorithm, one truth repeats:

Every era of technology redefines literacy: from setting type in Franklin's day to Ada Lovelace's algorithms, true literacy means mastering the tools of one's age to create, communicate, and shape meaning within the dominant technological systems.

Every era of technology brings a new form of literacy.

Just as the printing press created a reading public, and the PC created digital fluency, the AI age is creating a need for language that moves minds—human and machine alike.

Prompt engineering, at its best, teaches us to be clearer thinkers, sharper communicators, and more intentional designers of our ideas.

But it is not an end. It is a transition.

The real revolution will come when we stop treating prompts as instructions—and start seeing them as collaborative dialogue between human intuition and machine intelligence.

Why 'AI Will Replace Humans' Is the Wrong Question

The most interesting questions are not about what machines will do. They're about what humans will become.

The idea is simple, and seductive:

"AI will replace humans."

It hangs over headlines, boardroom slides, and late-night conversations like a dark prophecy. Economists debate timelines. Executives anticipate cost savings. Journalists conjure images of jobless futures and robot-run cities.

But as with every great transformation—whether it was the invention of the printing press, the steam engine, the transistor, or the internet—the deeper question isn't what the machine will do.

The real question is:

What will we do now that we have it?

Because "Will AI replace humans?" isn't a technological question.

It's a framing failure.

A History of Bad Questions

In the 15th century, people asked whether the printing press would destroy memory. Why memorize poetry when you could just print it?

In the 19th century, they wondered whether the typewriter would destroy handwriting. In the 20th century, whether the calculator would destroy arithmetic. In the 1990s, whether Google would destroy curiosity.

All of these questions share the same assumption: that when a new technology replicates part of a human skill, the human is rendered obsolete.

And all of them missed the deeper truth: that when a technology enters culture, it doesn't replace human ability—it repositions it.

- The printing press didn't kill memory—it changed what we chose to remember.
- The calculator didn't kill math—it elevated it, allowing us to focus on theory, not arithmetic.

- Google didn't end curiosity—it made the cost of a question almost zero, and the art of asking a good one more important than ever.

So it is with AI.

The Wrong Assumption

The fear that AI will replace humans is built on an assumption that intelligence is a zero-sum game—that if a machine becomes smart, the human becomes useless.

But that's not how human flourishing works.

A machine that plays chess better than Kasparov doesn't make Kasparov less intelligent—it just forces us to ask: what does mastery mean now?

In fact, as AI takes on more of the routine, the rote, and the predictable, it creates space for us to focus on the uniquely human:

- Creativity
- Empathy
- Ethics
- Judgment
- Storytelling
- Leadership
- Moral reasoning

We don't lose purpose—we redefine it.

The Real Question: Will We Evolve Fast Enough?

What we should be asking is not "Will AI replace humans?" but:

- How do we design AI systems that augment human dignity rather than diminish it?
- How do we retrain and reposition workers before disruption hits?
- How do we ethically distribute the gains of AI-driven productivity?
- How do we rethink education for a world where knowledge is abundant, but discernment is rare?
- How do we retain agency in a world where decisions are increasingly automated?

These are not questions for engineers alone.

They are questions for philosophers, educators, designers, policy makers, parents, and citizens.

Because the future of work is not binary—human or machine.

It is hybrid.

Reflection Point: The Machine and the Mirror

What do the lives of Einstein, Da Vinci, Franklin, and Jobs teach us: it is that the story of innovation is never about the machine.

It is about the mirror the machine holds up to us.

AI is not asking, "Can I do what you do?"

It's asking, "Do you still know what makes you you?"

To say that AI will replace humans is to miss the deeper transformation underway. We are not at the end of something. We are at the threshold of reinvention—of our work, our institutions, and our imagination.

Whether that becomes a chapter of loss or a renaissance of potential is not up to the algorithm.

It's up to us.

PART II: AI ACROSS INDUSTRIES – A SECTOR-BY-SECTOR CHRONICLE

Part II

AI Across Industries – A Sector-by-Sector Chronicle

The steam engine reshaped factories. Electricity rewired cities. Artificial intelligence is rewiring industries—not by breaking them, but by reimagining what they're for.

There's a famous story about the early days of electrification. When factories first replaced steam with electric motors, productivity didn't spike. Why? Because they kept placing the new motors in the exact spot where the old engines had been. It wasn't until they redesigned the entire factory layout—rethinking workflow, structure, even purpose—that electricity became revolutionary.

Today, we're witnessing the same hesitation with artificial intelligence.

Executives plug in AI where the spreadsheet used to sit. Teams ask it to do what interns once did. Doctors treat it as a smarter search bar. Writers as a faster assistant.

But the industries that will truly thrive are not the ones that add AI to existing workflows. They're the ones that reshape what the industry is for—from first principles, through the lens of intelligent systems.

From Infrastructure to Intelligence

What makes this transformation different from previous tech shifts is that AI is not a tool of one trade. It is fluid, cross-disciplinary, and industry-agnostic.

It doesn't just live in labs. It lives in:

- The operating room
- The call center
- The trading desk

- The classroom
- The tractor
- The courtroom
- The film edit suite
- The pharmaceutical pipeline

Wherever there is data, repetition, complexity, or language, AI finds a foothold. And the result isn't uniform automation. It's divergent reinvention.

In finance, AI becomes a risk whisperer.

In healthcare, a pattern detector.

In education, a personalized tutor.

In agriculture, a predictive prophet of soil and season.

In entertainment, both muse and mimic.

Each sector responds differently because it is built on distinct types of knowledge, traditions, and resistance.

Industry as Canvas

Consider this: If you were painting this chapter, you might not start with a line of code. You'd better begin with a human.

Picture this: Perhaps a doctor in Mumbai who uses AI to triage patient data during a dengue outbreak. Or a music producer in Seoul who builds beats with an algorithm trained on 70 years of jazz. Or a farmer in Kansas whose tractor now reads satellite data as it plants.

You would find that innovation, when it truly lands, doesn't feel like science fiction. It feels like work changing—quietly, then all at once.

And that's the story of Part II.

Not abstract forecasts. Not technological theory. But a ground-level chronicle of how industries are being reshaped—sector by sector, worker by worker, question by question.

What You'll Find in This Part

Each chapter in this section focuses on one industry, and each follows a common structure:

- A snapshot of the industry before AI
- How AI is now being used—tools, use cases, and frontier innovations
- The opportunities unlocked and the jobs reshaped
- The risks, blind spots, and ethical tensions
- A look ahead at what the industry might become

But this is not just a taxonomy of technologies. It's a biography of impact.

Because when AI meets industry, it doesn't just optimize. It questions fundamentals.

What does it mean to diagnose?

To teach?

To govern?

To design?

To serve?

Reading the Chronicle Ahead

You may want to start with the industry you know. Perhaps you're in pharma, or law, or logistics. But keep reading.

Because the secret of AI's disruption is not confined to any one field—it's the pattern of change, the rhythm of resistance, and the language of adaptation that repeats across domains.

That's where the insight lies not just in what AI can do—but in how humans in each domain choose to respond.

So let us begin.

From hospitals to hedge funds, factories to film studios, courtrooms to classrooms—AI is not coming.

It is already here.

And the industries that understand that best will not merely survive.

They will lead.

Chapter 4

Healthcare and Pharma – From Molecules to Models

When AI enters medicine, it doesn't just change how we treat disease. It changes how we understand life.

In 1928, Alexander Fleming came back from vacation and found mold killing bacteria in his petri dish—accidentally discovering penicillin.

Nearly a century later, an AI system discovered an entirely new antibiotic, halicin, by screening millions of molecules in silico—in hours, not decades.

In that shift lies a parable of our time: from serendipity to simulation, from Eureka to algorithm.

The field of medicine—long considered sacred, methodical, and human—has now become one of the most ambitiously disrupted by artificial intelligence. And not just in one place. Across the entire chain of care—from bench to bedside, from molecules to models, and from diagnosis to delivery—AI is being woven into the fabric of healthcare and pharmaceutical innovation.

But while the transformation is technological, the stakes are not.

They are human.

Drug Discovery: Cracking the Code of Chemical Space

The traditional path of drug development is famously long, expensive, and inefficient. It can take 10–15 years, cost over $2 billion, and result in 90% of drugs failing in clinical trials.

Enter AI.

- Startups like Insilico Medicine, Atomwise, and BenevolentAI now deploydeep learning to predict molecular interactions, design novel compounds, and even prioritize targets that would have been invisible to the human eye.

- DeepMind's AlphaFold, in 2021, predicted the 3D structures of over 200 million proteins—a seismic leap that would have once taken a generation.
- Pfizer utilized AI modeling to expedite vaccine design during the COVID-19 pandemic. What would have taken months in wet labs was simulated in days.

When you think about it, this marks a shift as fundamental as the invention of the microscope: from observing biology to programming it.

Clinical Trials and Real-World Evidence

AI isn't just redesigning the molecules—it's rewriting the method of testing them.

- Natural language processing tools now scan patient records to identify ideal trial candidates, particularly for rare diseases.
- Digital twins—virtual models of patients—simulate how a person might respond to a drug, enabling adaptive trials and personalized protocols.
- Wearable data and real-world evidence platforms, such as those pioneered by Roche and Apple, track patient outcomes outside the clinic, enriching datasets with unprecedented granularity.

The traditional linear trial model—Phase I, II, III—is giving way to continuous, dynamic learning systems. AI doesn't just measure—it adapts.

And that changes not just the trial. It changes how trust is built.

Diagnostics: The Machine that Sees

If a picture is worth a thousand words, then an AI trained on a million images can spot what no radiologist might.

- Lunit in South Korea and Qure.ai in India have trained algorithms to detect tuberculosis, lung nodules, and strokes with comparable or superior accuracy to human specialists.
- AI tools are now used in dermatology, retinopathy, cardiology, and even mental health, where voice analysis may detect early signs of depression.

But even the most accurate system raises the same question:

"What is the role of human judgment when machines outperform intuition?"

For many physicians, AI is not a threat—it's a second set of eyes. But it's also a mirror, reminding them of their own fallibility.

Patient Engagement and the AI Bedside Manner

In a quiet corner of a hospital in Boston, an AI assistant helps a Parkinson's patient manage medications, answer questions, and schedule appointments—all via voice.

Elsewhere, GPT-based health chatbots answer thousands of patient queries per day, lightening the administrative load on overstretched doctors.

But what happens when patients bond with a chatbot when the AI's bedside manner is more consistent than the doctor's?

We enter a strange frontier—where empathy is simulated, and connection is mediated by code.

Can a machine care?

Or is it merely convincing us that it does?

Pharma Marketing: From Push to Precision

AI is reshaping how drugs are not only developed, but also delivered to the market.

Next-best-action algorithms personalize outreach to physicians based on prescribing behavior and patient demographics.

ChatGPT-powered content engines generate tailored messaging for various stakeholders, including HCPs, payers, and patients.

Predictive analytics forecast demand, optimize launch sequencing, and simulate price sensitivity across geographies.

We are moving from mass promotion to micro-personalization. However, it also comes with the risk of manipulation—reducing patients to datasets and care into conversion funnels.

Here again, the line between optimization and exploitation demands scrutiny.

Ethical Frontiers: From Bias to Bioethics

AI in healthcare raises uniquely urgent ethical questions:

- What happens when an algorithm is trained on biased clinical data—and misdiagnoses underrepresented populations?
- Who is liable when an AI-assisted diagnosis is wrong—the model, the hospital, the doctor, or the developer?
- Should patients be told when their treatment is algorithmically guided?

And perhaps most deeply: how do we balance the efficiency of machines with the dignity of care?

Mind you, these aren't peripheral concerns. They are central to the story.

Because medicine is not just about what works, it's about what matters.

The Future: From Healing to Human Augmentation

We are approaching a future where:

- AI predicts illness before symptoms arise
- Virtual health coaches guide daily behavior
- Drugs are designed for your genes, not the average genome
- Hospitals are decentralized, and care happens at home, on devices that learn from you
- Models anticipate pandemics, triage crises, and suggest interventions faster than human systems can

The end goal is not replacement. It is reinvention.

Of the clinic. Of the drug pipeline. Of the very nature of health itself.

Reflection Point: Intelligence Meets Compassion

Remember: true innovation fuses knowledge with humanism.

The risk in AI-powered healthcare is not the rise of cold machines.

It is the abdication of care to algorithms.

The opportunity is not just faster diagnosis or cheaper trials.

It is the chance to redistribute attention—to let machines do what they're good at, so humans can do what only they can: listen, touch, reassure, and choose wisely.

As we move from molecules to models, we must ask not just what we can build.

But why are we building it—and for whom?

AI in Drug Discovery: From Serendipity to Simulation

If the 20th century was about discovering new drugs, the 21st is about designing them—with algorithms that think like chemists, and sometimes better.

For most of modern pharmaceutical history, drug discovery was part science, part luck, and part long, expensive waiting.

Penicillin was discovered by accident. Statins were stumbled upon. Even blockbuster drugs like Viagra began their lives chasing one ailment and ended up curing another.

It was a world built on trial and error, petri dishes, animal models, and multi-year pipelines—where it could take a decade, billions of dollars, and thousands of failures to bring one drug to market.

But in recent years, a different story has begun to unfold—quietly at first, then unmistakably—with the rise of AI-powered drug discovery platforms.

Two names stand out: Exscientia and Atomwise.

And their stories are not just about technology. They are about the transformation of how we search for cures—from randomness to reason, from laboratories to learning systems.

Exscientia: The Philosopher-Scientist's Algorithm

Founded in Oxford in 2012 by Dr. Andrew Hopkins, a biologist who once dreamed of a world where design replaced discovery, Exscientia was built on a simple but radical idea:

What if we could use AI to design drugs from first principles, just like an architect draws blueprints?

Instead of testing thousands of compounds in a lab, Exscientia uses deep learning models to simulate how molecules might interact with biological targets. The platform learns from vast datasets of chemical and genomic information, predicts efficacy and safety, and optimizes for multiple variables—potency, selectivity, toxicity, metabolism—all at once.

In 2020, Exscientia made headlines by developing the first AI-designed drug molecule to enter clinical trials—a compound targeting obsessive-compulsive disorder, in collaboration with Sumitomo Dainippon Pharma. The molecule, DSP-1181, was identified in under 12 months—a process that typically takes five years.

And that wasn't an anomaly.

- In 2021, Exscientia announced a molecule for oncology, which was again discovered using AI.
- By 2023, it had over 25 AI-designed drugs in its pipeline, spanning cancer, inflammation, virology, and other areas.
- In 2024, it unveiled a precision oncology platform that used patient-specific data to match tumor profiles with custom-designed molecules.

Hopkins called it a step toward "autonomous drug design." But his goal wasn't speed alone—it was creativity.

"The machine is not replacing the chemist," he said. "It is the chemist's imagination—at scale."

Atomwise: The Digital Chemist in the Cloud

Across the Atlantic, in San Francisco, another pioneer was taking a different but complementary path.

Founded in 2012 by Abraham Heifets and Izhar Wallach, Atomwise focused on one of the oldest and hardest problems in drug discovery:

How do molecules actually fit together?

Using a deep learning model called AtomNet, Atomwise developed a platform that can simulate how small molecules interact with protein targets. Rather than physically testing tens of thousands of compounds, AtomNet can virtually screen billions, identifying promising candidates in days.

It's a bit like finding the right key for a molecular lock—not by hand, but by unleashing a swarm of digital locksmiths who can test every key in existence, and many that don't exist yet.

And the results have been striking:

- Atomwise partnered with Merck, Bayer, and Eli Lilly, tackling diseases from Ebola to leukemia.
- It helped identify novel inhibitors for proteins that were once considered "undruggable."
- In one case, its AI platform proposed 78 promising compounds to combat multiple sclerosis within 10 days, a task that might have taken a human lab over a year to accomplish.

Heifets often says:

"We're not just speeding up discovery. We're discovering things we would never have found at all."

This is not AI as an optimizer. It's AI as explorer—navigating the chemical universe faster than human cognition can map.

From Data to Drugs: A New Scientific Language

Both Exscientia and Atomwise signal a shift in how we think about thinking in science.

Traditionally, drug discovery has required wet lab experiments, animal testing, and intuition gained from years of experience at the bench. Now, data-rich AI systems can identify subtle correlations, multi-target effects, and toxicity risks before a compound is even synthesized.

And that shift—from reactive testing to proactive simulation—may be as revolutionary as the discovery of DNA.

It changes not just what we can discover, but who can do it. Startups, university labs, and low-resource countries can now leverage cloud-based AI models that were previously limited to pharmaceutical giants.

Reflection Point: Tools and the Soul of Science

In *The Innovators*, Walter Isaacson describes Ada Lovelace's insight that the beauty of the machine lies not in its power, but in its partnership with the human imagination.

The same applies here.

AI will not dream of cures. It will not feel the urgency of a dying patient or the awe of a new compound under a microscope.

But it will help those who do.

It will narrow the search.

It will test the hypotheses.

It will redraw the boundaries of what we can know—and how fast.

And it will force us to ask:

What becomes of science when the spark of discovery is shared with a machine?

Digital Twins & Personalized Medicine

When medicine stops treating the average and begins treating you, the story of healing becomes profoundly personal and beautifully precise.

In the early 2000s, the Human Genome Project was hailed as the Rosetta Stone of modern biology. For the first time, we had the full script of our DNA—a play in 3 billion letters. Scientists hoped it would unlock the secrets of cancer, heart disease, mental illness, and more.

But there was a problem. The genome was like a piano. It told us what could be played, but not what was being played.

What we needed was not just a map, but a model—not just a snapshot of our biology, but a living, breathing replica that could evolve, respond, and help us simulate the consequences of every decision, every treatment, every mutation.

And so, from this need emerged one of the most transformative ideas in the future of healthcare:

The digital twin.

Not a metaphor. Not a metaphorical double.

But an actual computational mirror of you—your genes, your biomarkers, your habits, your physiology—rendered in code.

And with it, the promise of personalized medicine finally became real.

From One-Size-Fits-All to One-in-8-Billion

For decades, medicine has been built on averages.

- The "normal" blood pressure.
- The "typical" dose.
- The "standard" response rate.

But no patient is average. And no disease behaves the same way in two bodies.

When you think about it, genius innovators like Leonardo and Einstein sought the universal through the particular but digital twin does the opposite: it finds the particular in a sea of generalities.

With enough data, a digital twin can simulate:

- How your body will react to a specific cancer drug
- How a surgical intervention might alter your cardiac rhythm
- How changes in diet, sleep, or exercise affect your risk of relapse
- How a rare genetic mutation might express under environmental stress

It is trial and error without the error.

How it Works: The Anatomy of the Twin

Creating a digital twin starts with data but not just any data.

- Genomics: Your inherited blueprint
- Proteomics: How your proteins behave in real time
- Metabolomics: How your body processes fuel and waste
- EHRs: Your entire medical history
- Wearables: Sleep, heart rate, glucose, stress
- Lifestyle factors: Nutrition, environment, stress exposure

This data is fed into multi-scale models algorithms that mimic the behavior of organs, tissues, and cells. These are cross-referenced with population data and machine learning insights to make predictions.

Companies like Siemens Healthineers, Dassault Systèmes, and Philips have pioneered digital twin platforms for cardiology, oncology, and neurology.

One example: A patient with arrhythmia is given a digital model of their heart. Before a procedure is done, simulations are run in milliseconds to determine the optimal intervention point, minimizing risk and maximizing effectiveness.

Another: A twin of a cancer patient is used to simulate different chemo regimens, helping doctors choose the one with the fewest side effects and the greatest survival odds.

This is no longer science fiction.

It is real-world forecasting inside the body.

The Ethics and the Edge

A word of caution here: every innovation comes with a tradeoff.

The power of the digital twin is also its vulnerability. It requires deep access to personal data, continuous surveillance, and trust in algorithmic interpretation.

- Who owns your twin?
- Who insures against its misuse?
- Can a model built on biased data lead to biased treatment?

And deeper still: Can we reduce a human being to a model? Even if that model is stunningly accurate?

The answer lies not in rejecting the technology but in embedding it within the ethical architecture of care.

Toward a World of Personal Medicine for All

Today, most digital twin platforms are primarily found in elite clinics or well-funded trials. But the potential extends far beyond.

In the future:

- A child in rural Africa could have a twin that predicts vaccine response
- A patient in Mumbai could simulate diabetes progression and tailor lifestyle interventions
- An elderly woman in Sweden could model her response to arthritis medication before ever swallowing a pill

This is democratized precision medicine—if we choose to build it that way.

Reflection Point: The Mirror that Heals

Remember: the digital twin is not a replacement for care, but as a mirror crafted by science to better understand ourselves.

In the Renaissance, mirrors were luxury objects symbols of wealth and vanity.

But in the AI age, the most valuable mirror may be one inside us, built of data, models, and insight.

It won't show us how we look.

It will show us how we heal.

And that might be the most human technology of all.

Pharma Marketing Automation and the Ethical Challenges

When the machine learns to persuade, we must ask—not just what it sells, but how, to whom, and why

There's a scene that repeats itself now in pharmaceutical boardrooms and brand strategy meetings around the world.

A product manager opens a dashboard. She sees predictive scores on physician behavior, segmented patient profiles, real-time sentiment from online communities, and a next-best-action algorithm that already suggests which cardiologist in which city should receive a message, via which channel, at what time, with what tone.

She clicks "deploy."

And in milliseconds, thousands of personalized nudges go live—emails, SMS messages, chatbot follow-ups, LinkedIn ads, educational videos tailored to each stakeholder.

No rep, no writer, no traditional approval workflow. Just a machine-driven engine of persuasion—trained on data, optimized for response, automated for scale.

It's efficient. It's effective. And it's already here.

But the key question to ask:

"Is this innovation merely elegant or is it also ethical?"

The Rise of the Algorithmic Marketer

Over the last decade, pharma marketing has undergone a quiet revolution. Once dominated by field reps, printed brochures, and broad-segment campaigns, it is now increasingly powered by AI-based marketing automation platforms.

- Omnichannel orchestration tools, such as Veeva, Salesforce Health Cloud, and Aktana, analyze physician behavior and automate outreach with precision.
- Natural language generation engines draft emails, patient education materials, and promotional content tailored to specialty, geography, and prescribing history.

- Chat GPT-based co-pilots for marketers help create compliant, tone-specific, and even multilingual campaigns in minutes.
- Predictive analytics forecast script lift, sentiment response, and channel fatigue guiding strategy in real time.

This is no longer just about reaching the customer. It's about knowing them deeply, digitally, sometimes intimately.

In the words of one pharma CMO:

"We've gone from marketing to personas to marketing to fingerprints."

From Mass Promotion to Micro-Precision

In the past, a brand campaign might be designed for "Cardiologists, 40–65, urban settings."

- Today, AI marketing systems can create 1:1 adaptive journeys for each physician:
- Which clinical study are they most influenced by?
- What is their preferred channel email, rep visit, podcast, CME portal?
- Are they early adopters or therapeutic conservatives?
- Do they respond to patient-centric messaging or data on the mechanism of action?

Each interaction becomes a data point, each response a signal, each silence a calibration.

The result? Fewer wasted impressions. Greater script lift. Faster time-to-impact.

But also less visibility, less friction, and fewer human gatekeepers.

The Ethical Tensions: Personalization vs. Manipulation

Marketing is, by nature, persuasive. However, when AI systems learn not only what persuades, but also who is most persuadable, a line begins to blur.

- When does segmentation become profiling?
- When does adaptive messaging become behavioral targeting?
- When does "next best action" become predictive influence?

In pharma where the stakes involve life-altering decisions, vulnerable patients, and trusted healthcare professional relationships the ethical weight is heavier.

And the questions are urgent:

- Should a machine suggest which physicians are most likely to switch based on past compliance with detailing?
- Should it detect when a doctor is burned out and adjust the tone of messaging to achieve emotional resonance?
- Should it know when a cancer patient is most receptive to a clinical trial invitation and automate the outreach?

These are not abstract questions. These are now.

And they are rarely answered in product demos.

Regulatory and Trust Frontiers

The current compliance frameworks FDA, EMA, IFPMA codes—were not designed for autonomous systems that learn and adapt.

- Can AI-generated promotional copy be pre-approved if the output varies by user?
- Who is accountable for off-label inference in an AI-generated reply?
- How do you audit a system trained on proprietary physician behavior data?

What we're seeing is not just a tech disruption but a regulatory lag.

And as history shows from the unregulated days of tobacco advertising to the data-hungry days of social media when regulation lags persuasion, trust collapses.

It is important to remember that:

"Innovation without ethical design is not progress. It's a prelude."

Designing for Integrity

The challenge is not to abandon automation. It is to humanize it through transparency, accountability, and design ethics.

Some companies are taking steps:

- AI audit trails to log why a message was sent, and to whom.
- Digital marketing ethics boards to review personalization thresholds.
- Human-in-the-loop systems where AI suggests, but humans decide.
- Consent architectures that allow physicians to shape their own experience.

But these are early efforts. What's needed is a shared code of conduct an ethical "label" on AI-driven marketing akin to informed consent.

Because at its best, pharma marketing automation can educate, empower, and enhance relationships.

However, at its worst, it can exploit vulnerabilities in ways that no human marketer would dare—not out of malice, but out of necessity, driven by optimization.

Reflection Point: Selling with Conscience

It is essential to recall that Steve Jobs fused technology with humanity—not just asking "Can we build it?" but also "Should we?"

In the same spirit, we must ask:

- What is pharma marketing for in the age of AI?
- Is it to move product, or to build understanding?
- Is the physician a target, or a partner?
- Is the patient a segment, or a soul?

If we get the answers wrong, AI will amplify our worst habits.

But if we get them right, AI could help usher in a new kind of marketing responsible, relational, and rooted in care.

Not just smarter.

But wiser.

A Code of Conduct for Ethical Pharma Marketing Automation

"The measure of intelligence is not just in what we build, but how we wield it—with restraint, respect, and responsibility."

When you chronicle the rise of the digital age from Steve Jobs to Jennifer Doudna you return often to a moral inflection point: the moment when capability outpaces conscience.

In pharmaceutical marketing, AI-based automation is reaching a critical point.

It can now identify physician sentiment from social posts.

It can predict which HCPs are likely to switch prescribing behavior.

It can craft hyper-targeted messages in seconds.

It can personalize at scale, optimize in real-time, and measure across touchpoints.

But can it do all this ethically?

To answer that, we don't just need policies. We need principles—a modern-day Hippocratic Oath for machines that persuade.

The Ethical Automation Charter: A 10-Point Code of Conduct

1. **Human-in-the-Loop by Design**

   AI can suggest.

   Humans must decide.

   Every automated touchpoint be it content, targeting, or channel—should offer human oversight before deployment, not as an afterthought, but as the default.

2. **Informed Consent as a First Principle**

   Just as patients consent to treatment, HCPs and patients should consent to engagement.

   Offer transparency into:

   - How their data is used
   - What content they will receive
   - How frequently they'll be contacted

   Consent isn't a checkbox. It's a contract.

3. **Transparency of Algorithms**

   Black-box models undermine trust.

Explainable AI — why a certain HCP was targeted or a message was chosen—must be documented and auditable.

Build for clarity, not just cleverness.

4. **Contextual Sensitivity**

   A cancer diagnosis.

   A child in critical care.

   A physician navigating burnout.

   Marketing automation must recognize emotional context and decelerate when sensitivity is required.

   Optimization without empathy is exploitation.

5. **Guardrails Against Manipulation**

   AI can learn what makes people click. However, it should never exploit vulnerabilities whether it be fear, urgency, or cognitive bias.

   Prohibit:

   - Emotionally coercive copy
   - Fake scarcity or misleading claims
   - Hyper-targeting based on psychological fragility

   This isn't retail. This is healthcare.

6. **Bias Audits and Equity Reviews**

   If your data reflects historical inequities, your AI will replicate them.

   Conduct regular audits for:

   - Bias against rural or underserved populations
   - Language bias in message delivery
   - Over-targeting high-prescribing physicians over newer voices

   Inclusion isn't optional. It's ethical hygiene.

7. **Patient-Centric Messaging**

   Even when marketing to HCPs, the patient voice must be honored.

   Avoid:

   - Over-medicalized, jargon-heavy language
   - Content that minimizes risk for the sake of persuasion
   - DTC campaigns that feel like "ads," not support

   Speak with, not just to.

8. **Audit Trails and Accountability Logs**

   Every AI-driven campaign must leave a digital breadcrumb trail.

   Log:

   - Who approved it
   - What data triggered it
   - What changes were made by the algorithm

   If it can't be reviewed, it shouldn't be deployed.

9. **Continuous Learning, Not Just Continuous Targeting**

   Pharma AI systems should not only learn from user behavior but also from ethical incidents, flagged errors, and feedback loops.

   Incorporate:

   - Ethics dashboards
   - Internal red flag systems
   - Learning cycles that include human values

10. **Purpose-Driven Use, Not Just Performance-Driven Use**

    The fundamental question isn't "How well did it work?"

    It's "Was it right to use?"

    Tie every automation decision back to the core purpose:

    "To educate, to support, and to improve human health."

    When in doubt, pause.

    Remember: Steve Jobs insisted the circuit boards inside the original Mac be beautiful, even though users would never see them.

    That is the spirit this charter invites:

    Ethics as internal architecture.

    Not because it's visible. But because it's right.

Predictive Analytics in Real-World Evidence and Trial Design

We used to find answers in controlled labs. Now we find truth in the messy, magnificent wildness of the real world.

For decades, the gold standard in pharmaceutical research was the Randomized Controlled Trial (RCT) – rigid, pristine, and often disconnected from the real world.

RCTs were designed for internal validity. But they rarely captured diversity, variability, and complexity.

They told us how drugs worked in theory, not always in practice.

Then came real-world evidence (RWE).

And now, AI-powered predictive analytics is turning RWE into a compass—reorienting drug development, trial design, and regulatory strategy.

The RWE Data Boom

Sources like:

- Electronic Health Records (EHRs)
- Claims data
- Wearables
- Genomic datasets
- Social health platforms
- Patient-reported outcomes

...have exploded in scale. But data alone isn't a transformation.

Prediction is.

Enter AI.

Machine learning algorithms can now detect:

- Early efficacy signals across populations
- Patterns of off-label use and outcomes
- Predictors of dropout in clinical trials
- Regional variations in drug response
- Socioeconomic factors influencing adherence

And more importantly:

They can simulate trial outcomes before the trial even begins.

Case in Point: Pfizer's AI-Augmented Trial Simulation

In its COVID-19 vaccine development, Pfizer used AI modeling on RWE datasets to simulate different population responses, estimate dropout rates, and adjust trial designs dynamically cutting timelines without compromising rigor.

The result? A process that used to take years was compressed into months without sacrificing safety.

How Predictive Analytics Reinvents Trial Design?

1. **Synthetic Control Arms**

   Instead of assigning half of the trial patients to a placebo, RWE can simulate their expected outcomes, thereby reducing risk, cost, and ethical dilemmas.

2. **Dynamic Eligibility Criteria**

   AI can predict who is likely to benefit or drop out based on EHR and behavioral data, helping optimize recruitment.

3. **Site Selection Optimization**

   Machine learning models identify regions with higher patient concentrations, better adherence rates, and lower attrition.

4. **Real-Time Protocol Adaptation**

   Using streaming data from wearables or digital endpoints, trials can adapt dosing, frequency, or cohort segmentation in real-time.

Regulatory and Ethical Evolution

Agencies such as the FDA, EMA, and PMDA are now issuing frameworks for the acceptable use of RWE in regulatory submissions. The 21st Century Cures Act opened the door but AI is pushing it wide open.

However, ethical caveats remain:

Is the RWE data representative, or biased by access and geography?

- Can predictive models be audited for fairness?
- Are patients aware that their data is shaping trials they never joined?

The solution isn't to halt progress.

It's to embed reflection into design.

Reflection Point: From Certainty to Complexity

Some of the best minds thrived in ambiguity—Da Vinci, Franklin, Doudna. Those who embraced messiness as insight.

RWE is messy.

Real patients don't follow protocols.

They forget doses. They move cities. They switch physicians.

But within that noise is the truth of medicine in motion.

AI doesn't make the world neater.

It helps us learn from its chaos.

And in doing so, we don't just build better trials.

We build more humane science.

AI in Medical Affairs and MSL Transformation

When machines learn to listen more effectively than we speak, and to speak with greater empathy than we expect, the role of the medical expert must evolve not vanish.

In every technological revolution, there are those roles we assume will be eliminated and those we assume are untouchable.

For decades, Medical Science Liaisons (MSLs) belonged to the second category.

They were trusted scientific bridges. Relationship builders. Peer-to-peer educators.

Not sales reps. Not marketers. But the conscience of the company, bringing evidence, nuance, and clarity to physicians who didn't want a pitch, but a partner.

But then came AI. Not the cold, robotic kind.

The kind that could read 100,000 clinical papers overnight.

The kind that could predict a KOL's interest before the first email was sent.

The kind that could simulate a medical conversation before a real one began.

Suddenly, the MSL's world was no longer untouched.

From Field Force to Intelligence Force

For years, the MSL role was defined by the time spent in the field and the depth of knowledge.

The best MSLs were those who knew both the data and the doctor.

But AI flipped the script.

At Novartis, an internal experiment with natural language processing (NLP) tools allowed MSLs to auto-generate personalized scientific decks based on HCP preferences, prior interactions, and recent publications. What took a day now took a minute.

At AstraZeneca, predictive analytics helped MSL teams prioritize KOL engagement not by geography or territory, but by influence networks—who other doctors listened to.

MSLs were no longer just delivering knowledge.

They were becoming part of a knowledge engine.

Four Shifts in the AI-Powered Medical Affairs World

1. **From Reactive to Predictive Engagement**

   Before:

   An MSL met with an oncologist and then followed up if the doctor showed interest in the Phase III trial.

   Now:

   AI tools analyze the oncologist's publication history, social sentiment, and network affiliations, predicting interest before the meeting occurs.

   One startup, QuantHealth, even models how a given KOL is likely to interpret trial data based on prior decision behavior. MSLs use this to tailor conversations before the first "hello."

2. **From Content Delivery to Contextual Co-Creation**

   MSLs used to rely on slide decks approved months ago.

   Today, AI co-pilots like Microsoft's BioGPT or Med-PaLM can instantly summarize recent journal articles, identify gaps in evidence, and suggest analogies to explain complex mechanisms to different specialties.

   MSLs now walk into meetings with living content adaptable, interactive, and hyper-relevant.

   They're no longer messengers. They're sense-makers.

3. **From HCP Segmentation to Influence Mapping**

   AI-powered network analysis tools (like those used by BenevolentAI and H1 Insights) allow medical affairs teams to map not just KOLs, but KOL constellations — the entire web of influence, conversation, and knowledge flow.

   Suddenly, a physician in a rural area who writes few papers but influences 40 others becomes more critical than the most published voice in Manhattan.

   AI reveals quiet power, not just loud prestige.

4. **From Meeting Logs to Insight Engines**

   Previously, MSLs filed post-meeting notes into CRMs.

Today, voice-to-text AI transcribes conversations, extracts key themes, and flags emerging unmet needs.

Medical Affairs can now aggregate insights across thousands of interactions to detect trends in resistance, formulation challenges, or patient-reported outcomes well before the commercial team or R&D sees them.

Insight becomes proactive, not retrospective.

The Role Redefined, Not Replaced

When you think about it, the best innovation stories are not about replacement—but reimagination.

The violin did not replace the human voice.

The iPhone did not replace relationships—it rechanneled them.

Likewise, AI will not replace the MSL.

However, it will require that the MSL become more than just a field scientist.

The new MSL is part:

- Data interpreter
- Strategic communicator
- Digital co-pilot operator
- Real-time insight synthesizer
- Ethical steward

This isn't a downgrade. It's an upgrade—in depth, scope, and impact.

Ethical Front lines: Conversations with Consequence

But with power comes ethical tension.

- What happens if an AI biases outreach toward only top-tier institutions, ignoring community doctors?
- If an MSL uses AI-generated literature summaries, who ensures accuracy and neutrality?
- When real-time dashboards show who's prescribing what, how do you avoid the slippery slope into promotional pressure?

To mitigate this, leading firms are building AI Governance Boards within Medical Affairs. These include ethicists, physicians, data scientists, and patients.

Because when the message matters as much as the molecule, how you engage becomes as important as what you say.

Reflection Point: Humanity in the Loop

In his biography of Jennifer Doudna, Isaacson described how CRISPR gave us the ability to edit life itself, but it was the human debates—the ethics, the pause, the perspective that gave the story its gravitas.

The same is true here.

Medical Affairs may become more data-driven, more efficient, more predictive.

But its soul, the commitment to science, trust, and care—must remain human.

The MSL of tomorrow will use AI not to replace their voice, but to refine its clarity.

Not to accelerate blindly, but to engage wisely.

Not to scale indiscriminately, but to listen better.

And that at the intersection of technology and trust—is where medicine's next great storytellers will live.

AI in Diagnostics and Clinical Decision Support

It was not about teaching machines to think like doctors. It was about teaching doctors to think with machines.

Every era of medicine has been marked by one key advance in how we see.

The stethoscope let doctors hear what was once inaudible.

- The X-ray made the invisible visible.
- The CT scan gave cross-sectional truths to complex puzzles.
- And now, AI gives us something even more elusive: the probable.

Not just what is seen or heard. But what is likely?

Not just what is true today. But what may be true tomorrow?

And in that shift from sensing to synthesizing AI is transforming diagnosis and clinical decision support from art alone to augmented intelligence.

The New Diagnostic Partner: Pattern Overload Meets Pattern Recognition

In 2016, a Japanese woman baffled her physicians. Months of misdiagnoses, a constellation of nonspecific symptoms. Finally, her genome was uploaded into IBM Watson's prototype diagnostic engine. Within minutes, Watson flagged a rare leukemia subtype, along with evidence citations and potential treatment paths.

It wasn't magic. It was machine reading at scale.

AI excels where human cognition buckles:

- Parsing hundreds of variables
- Recognizing invisible correlations
- Remembering millions of prior cases
- Staying current with thousands of weekly publications

What once took hours of literature searching or trial and error now takes seconds.

The differential diagnosis no longer ends with "best guess"—but with a ranked probability distribution.

In radiology, AI systems like Aidoc, Viz.ai, and Qure.ai now outperform junior doctors in detecting brain bleeds, pulmonary embolisms, and lung nodules on scans.

But perhaps the real story is not AI replacing the radiologist, but redirecting them from sifting to synthesizing, from reading to reasoning.

Clinical Decision Support: Second Opinions at Machine Scale

CDS systems aren't new. However, they were often clunky—interruptive pop-ups in EHRs, generic alerts that were easily ignored.

Today's AI-powered CDS is different.

- It's context-aware: Adapting suggestions based on patient history, comorbidities, and physician specialty.
- It's real-time: Monitoring live vitals and labs to warn of deterioration before it happens.
- It's conversational: Integrated into voice assistants that communicate with doctors in natural language.

Companies like Tempus, Cleerly, DeepMind Health, and Atropos Health are reimagining how we guide medical judgment—not to override clinicians, but to nudge them with precision.

At Mayo Clinic, AI flagged sepsis hours before nurses noticed. At Mount Sinai, deep learning systems predicted COVID deterioration with 80% accuracy. In rural India, chest X-rays run through Qure.ai's algorithm detect TB faster than many overburdened clinicians can.

The net effect?

Doctors aren't losing agency.

They're gaining foresight.

The Judgment Layer: Why AI Still Needs the Human

Human history consistently reminds us: the most powerful tools are those grounded in judgment.

So it is with AI in diagnosis.

AI can spot pneumonia on a scan.

But only the doctor knows if it's pneumonia in a terminal cancer patient—and how aggressively to treat.

AI can predict stroke risk with uncanny accuracy.

But only the clinician sees the caregiver struggling at the bedside and decides what compassionate care actually means.

In this new paradigm, doctors don't abdicate judgment.

They refine it, informed by a data engine that never sleeps, never forgets, and sees the forest and the trees.

Myths, Realities, and Resistance

Some say:

"AI will replace the diagnostician."

As the history of inventions in every domain from the invention of the personal computer to CRISPR gene editing reminds us, the future belongs not to machines or humans, but to those who master the partnership.

The real risks are not robotic errors.

They are:

- Data bias (trained on the majority populations, misdiagnosing minorities)
- Over-reliance (clinicians trusting the machine over their own instincts)
- Liability ambiguity (when AI errs, who's responsible?)
- Black-box opacity (when algorithms make recommendations, but can't explain them)

The lesson?

Transparency, training, and ethics must be built into the diagnostic toolbox by design.

From AI-Haves to AI-for-All

Currently, many of these tools are available in elite hospitals, pilot programs, and cutting-edge startups.

But what happens when we scale?

- In Sub-Saharan Africa, where radiologists are scarce, AI readers could triage X-rays.

- In overburdened primary care clinics in Detroit or Delhi, AI CDS could flag urgent cases before it's too late.
- In elder care homes, continuous monitoring via AI could detect silent deterioration.

This isn't a technological fantasy. It's a public health imperative.

Reflection Point: Diagnosing with Empathy and Algorithms

When you think about it, the true beauty of AI in diagnostics is not in the machine's intelligence, but in its humility.

Because for the first time in history, medicine has a tool that says:

"I've seen this before, even if you haven't."

"I've read every paper on this subject, even if you couldn't."

"Here's what might be happening. But you, doctor, must decide what it means."

That is not replacing human judgment.

That is honoring it with deeper sight.

And as we stand at the cusp of this AI-infused future, perhaps the greatest diagnostic test we face is one for ourselves:

Can we harness this power not just to heal faster, but to care more effectively?

Because the best diagnoses don't just identify disease.

They illuminate the path to wholeness.

AI in Imaging and Pathology: The Lens of the Invisible

The great artists painted with pigments. The great scientists painted with light. Today, AI paints with data—revealing what the human eye missed and the human mind must now understand.

Somewhere in the heart of a busy hospital, a radiologist scrolls through hundreds of chest scans—each image a grayscale landscape of uncertainty. A missed shadow here, a faint opacity there—and a life can pivot toward tragedy or relief.

In another room, a pathologist peers through a microscope at a biopsy slide cells coalescing in shapes both familiar and deceptive. One blink, one moment of fatigue, and a cancer could be missed—or imagined.

This is not the failure of the human mind.

It is its limit.

And now, AI is expanding that limit.

From Roentgen to Resolution: A History of Seeing More

In 1895, Wilhelm Roentgen accidentally discovered X-rays. It was the first time in history that man could see inside himself without cutting flesh.

But while we've since leapt from X-rays to MRIs, from PET scans to digital pathology, the one constant has remained:

The image is only as good as the interpreter.

What AI offers is not new light, but new sight.

Where the human eye is biased toward symmetry and salience, AI detects patterns in chaos, discerns signals in noise, and identifies gradients of probability.

As Walter Isaacson chronicled in *The Innovators*, it's often the partnership between the visionary and the computational that triggers revolutions. In radiology and pathology, we are witnessing that moment now.

Imaging Revolution: Pixel by Pixel, Lesion by Lesion

AI in imaging is not one monolith. It's an ecosystem of capabilities:

- Detection: AI flags subtle anomalies such as lung nodules, brain bleeds, and breast microcalcifications that even senior radiologists might miss.
- Segmentation: It outlines the exact size and shape of tumors, vessels, or organs for surgical planning.Classification: It predicts whether a lesion is benign or malignant, based on texture, edge sharpness, and AI-learned features invisible to the naked eye.
- Progression Tracking: It compares images over time, pixel by pixel, to assess the rate of disease progression or regression.

Companies like Aidoc, Zebra Medical Vision, HeartFlow, Lunit, and Qure.ai have developed FDA-approved tools that now assist in the detection of strokes, pulmonary embolisms, bone fractures, and more with speed measured in seconds, not hours.

In a world where minutes mean life or death, this is not a luxury.

It is a lifeline.

Pathology: When the Slide Speaks to the Silicon

If radiology is about anatomy, pathology is about cellular truth.

For over a century, pathologists have used microscopes to study tissue. They've hunted for mitotic figures, nuclear pleomorphism, staining patterns—each detail a whisper of what lies ahead for the patient.

But these interpretations, while steeped in experience, are also susceptible to fatigue, subjectivity, and information overload.

Enter AI-powered digital pathology.

Whole slide imaging (WSI) turns a tissue biopsy into a high-resolution image. Deep learning algorithms then analyze these slides for:

- Cancer subtypes
- Grading and staging
- Margins of resection
- Molecular profile correlations
- Predictive biomarkers for therapy selection

At Google Health, an AI model achieved 94.6% accuracy in identifying metastatic breast cancer in lymph node biopsies, surpassing the average performance of pathologists.

At Paige.AI, algorithms trained on tens of thousands of slides now assist in detecting prostate cancer, even in ambiguous cases where human experts disagree.

At PathAI, platforms are being used not only for diagnosis but also to predict responses to immunotherapy by analyzing the tumor microenvironment.

This is not just a better diagnosis.

This is personalized prognostication—at scale.

What Machines Can See, But Humans Must Decide

However, remember that with every innovation comes the risk of overreach.

- Can an AI understand clinical context?
- Does it know the patient's story?
- Can it weigh a probabilistic risk against an anxious family or a patient's spiritual readiness?

The answer, as always, is no.

But that's not a weakness of AI.

It's the strength of the human.

The ideal future is not radiologist or AI.

It's radiologist + AI.

It's the pathologist with a second opinion in silicon.

It's the clinician who listens to both—the patient's breath and the algorithm's hum.

Equity, Bias, and the Ethical Gaze

A concern looms large: What if the algorithm sees wrong?

When models are trained on homogeneous datasets, they may miss disease patterns in underrepresented populations. Studies have shown that AI can underperform on scans from Black, Hispanic, or pediatric patients if not properly trained.

To see truly, AI must be trained not just on data, but on diverse data—spanning ethnicities, geographies, disease variations, and health systems.

As Isaacson reminds us, the greatest innovators Doudna, Jobs, Turing—understood that technology amplifies human values. If we want equity, we must encode it.

Reflection Point: Seeing Beyond the Image

The stories of all great inventors and inventions tell us that invention is not an end, but a mirror.

In that sense, AI in imaging and pathology is our modern mirror. It shows us what we've missed. It shows us what matters. Above all, it demonstrates the power of collaboration.

Where the machine sees pixels, the doctor sees people.

Where AI recognizes patterns, the human must provide meaning.

Where the code flags a lesion, the clinician must ask:

"What is the right next step for this person, at this moment, in this life?"

Because ultimately, even the most perfect image is just a starting point.

The real diagnosis happens in the heart not just in the eye.

AI in Surgical Robotics and Pre-operative Planning: When Machines Learn to Cut?

Every great leap in medicine comes when the hand becomes an extension of the mind. With AI in surgery, the hand now also holds memory, prediction, and the quiet hum of machine intelligence.

In the summer of 1999, an unusual partnership was forged between the surgeon's intuition and the engineer's ambition. That year, Intuitive Surgical introduced the da Vinci Surgical System. This robotic platform would enable a human surgeon to sit at a console and operate robotic arms to perform laparoscopy with stunning precision.

The promise then was stability. No tremor. No fatigue. Just precision.

But what if the robot could predict where to cut?

What if it could learn the soft resistance of tissue?

What if, over time, it could understand anatomy as well as a seasoned surgeon?

That's no longer science fiction.

That's AI-driven surgical robotics and it's rapidly becoming the new standard.

From Mechanics to Intelligence

The earliest surgical robots were no more than finely tuned machines—obedient arms that followed the surgeon's every command. They didn't make decisions. They didn't offer insights. They never asked questions.

Today, things have changed.

With the infusion of artificial intelligence, surgical robotics has entered a new era one defined not just by motion, but by cognition.

Take, for instance, CMR Surgical's Versius system, or Medtronic's Hugo, or the soon-to-arrive platforms from J&J's Verb Surgical, built in collaboration with Google's DeepMind. These are no longer just motion-control devices. They are learning systems.

Using thousands of hours of recorded surgeries, these robots train deep learning models to:

- Recognize anatomical landmarks in real-time
- Predict complications before they arise
- Adjust grip pressure or tool movement based on the texture or resistance of tissue
- Suggest optimal suturing paths
- Simulate outcomes based on intraoperative decisions

In short, they become more than tools. They become co-pilots.

Preoperative Planning: When AI Prepares the Battlefield

But before the scalpel or robotic scissors touches skin, AI has already been hard at work behind the scenes.

Preoperative planning is undergoing a transformation akin to what Isaacson once described about Steve Jobs: the genius wasn't just in building a sleek computer it was in rethinking the entire experience.

AI now plays a role in:

1. **3D Anatomical Modeling:**

   Patient scans — CT, MRI, ultrasound are fed into algorithms that build personalized anatomical maps. These are not static models. They breathe with predictive insight, showing how organs shift with respiration or how tissue might respond to pressure.

2. **Virtual Simulation and Rehearsal:**

   Just as flight simulators train pilots, AI-powered systems allow surgeons to virtually rehearse the procedure. What-if scenarios can be played out: What happens if blood pressure drops? What if the tumor's margins are broader than expected?

3. **Risk Stratification and Outcome Prediction:**

   AI uses patient-specific data such as age, BMI, comorbidities, and previous surgeries to predict outcomes and suggest adjustments. It helps address the surgeon's main concern: "Will this plan work for this patient?"

   In essence, AI personalizes the surgical blueprint, preparing the human team with precision that no chalkboard or textbook ever could.

Real-World Impact: From Brain to Bone

In neurosurgery, where micromillimeters matter, AI assists with preoperative mapping to avoid damaging cognitive centers during tumor resection.

In orthopedic surgery, companies like Zimmer Biomet integrate AI with robotic limbs to ensure the perfect alignment in knee replacements reducing recovery time.

In spinal surgery, Mazor Robotics uses AI-guided navigation to plan where to place rods and screws with spine-straightening accuracy.

And in each of these, the result is not just better outcomes it's fewer surprises in the operating room. In the world of surgery, that's a revolution.

Important Questions: Who Holds the Scalpel?

What happens to human creativity when machines become collaborators?

This is not just about automation. It's about amplification.

Surgeons aren't being replaced. They are being redefined.

They must now understand data science.

They must question the algorithm's assumptions.

They must decide when to trust the machine—and when to override it.

This is where ethics enters the room. If an AI-assisted robot makes an error, who is responsible? The programmer? The manufacturer? The surgeon?

And will patients consent to procedures where decisions are shaped, in part, by a black-box neural network?

These are no longer philosophical questions. They are being debated in surgical boards, hospital ethics committees, and regulatory bodies from the FDA to the EMA.

Looking Ahead: The Conscious Scalpel

We should end not with certainty but with curiosity.

What if, one day, a surgical AI is smart enough to learn from one surgeon and teach another?

What if it becomes a collective memory of all surgical wisdom—constantly updated, globally distributed?

What if it evolves from a tool… to a teacher?

That's the horizon AI is moving us toward—not just smarter machines, but wiser medicine.

And the question isn't whether AI will take over surgery.

The question is whether we, as humans, will rise to match its intelligence with empathy, its precision with judgment, and its efficiency with wisdom.

That, perhaps, is the next great chapter in the human story.

AI in Clinical Trials and Real-World Evidence

What if the greatest clinical discovery of our time wasn't a new molecule, but a new way to understand data already in plain sight?

In the story of scientific progress, some breakthroughs arrive in petri dishes. Others arrive in patterns visible only to those who know how to see.

For centuries, clinical trials were the gold standard of evidence. They were meticulous, expensive, and often painfully slow. Trials took years, recruited narrowly, and operated within a tightly controlled bubble that excluded more than it included.

But in the 2020s, as the pandemic turned the world into one giant experiment, a quiet revolution accelerated:

Artificial intelligence is beginning to change the way we test, track, and trust medicines.

Not by replacing the scientist.

But by giving the scientist better eyes.

From Lab to Life: RWE and the Rise of the Invisible Trial

Walter Isaacson once described how Leonardo da Vinci could perceive movement in the muscles before anatomists had a vocabulary to describe it. Similarly, AI in clinical research helps us see signals in chaos.

Where traditional trials were bounded, AI allows us to tap real-world evidence (RWE):

- Electronic health records
- Insurance claims
- Wearable data
- Social media sentiment
- Genomics + environmental exposure models

Companies like Flatiron Health, Tempus, and Verantos are using AI to harmonize fragmented, messy, and non-standardized patient data into structured insight. With machine learning, we can now simulate virtual control arms, shorten trial durations, and even predict dropout rates before enrollment begins.

This is not theory it's happening.

When Pfizer ran its COVID-19 vaccine trial, AI was used to:

- Accelerate recruitment
- Monitor safety signals in near real-time
- Analyze subpopulation effects faster than traditional review panels

The result? One of the fastest vaccine trials in history—with scientific rigor intact.

Intelligent Trial Design: From Guesswork to Guided Learning

Traditionally, trial design was a guessing game dressed in protocol.

You picked a dose. You picked endpoints. You hoped the math worked out.

Today, AI is changing that. It simulates multiple arms, multiple endpoints, and adaptive learning curves even before the first subject is enrolled.

Companies like Owkin and Unlearn.AI use synthetic control arms, where historical data replaces placebos. Others, like Deep 6 AI, mine EMRs with NLP (natural language processing) to find the right patient among millions of records cutting recruitment time by up to 80%.

In oncology, where survival is measured in months, this isn't just efficient. It's life-saving.

And the biggest shift?

We're moving from snapshot evidence to streaming evidence—constantly updating as the world evolves.

Important Questions: Can We Trust the Model?

But just as Einstein reminded us, "Not everything that counts can be counted." So too with AI in trials.

Bias is a risk. Algorithms trained on historical data can perpetuate inequalities if uncorrected.

Transparency is a must. Regulatory bodies, such as the FDA and EMA, are grappling with how to validate models that learn as they go.

And ethics must anchor innovation. Can we deny a patient treatment because a black-box model says "low response likelihood"? What if the model is wrong?

These are not just algorithmic challenges. They are human ones.

We must ask not just "What can AI do?"

But: "What should it do?"

AI in Pharma Commercial Strategy

"In the age of intelligence, selling a drug is no longer just about persuasion. It's about precision."

When Steve Jobs launched the iPhone, he didn't just create a phone. He created an interface between person and possibility.

Today, pharma marketers are learning a similar truth:

In a world of data-saturated decision-makers, the traditional broadcast model is no longer effective. The future belongs to those who can deliver the right message to the right stakeholder at the right time through the right channel.

Enter AI.

It is transforming every aspect of the commercial engine—from segmentation and targeting to campaign design, field-force effectiveness, and omnichannel orchestration.

Predictive Sales: From Spray-and-Pray to Surgical Precision

Imagine this: An oncology brand manager wants to identify 1,000 oncologists likely to prescribe a new checkpoint inhibitor. In the past, they would review past prescriptions, geography, and possibly a few specialty codes.

Today, platforms like Aktana, ZS Associates 'REVO, and IQVIA Orchestrated Customer Engagement (OCE) integrate:

- Claims data
- KOL influence graphs
- Content engagement metrics
- EHR notes via NLP
- Rep-to-HCP interaction transcripts

The result? Next Best Action recommendations that are updated daily, predicting not only who to call but also what message, which channel (email, video, face-to-face), and when.

McKinsey found that companies using AI in commercial operations saw a 5–10% lift in sales productivity within the first year.

This is not sales. This is an augmented strategy.

Omnichannel AI: Marketing that Learns in Real-Time

In the digital-first era, AI doesn't just predict what customers want. It listens.

By ingesting click-through rates, page dwell times, social media sentiment, and chatbot queries, AI models help pharma teams:

- Refine messaging dynamically
- Personalize educational journeys for HCPs and patients
- A/B test email campaigns at scale
- Trigger tailored content when a physician shows interest in a specific indication

Take Novartis: Their Data42 platform unifies over 2 million patient-years of data. Coupled with their AI-enabled campaign engines, they optimize brand content across more than 100 touchpoints per prescriber.

And what about compliance?

AI flags non-compliant wording, tracks promotional review processes, and even assists in automating approval workflows—all while keeping a real-time audit trail.

The AI-Powered Rep: Empowered, Not Replaced

A field rep, equipped with an AI dashboard, knows that:

- Dr. Gupta prefers peer-reviewed data sent by email
- Dr. Jackson tends to convert after a 2nd video call
- Dr. Perez hasn't seen the new MOA video despite prescribing similar drugs

Rather than replace reps, AI makes them super human. More informed, more relevant, and more trusted.

True innovation is not about eliminating the human. It's about elevating them. Always.

Strategy in the Age of Intelligence: Leading by Listening

In the past, commercial strategy was annual. Plans were made, budgets locked.

Now, strategy is real-time.

AI helps leadership teams run digital war rooms, visualize patient journeys, and reallocate budget based on campaign responsiveness not quarterly, but daily.

Those who listen closely to data move fast.

Those who move fast win.

Final Reflection: The Soul of Strategy

What remains constant even in this world of intelligence—is the human need to connect. AI can predict behavior, but only humans can inspire trust.

As Steve Jobs designed with empathy, so too must pharma leaders strategize with conscience.

The final advantage isn't in the model.

It's in the meaning.

That is where the future is shaped—not in machines, but in the minds that guide them.

AI in Patient Engagement and Digital Therapeutics

From compliance to connection: How AI is reshaping the patient experience.

In the mid-20th century, medicine was paternal. Doctors prescribed, patients obeyed or didn't. The human body was a passive recipient of pills, and behavior change was a matter of chance, not science.

But today, in a world where smartphones sit in our palms and biosensors wrap around our wrists, a different kind of revolution is unfolding—not in hospitals, but in homes.

Artificial intelligence is giving patients something medicine has never been able to provide before: agency.

From Passive Patients to Digital Participants

When Walter Isaacson chronicled the rise of Steve Jobs, he emphasized not just the device but the interface. Jobs didn't invent the smartphone; he reimagined how we relate to it.

Steve Jobs did far more than simply oversee the invention of the iPhone he fundamentally reimagined the interface and, in doing so, transformed our relationship with technology. Before the iPhone, phones were cluttered with physical buttons and static controls; Jobs insisted on an elegant user experience, featuring a touch-based interface that was intuitive, minimal, and flexible.

Revolutionizing User Interaction

Jobs's belief was that technology should serve people through simplicity and delight, not intimidation. His influence led to the elimination of the physical keyboard in favor of an adaptive touchscreen, allowing each app to present its own custom interface. This made technology accessible to everyone, regardless of technical skill.

Digital therapeutics (DTx) are similar to healthcare in their approach.

Take Pear Therapeutics, whose FDA-approved app for opioid addiction uses cognitive behavioral therapy algorithms, adaptive nudges, and gamified modules to reduce relapse. Or Akili Interactive, whose video game treatment EndeavorRx cleared for ADHD doesn't just teach kids focus; it learns how each child focuses and adapts in real-time.

These aren't apps.

They are software as medicine, coded with empathy and powered by AI.

Precision Nudging: The Rise of Behavioral AI

Remember when Fitbits simply counted steps? Today, AI can tell if you're spiraling into a depressive episode based on sleep, speech, and swipe patterns.

Startups like Woebot Health use conversational AI trained on cognitive therapy to offer on-demand support, guiding users through distress with clinically validated language. Unlike a therapist, Woebot is available at 2 AM when anxiety strikes hardest.

Meanwhile, Propeller Health equips asthma inhalers with AI-powered sensors. If a patient skips a dose, the app checks weather, pollen count, and emotional cues to understand why then suggests personalized nudges.

Think about it: innovation doesn't just answer questions it reframes them.

The old question was: "Did the patient take their meds?"

The new question is: "How can we help them want to?"

Human Touch, Augmented

Critics worry about a dystopian future where robots replace humans. But the most effective AI-powered patient engagement platforms don't replace care—they scale empathy.

Chatbots triage thousands of patient queries, enabling nurses to spend more time on complex care.

AI analyzes speech tone during virtual check-ins to detect loneliness or suicidal ideation.

Virtual assistants read aloud in native languages, reducing disparities for non-English speakers.

Consider Babylon Health, which has deployed AI symptom checkers in refugee camps and underserved areas. The result? Access, equity, and dignity—without needing to build a hospital.

Remember: where innovation is always paired with moral imagination, this is the kind of human-centered intelligence that changes history.

AI in Market Access and Value-Based Pricing

The currency of the future isn't just dollars. It's data that proves value.

The pharmaceutical industry has long been caught in a tug-of-war.

On one end: the cost of discovery, protected by patents and justified by science.

On the other hand, the demand for affordability, driven by payers, governments, and patients.

In this battleground, the most decisive weapon isn't lobbying.

It's evidence of value and that's where AI is shifting the power dynamic.

From Static Pricing to Dynamic Value

Traditionally, pricing in the pharmaceutical industry was part art, part actuarial math. Drugs launched at prices that reflected R&D costs, market demand, and competitive positioning.

Today, however, value-based pricing (VBP) is the new frontier—linking reimbursement to real-world outcomes, not just theoretical efficacy.

And AI is what makes it possible to measure those outcomes in real-time across populations.

Take Novartis 'agreement with NHS England for inclisiran, a cholesterol-lowering drug. The deal? Payment was tied to actual LDL reduction in the population tracked using AI-fed NHS databases.

Or consider Spark Therapeutics, whose gene therapy for a rare form of blindness (priced at $850,000) came with outcome-based rebates. If the therapy failed to work? No full payment.

In the analog era, such contracts were pipe dreams. Today, with AI-driven RWE platforms, they're auditable, traceable, and scalable.

AI as a Pricing Strategist

Firms like Amgen and Sanofi now use AI models to simulate:

- Budget impact scenarios
- QALY-adjusted cost thresholds
- Geographic pricing segmentation
- Longitudinal health outcomes in diverse populations

With these models, pricing isn't a decision.

It's a simulation, tested a thousand times before launch.

Think about it: the key to great leaps lies in seeing invisible patterns—just as relativity revealed the invisible fabric of spacetime, AI reveals economic gravity in pharma: What price leads to sustainable adoption? Where does payer resistance peak? What outcomes are worth paying for?

Value to Whom? The Ethical Dimension

But the AI-driven pricing era comes with its own paradoxes.

- What if AI determines a rare disease treatment is "not cost-effective"?
- Will value-based pricing exclude patients who don't meet the algorithm's profile?
- How do we ensure that AI doesn't encode bias against marginalized groups?

As with all great advances, the challenge is not just building the machine—but steering it wisely.

AI gives us a sharper lens. But what we choose to see—and what we ignore—remains a human choice.

From Access to Equity

Ultimately, AI is not just about maximizing revenue. It can be a force for health equity.

By modeling disease burden across ZIP codes, analyzing social determinants of health, and flagging reimbursement barriers in real time, AI helps pharma:

- Expand patient assistance programs
- Design differential pricing
- Collaborate with payers and regulators on smarter access pathways

Think of it this way:

Where Steve Jobs gave us the tools to communicate better, AI gives us the tools to coordinate better between science, business, and society.

And if we use it right, we won't just sell more drugs.

We'll heal more people.

AI in Supply Chain and Pharma Operations

The veins of the pharmaceutical world are no longer just physical. They are digital, adaptive, and increasingly intelligent.

When a vaccine was developed in record time during the COVID-19 pandemic, the miracle didn't end in the lab. It had to travel—from a factory in Belgium to a clinic in Boston, through a cold chain of unforgiving precision. In this vast network of vials and variables, one force held the entire system together: real-time intelligence.

This is the unsung revolution of artificial intelligence—not in the pill, but in the path the pill takes.

We might begin here not with a machine, but with a map—a global dance of APIs, warehouse scanners, satellite sensors, and blockchain timestamps. In the AI era, logistics is no longer just about moving goods. It's about predicting friction.

The Pre-AI Problem: Fragile and Fragmented

Pharmaceutical supply chains have always been a paradox.

- Highly regulated, yet full of blind spots.
- Global in reach, but siloed in function.
- Mission-critical, but slow to digitize.

Before AI, much of pharma's operational machinery relied on:

- Historical forecasts that assumed past = future
- Spreadsheet-based demand planning
- Human buffers (more inventory, more cost)
- Reactive issue management

The result? Expired stock, delayed shipments, drug shortages, and during crises, full-blown collapses.

Intelligence at Every Node

Now enter AI.

In the hands of companies like Pfizer, GSK, and Roche, AI is transforming the pharma supply chain from linear pipelines to adaptive ecosystems.

Consider predictive demand modeling. Algorithms ingest data from prescriptions, clinic reports, flu forecasts, and even social media trends to predict where medicine will be needed—weeks before human planners would notice.

Or AI-powered warehouse automation:

- Robotic pickers coordinate with machine-learning platforms.
- Computer vision checks packaging integrity in milliseconds.
- IoT sensors feed temperature logs to AI that can halt shipments mid-route if a cold chain breach is imminent.

Consider this: it's the convergence of disciplines—biology, logistics, data science, and ethics—that defines this moment.

End-to-End Visibility: From Molecule to Market

One of the most ambitious transformations is end-to-end traceability. No longer is pharma content with tracking shipments. Now, AI tracks:

- The origin of raw materials (Was that active ingredient from a compliant supplier?)
- The precise environmental conditions of every shipment (Was the insulin vial ever above 8°C?)
- The carbon footprint per SKU
- The probability of disruption in each logistics node due to geopolitical risk, weather, or local regulation changes

Platforms like Blue Yonder, Kinaxis, and NVIDIA's Omniverse Digital Twins now simulate entire supply chains, much like flight simulators, helping operations teams stress-test scenarios before they occur.

From Efficiency to Resilience

In a post-pandemic world, resilience has replaced just-in-time efficiency as the new gold standard.

AI helps pharma:

- Identify dual-sourcing opportunities

- Optimize route changes dynamically based on port congestion
- Predict machine failure in manufacturing (using predictive maintenance AI)
- Balance regulatory risk in different countries

Take Novartis: its "Insight Center" uses AI to track every step of its manufacturing and logistics in real time. If a batch is delayed in Germany, the system suggests which production lines in Slovenia can speed up to compensate—automatically.

This is not efficiency. This is cognitive orchestration.

AI in Manufacturing: The Smart Factory

On the factory floor, AI becomes the heartbeat of continuous manufacturing.

- It tunes bioreactors for cell therapy manufacturing
- It detects anomalies in tablet coatings via high-resolution image analysis
- It runs simulations of process tweaks that might yield higher quality or purity
- It works with digital twins of manufacturing lines to experiment safely in silico

Companies like Sanofi have launched "Factories of the Future"—AI-run plants that reduce deviation by 50%, optimize energy consumption, and retrain models every week with new data.

You might compare this to the early days of the semiconductor fabs—precision meeting iteration, craft meeting code.

Ethical Logistics: Fairness, Access, and Sustainability

But AI also poses operational questions of ethics:

- Should delivery priority go to more profitable markets or more vulnerable populations?
- Will AI-based cost optimization reduce access in rural or underserved regions?
- Can AI help reduce pharmaceutical waste, not just for cost but for the climate?

Startups like PharmAccess and Zipline are using AI to power drone delivery networks in sub-Saharan Africa, optimizing the distribution of critical medications to remote clinics in minutes, not days.

Others are using AI to redistribute near-expiry stock before it's wasted—ensuring better stewardship of resources and improved health equity.

This is where innovation meets responsibility.

From Backend to Boardroom

AI in supply chain is no longer a "back-office" function.

- It's shaping the launch strategy
- Informing market timing
- Redefining competitive advantage

The companies that succeed in this AI-powered world will not just have better products. They will have better systems for delivering those products, faster, fairer, and more efficiently than ever before.

In pharma, as in history, the unsung logistics win wars.

Now, they are winning health.

Timeline: The Intelligent Molecule – AI's Journey Across the Pharma Value Chain

Great revolutions don't arrive all at once. They ripple. And the most profound ones quietly transform every link in the chain until the entire system begins to think.

2012 – Deep Learning's Spark Meets Drug Discovery

In a Montreal lab, Geoffrey Hinton's breakthroughs in deep learning suddenly made pattern recognition machines smarter than ever. Across the Atlantic, scientists at startups like Atomwise and Exscientia began asking a radical question:

Could we train AI to sift through molecular libraries the way Google sifts through webpages?

That year, Atomwise developed the first deep learning model for structure-based drug design. For the first time, neural networks were able to predict how molecules bind to proteins.

Value Chain Impact: Discovery & Preclinical

Insight: When intuition meets iteration, the blackboard gives way to the neural net.

2015 – AI Enters Clinical Trial Design

At a Janssen R&D meeting, a recurring frustration echoed: patient recruitment delays.

That year, Trials.ai and Antidote emerged, utilizing AI to optimize trial protocols and match real patients to inclusion criteria—faster, cheaper, and more fair.

Meanwhile, IBM Watson Health launched bold trials in oncology trial design. Some stumbled, but the idea was planted: data could redesign experimentation itself.

Value Chain Impact: Clinical Trials

Insight: It wasn't just about accelerating trials—it was about teaching trials to learn.

2017 – Logistics Gets a Brain

At Pfizer's Global Supply Chain Control Tower, AI models began predicting supply chain bottlenecks based on weather, labor, and demand signals.

Around the same time, Sanofi launched its "Factory of the Future" in Framingham, where robots, IoT sensors, and machine learning algorithms produced biologics in a digitally twinned environment.

Value Chain Impact: Manufacturing & Distribution

Insight: Just as Henry Ford once streamlined production, AI now simulates every node—before reality catches up.

2018 – Pharma Marketing Meets the Algorithm

Sales reps once carried samples. Now, they carried data.

With Salesforce Einstein, Veeva Systems, and other platforms, reps were told which HCP to call, what message to say, and when—not by their managers, but by an algorithm trained on prescription behavior, location, and engagement patterns.

Pharma brand teams began using AI for message personalization, sentiment analysis, and campaign optimization.

Value Chain Impact: Marketing & Commercial Strategy

Insight: Where Madison Avenue met Cambridge Analytica, pharma found a new persuasion tool—but also a new ethical boundary.

2019 – Real-World Evidence Gets Real-Time

The FDA's growing acceptance of real-world evidence (RWE) opened a new frontier.

Companies like Aetion, Flatiron Health, and Tempus began using machine learning to draw insights from EHRs, claims, and wearable data—transforming post-marketing surveillance into predictive vigilance.

RWE wasn't just retrospective. It was becoming prospective, predictive, and proactive.

Value Chain Impact: Post-Market Safety, Evidence Generation

Insight: When the real world becomes the dataset, the lab becomes the living patient.

2020 – Personalized Medicine + Digital Twins

The pandemic accelerated everything.

AI models were built in days to predict ventilator demand. mRNA vaccine candidates were modeled using predictive bioinformatics.

Simultaneously, digital twins of patients—using multi-omic data and simulations—emerged in oncology and rare diseases.

Quris AI developed patient-on-a-chip systems with AI predicting drug toxicity before animal or human trials.

Value Chain Impact: Personalized Care & Precision Medicine

Insight: It's no longer about treating disease—it's about simulating the patient before the first symptom appears.

2021 – The Rise of the AI Medical Affairs Copilot

Medical Science Liaisons (MSLs), once burdened by literature, now have NLP-powered summarizers, AI slide builders, and chatbot support for HCP queries.

Companies began integrating GPT-style LLMs into medical information (Med Info) platforms, delivering personalized, evidence-backed, and compliant responses at scale.

Value Chain Impact: Medical Affairs

Insight: The new scientific storyteller isn't just trained in medicine—it's fine-tuned on billions of words.

2022 – Market Access and Pricing Models Go AI-Native

As value-based pricing gained ground, AI was deployed to predict budget impact, assess value pathways, and simulate payer negotiations.

Companies like IQVIA and BresMed used ML for health economic modeling, scenario forecasting, and budget impact visualization.

Value Chain Impact: Market Access & HEOR

Insight: Pricing, once a black art, was becoming a white-box simulation.

2023 – Generative AI Becomes the Interface

With the arrival of ChatGPT, Med-PaLM, and Claude, everything changed.

Patient support? AI chatbots.

Regulatory writing? AI copilots.

Clinical documentation? Transcription + summarization by LLMs.

Some firms even tested generative AI to write study protocols, design visual abstracts, or simulate virtual advisory boards.

Value Chain Impact: Every vertical

Insight: The interface changed. Now, you could talk to the machine—and it talked back.

2024–2025 – The Shape of What's Next

We now stand on the edge of an AI-native pharma industry, with:

- Autonomous trial design (TrialJectory)
- Supply chain digital twins (NVIDIA Omniverse + SAP)
- Multimodal drug discovery (language + protein + imaging models)
- Predictive health journeys (opt-in patient navigation from screening to treatment)
- AI governance frameworks (EU AI Act, FDA Algorithmic Transparency pilot)

And perhaps most transformative: the shift from "pharmaceuticals" to "pharmatechnology"—where pills, data, and platforms are co-developed.

Final Insight:

The story of AI in pharma is not about machines taking over.

It's about machines making the invisible visible: patterns in disease, inefficiencies in process, and signals in silence.

It's about how the arc of health innovation is bending—not only toward cure, but toward prediction, personalization, and prevention.

Reskilling for the Age of Intelligence: How Medical Professionals and Brand Managers must Evolve?

Revolutions are not merely about machines. They are about minds adjusting to new realities.

In 2025, a young oncologist in Hyderabad reviews a patient's tumor genomics. An AI model suggests three personalized therapies, ranked by efficacy and predicted side effects. She glances at the recommendations, nods—but then pauses. She still needs to explain this to the patient, anticipate insurance approval, and decide what to do if the AI misses something rare. The machine has given her information. Now, her job is to bring judgment.

Across the world, a brand manager in Basel stares at a dashboard. Engagement metrics are up. A natural language model has generated a comprehensive campaign for a new diabetes therapy, with messaging tailored to physicians, patients, and payers. But something feels…off. The tone is polished, yet too sterile. The science is sound, but lacks soul. The brand's essence is lost in translation. She rolls up her sleeves.

The AI has spoken. But the human is still accountable.

This is the shape of the new workplace. One where doctors, MSLs, and marketers no longer compete with AI—but collaborate with it.

But to thrive in this future, they must first reskill.

For Medical Professionals: From Experts to Orchestrators

Doctors once relied on knowledge. Now they are stewards of systems intelligence.

What Must Change:

- From memorizing guidelines → to interpreting real-time, AI-curated clinical pathways.
- From static diagnoses → to dynamic risk predictions powered by genomics, lifestyle, and wearable data.
- From solo decision-makers → to collaborative interpreters of machine outputs.

The New Toolkit:

- Data Literacy: Understand AI model outputs, confidence intervals, bias risks, and limitations.
- Conversational AI Use: Integrate tools like Med-PaLM and Glass AI into consultations and literature reviews.
- Ethical AI Judgment: Know when to trust the machine—and when to override it.
- Human Skills, Elevated: Empathy, communication, shared decision-making—what the AI can't automate.

Learning Pathways:

- Harvard's AI in Health Care certification.
- Stanford's Augmented Clinical Decision-Making short course.
- On-site hospital programs integrating EHR AI tools and predictive dashboards.

Insight:

"The best physicians of the AI age won't be those who beat the machine—but those who know what it means when the machine wins."

For Brand Managers: From Storytellers to Strategy Scientists

Pharma marketing used to be about positioning and promotion. Now, it's about prediction, personalization, and platform integration.

What Must Change:

- From segment-based marketing → to real-time behavioral targeting across channels.
- From campaigns once a quarter → to AI-orchestrated content variations tested hourly.
- From product pushers → to ecosystem designers: integrating apps, devices, and therapies into the patient journey.

The New Toolkit:

- Prompt Engineering: Crafting precise queries to extract insights from large language models.
- Predictive Analytics: Understanding churn models, next-best-action engines, and forecasting dashboards.

- Customer Experience (CX): Journey mapping tools, empathy-based design, and AI-driven CX personalization.
- Ethical AI Governance: Ensuring messaging compliance, transparency, and fairness in AI-generated content.

Learning Pathways:

- MIT's AI for Pharma Commercial Leaders course.
- Kellogg's Marketing Analytics & AI bootcamps.
- Internal upskilling with tools like Veeva Nitro, IQVIA OrchestratedCustomer Engagement (OCE), and Salesforce Einstein.

Insight:

" Great brand managers used to ask: What is the message? Now they must ask: What does the machine know—and how can I make it resonate?"

The Crossroads: Human + AI

Neither medical professionals nor brand managers need to become data scientists. But they must become AI-fluent.

They must learn to:

- Ask smarter questions.
- Detect flawed inferences.
- Recognize machine bias.
- Use AI as a co-pilot, not an autopilot.
- Reclaim time from the repetitive and invest it in the relational, the strategic, and the ethical.

Reskilling Programs: The Blueprint

Role	Key Skill Focus	Program Examples
Doctors & MSLs	Data literacy, AI judgement, Genomic AI	Mayo Clinic AI CME, Coursera AI in Healthcare, OncoKB tools
Brand Managers	Prompt engineering, Matech AI, CX design	INSEAD Digital Strategy, ChatGPT for Marketers (LinkedIn)
Regulatory Experts	Explainability, AI compliance, labeling	EU AI Act Workshops, DIA AI in Regulatory Affairs Forum
All Roles	AI ethics, bias, fairness, future readiness	Stanford HAI, WHO AI Ethics Framework Workshops

Final Reflection: The Renaissance Professional

Some of the world's greatest innovators—whether Leonardo, Steve Jobs, or Jennifer Doudna—weren't just masters of tools. They were masters of synthesis. They bridged disciplines, learned from machines, and turned science into storytelling.

So too must today's professionals.

Because AI won't replace the doctor.

But the doctor who understands AI will replace the one who doesn't.

The same applies to the brand manager, the regulatory officer, and the supply chain analyst.

The new Renaissance is not in Florence or Silicon Valley.

It's in the interface between human and machine.

And it starts with a question, not of what we must learn,

But of who we are becoming as we learn it.

Chapter 5

Finance – The Algorithmic Trader's Empire

In the high-frequency hum of Wall Street's server rooms, finance met its destiny with code.

It began, as many revolutions do, in the shadows.

In the late 1980s, a small group of physicists, engineers, and renegade mathematicians peeled away from academia and hedge funds to forge something new. They weren't trying to beat the market by instinct or charm, but by instruction sets—coded formulas that could act faster than any human, fueled not by emotion, but by data.

By the time the 21st century arrived, they had achieved their goal.

The Quants Take Over

In 2009, Jim Simons, a former IBM researcher who ran Renaissance Technologies, posted annual returns that traditional portfolio managers could only dream of. His Medallion Fund became a near-mythical benchmark—not just because of the returns, but because of how they were achieved: by algorithms devouring terabytes of market signals, economic data, and microstructure trends. No TV appearances. No CNBC soundbites. Just code that whispered before the world roared.

These were the quants—and they had rewritten the rules of the financial game.

Then came AI. And with it, a new dimension of change.

From Quants to Machines that Learn

The classic quantitative approach depended on structured models, including assumptions about volatility, mean reversion, and correlation. However, in the 2010s, deep learning emerged. Now, AI can learn patterns without needing to be explicitly instructed on what to look for. Sentiment analysis from tweets. Satellite images of store parking lots. Voice tone of CEOs on earnings calls. Neural networks turned noise into a prediction.

Two Sigma, Citadel, and Bridgewater began pouring billions into AI talent, poaching from Google and MIT, offering seven-figure salaries to those who could train machines not just to trade, but to understand markets.

The line between a hedge fund and a tech lab blurred.

Welcome to the Real-Time, Reinforced Future

Today's cutting-edge funds run reinforcement learning agents—algorithms that evolve through trial and error, like a chess bot facing millions of hypothetical markets. They adjust positions not monthly, not daily, but microsecond by microsecond, reacting to liquidity, latency, and the faintest signals of arbitrage.

The age of "quantamental" investing—where machine insight augments human judgment—is in full swing.

AI doesn't just predict stock movement. It:

- Forecasts central bank decisions from macroeconomic text data.
- Anticipates credit default using alternative data (like browser metadata and call center logs).
- Detects fraud and market manipulation using anomaly detection models.
- Powers ESG risk engines that scan climate impact, diversity metrics, and ethical red flags.

Case Study: Kensho and the Real-Time Answer Machine

When S&P Global acquired Kensho Technologies in 2018 for $550 million, many wondered why a traditional ratings agency needed a Silicon Valley AI startup. The answer lay in Kensho's ambition: to become the "Siri for Wall Street."

Ask it:

"What happens to gold prices when North Korea fires a missile?"

Within seconds, it would scour decades of data and give a probabilistic answer.

It was no longer about hindsight. Kensho brought the power of contextual reasoning to real-time decision-making—a compass in the storm.

Myth: The Machines have no Masters

There's a belief that AI now controls finance, leaving humans behind. That's part truth, part myth.

Yes, machines execute more than 75% of trades on U.S. exchanges. However, behind every algorithm is a team of researchers, compliance officers, and strategists. When GPT-like models were tested for forecasting stock movements, they revealed unexpected biases, including the reinforcement of previous market cycles, racial bias in credit scoring data, and occasional hallucinations.

Think about it, "The algorithm is never truly independent. It is a mirror—reflecting the values and blind spots of its creators."

Regulators Chase the Machine

The challenge now is speed.

Regulators like the SEC and European Securities and Markets Authority (ESMA) are scrambling to understand AI-driven trading. Flash crashes, adversarial attacks, and model opacity pose real threats. In 2010, one rogue algorithm helped wipe out nearly $1 trillion in minutes. What happens when deep learning models go haywire?

The EU's AI Act has designated high-frequency trading as a "high-risk AI system," requiring transparency, auditability, and human override. But can humans still override?

Reskilling the Financial Braintrust

The Wall Street workforce is transforming. The archetype of the cigar-chomping trader is vanishing, replaced by the Python-wielding quant, the ethics-savvy AI auditor, and the "explainability" specialist. JPMorgan Chase alone launched an internal AI certification for over 5,000 employees. Goldman Sachs added prompt engineering to its investment banking curriculum.

The future isn't human versus AI. It's human empowered by AI—where understanding causality, building ethical models, and asking the right questions matter more than ever.

What Comes Next? The Edge of Autonomy

We may soon see fully autonomous hedge funds—LLMs that read 10-Ks, digest geopolitical news, simulate market reactions, and allocate capital, all without human input. But the question isn't whether they can.

The real question is: Should they?

Remember that" Every leap in intelligence—natural or artificial—carries both light and shadow. The future of finance will not be written in code alone. It will be written in the values we embed in that code."

In the age of AI, the algorithmic trader's empire is not just an economic engine. It is a mirror to our ambitions, our blind spots, and our evolving definition of trust.

AI in Finance: Timeline and Real-World Casebook

Tracking the rise of algorithms, intelligence, and innovation in the financial world

1987 – Black Monday and the Birth of Fear

The global markets crashed in a single day, wiping out nearly a quarter of the Dow Jones Industrial Average. Analysts blamed automated "portfolio insurance" programs, rudimentary precursors to today's algorithmic trading. It was a loud warning: automation had arrived, but it wasn't yet wise.

1998 – Renaissance Technologies and the Quant Holy Grail

Jim Simons and his team at Renaissance Technologies scaled up the Medallion Fund, utilizing a blend of statistics, pattern recognition, and early AI to outperform the markets consistently. They hired physicists and mathematicians—not MBAs. The age of the quant empire had begun.

2006 – Machine Learning in Risk and Fraud

Major banks have begun embedding machine learning models into their credit risk scoring and fraud detection processes. These algorithms began learning from data far more rapidly than traditional scoring models could adapt.

2010 – Flash Crash and the Limits of Speed

On May 6, 2010, U.S. equity markets experienced a sudden collapse and rapid recovery within minutes. A rogue algorithm helped trigger the drop, exposing the limited human oversight that remained in the age of high-frequency trading (HFT). It was a visceral reminder: AI can move faster than we can comprehend.

2013 – Kensho: Financial Siri Is Born

Founded in Cambridge, Kensho built an engine that could answer complex financial questions in natural language—something like "What happens to oil prices when hurricanes hit the Gulf?" The answers were rooted in vast historical datasets, processed at machine speed.

2016 – JPMorgan COiN

JPMorgan Chase launched Contract Intelligence (COiN), an AI system capable of reviewing thousands of legal loan agreements in seconds—a task that had previously taken lawyers 360,000 hours annually. The shift was seismic: AI wasn't just supporting analysts. It was replacing repetitive white-collar tasks.

2017 – Deep Learning Goes Sentimental

Financial firms have adopted deep learning to parse earnings calls, CEO tone, global news sentiment, and even Twitter data to inform market decisions. The language of finance was no longer a barrier for machines.

2018 – Kensho Acquired for $550 Million

S&P Global's acquisition of Kensho wasn't just a business deal—it was symbolic. It marked the merging of two worlds: traditional financial infrastructure and Silicon Valley's AI futurism.

2020 – GPT-3: Market Whisperer?

When OpenAI released GPT-3, hedge funds began testing it for financial analysis. Could it write research reports, parse SEC filings, or predict stock moves based on language? The answer: yes, but with nuance. Its potential was vast—but hallucinations and opacity risks remained.

2023 – BloombergGPT Arrives

A domain-specific language model trained on financial documents, news articles, and market data, BloombergGPT showed what was possible when LLMs were pointed toward a single goal: mastering the language of capital.

2024 – AI Dominates Trading Floors

Today, over 75% of trades on U.S. stock exchanges are executed by AI-powered systems, which often utilize deep reinforcement learning, sentiment mining, and market simulation. Speed, scale, and subtlety now define financial edge.

Casebook: Real-World Companies Leading the AI Finance Frontier

1. **Renaissance Technologies:** A legendary hedge fund run by code and quants. Renaissance's Medallion Fund continues to outperform every benchmark—despite being a black-box system. It remains a paragon of predictive modeling and algorithmic secrecy.
2. **Kensho:** Dubbed the "Siri for Wall Street," Kensho turned natural language questions into real-time, data-driven answers. Its acquisition by S&P Global provided the financial world with its first serious AI-native analytics platform, integrating news, economic events, and structured market data.
3. **JPMorgan Chase:** A pioneer in deploying AI internally, JPMorgan's COiN (Contract Intelligence) uses NLP to process financial agreements at scale. Their internal AI teams now focus on fraud detection, equity research, customer service, and internal compliance.
4. **Bloomberg:** With the launch of BloombergGPT, Bloomberg has trained a finance-specific LLM that can summarize earnings calls, write headlines, and predict market sentiment. This is the Bloomberg Terminal reimagined through AI.
5. **Two Sigma:** An epitome of science-meets-finance, Two Sigma relies on machine learning, cloud computing, and big data to build diversified, adaptive portfolios. Their data scientists outnumber traditional traders—and their models learn continuously.

6. **Goldman Sachs:** Once the bastion of old-school investment banking, Goldman is now one of the biggest recruiters of AI talent. Its LLM-based pilots explore productivity enhancement, while its algorithmic trading arms dominate in execution speed and spread optimization.
7. **Upstart:** By applying machine learning to credit underwriting, Upstart uses alternative data like employment history and education to assess borrowers. The result: expanded credit access and lower default rates—without the legacy bias of FICO scores.
8. **Zest AI:** Focused on fairness and transparency, Zest AI builds explainable credit scoring models. Used by lenders across the U.S., Zest's models outperform traditional systems and help mitigate bias—making a strong case for ethical AI in finance.

The Great Shift — Jobs in the Age of AI

It was a moment reminiscent of the arrival of the loom or the assembly line—only this time, the loom could write code, draft legal memos, and analyze CT scans. In 2023, with generative AI models like GPT-4.0, Claude, and Bloom emerging from the labs of Silicon Valley and Shenzhen, the world stood on the cusp of an employment transformation unlike any before.

The headlines were dramatic. “AI will take your job.” “Code is dead.” “The 9-to-5 is obsolete.” But behind the noise, the data painted a more nuanced and, in many ways, more hopeful story.

From Anxiety to Analytics: The WEF and McKinsey Lens

According to the World Economic Forum’s Future of Jobs Report, by 2025, approximately 85 million jobs may be displaced, primarily those involving repetitive administrative or manual tasks. Yet, the same report forecasts that 97 million new roles—focused on AI supervision, data strategy, green economy transitions, and human-centric care—could emerge.

That same year, McKinsey Global Institute published a comprehensive review suggesting that between 400 million and 800 million jobs globally could be impacted by automation by 2030. Not eliminated, but transformed. Modified. Reborn.

One startling figure stood out: up to 30% of working hours in the U.S. economy might be automated by the end of the decade. And yet, productivity gains from this shift could add $13 trillion to the global economy.

This shift points out the historical resonance. Like how the advent of the printing press didn’t destroy reading, it created mass literacy. Or how electricity didn’t simply remove factory hands, it gave rise to engineers, electricians, and an era of innovation. The same principle applies now. AI isn’t the end of human labor. It is the reconfiguration of it.

McKinsey & WEF Projections (2023–2030)

The Great Shift: Jobs and Transformations

By 2030, 30% of current working hours in the U.S. could be automated thanks to generative AI—a leap enabled by predictive systems, natural language processing, and machine learning models that increasingly handle routine and data-driven tasks.

The McKinsey Global Institute projects an even larger scale—between 400 million and 800 million jobs worldwide may be transformed or displaced by automation by 2030, depending on the speed of adoption.

Not all change spells doom. The World Economic Forum makes the case for adaptation rather than replacement: by 2025, around 85 million jobs may vanish, but 97 million new ones could emerge—especially in data analysis, AI oversight, content creation, and digital strategy roles.

Yet the policy and societal challenge is vast. McKinsey estimates that 75 million to 375 million workers could need full reskilling to transition into new areas.

"We stand at the cusp of a workforce renaissance, "where every administrative task, every clerked form, risks obsolescence—not because humans failed, but because the machine learned faster."

History reminds us—like how the printing press didn't kill reading, but demanded a new kind of literacy. Here too, the old jobs aren't vanishing—they're asking to be reimagined.

Look at the roles that will be flourishing by 2030: AI specialists, Big Data wizards, UI designers, and autonomous technicians. These are not inhuman roles. They are deeply human—engineering empathy, designing trust, harvesting insight from chaos.

And the jobs in decline? They remind us of the fragility of routine in an age where code can replicate a dozen clerks' worth of output in seconds.

The Human Layer: Policy, Reskilling, and Creativity

The numbers are staggering. But the real story lies in how societies respond.

Companies must invest in reskilling—utilizing micro-credentials, internal boot camps, and interdisciplinary on-ramps.

Governments must create safety nets and employment transition structures.

Workers must adapt, learn to be fluent in AI, and refuse to accept that automation is their fate.

Because beyond the spreadsheet lies a fundamental promise: automation doesn't replace imagination. It reveals its value.

Winners, Losers, and the Rewired Resume

Across a global heatmap of projected job roles, the WEF infographic drew a sharp contrast between rising and declining domains:

Fastest Growing Roles (by 2030):

- AI and machine learning specialists
- Big data analysts
- FinTech engineers
- Cybersecurity experts
- Autonomous vehicle technicians
- UI/UX designers
- Environmental engineers
- DevOps professionals
- Renewable energy system installers

Fastest Declining Roles:

- Data entry clerks
- Bank tellers
- Postal workers
- Administrative assistants
- Print machine operators
- Telemarketers
- Claims adjusters
- Stock clerks and order fillers

In this rapidly changing scenario, you'd meet Maria—a call center agent in Mexico who now works as a conversational AI trainer. Or Ravi, a former bank clerk in India, now helping to supervise algorithmic loan tools using real-world context to improve fairness. These aren't hypotheticals. They're already happening.

The Myth of Total Replacement

One of the most dangerous myths is the belief that AI will replace humans. That's the wrong question. The right one is: How will AI redefine what it means to be valuable in the workplace?

It's not automation vs. employment. It's automation plus augmentation. The machines take over the routine. Humans double down on what machines can't: judgment, empathy, creativity, context.

Look at the numbers again. McKinsey estimates that up to 375 million workers globally will need to be reskilled by 2030. But if done right, this won't just save jobs—it will create more resilient economies.

A Renaissance in Reskilling

The challenge now isn't to slow down AI. It's to speed up adaptation.

Governments must build transition safety nets, including wage support, lifelong learning grants, and AI literacy in public education.

Corporates must invest in upskilling bootcamps—not just for coders, but for warehouse workers, nurses, and bank clerks.

And individuals must adopt a growth mindset. Learn to work with AI, not fear it. Develop AI fluency. Practice prompt engineering. Blend domain expertise with digital agility.

In this new age, soft skills aren't secondary—they're central. The most in-demand leaders will be those who can bridge disciplines: the healthcare AI ethicist, the fintech behavioral scientist, the public policy + data hybrid thinker.

Beyond Statistics, Toward a Human Story

The timeline is clear: 2023–2030 will be the decade that decides whether AI becomes a net enabler or divider.

However, history has shown us something powerful: each time technology has threatened to outpace society, humans have risen to the challenge with ingenuity, adaptation, and courage.

The machines may be learning faster. But we, the humans, must learn wiser.

AI-Powered Finance: From Fraud to Freedom

The Watchers in the Code: AI-Powered Fraud Detection

In a quiet glass tower in Manhattan, the war on financial crime doesn't happen with guns or guard dogs. It happens in real time, in lines of code. At JPMorgan Chase, a neural network nicknamed "HawkEye" sifts through billions of transactions a day—flagging anomalies faster than any human compliance officer could dream of.

But it didn't start that way.

In the early 2000s, fraud detection was largely a reactive process. Banks waited for a breach, then tried to clean up. But with the 2008 financial crisis exposing systemic failures, and cybercrime rising like a tide, a different kind of sentry was needed—one that didn't sleep.

Enter machine learning.

Unlike static rule-based systems that failed to adapt, AI models could learn patterns, evolve, and catch the clever fraudster hiding in the noise. Today, Mastercard's Decision Intelligence system evaluates 1.9 billion transactions daily in real-time, identifying fraud with 300% greater accuracy through the use of AI.

In this new regime, a small charge from an unknown vendor in an unusual time zone might be all it takes for an AI to whisper: "This doesn't look right." And more often than not, it's correct.

It's not just fraud detection—it's financial immune surveillance, built not on instincts, but on inference.

Robo-Advisors: The Gentle Rise of Machine Wealth Managers

In a WeWork space in San Francisco circa 2011, two former bankers had an idea: why not make investing as easy as a Spotify playlist?

They called it Wealthfront, and soon after, competitors like Betterment, Schwab Intelligent Portfolios, and SoFi joined the fray. Their goal wasn't to replace human advisors with cold logic, but to give everyday investors access to optimized, personalized portfolio management—without the intimidating jargon or 1% fees.

The key? Algorithms.

These robo-advisors didn't just offer cheaper ETFs. They utilized AI-powered rebalancing, tax-loss harvesting, and even behavioral nudges—such as gently encouraging users not to panic-sell during a market dip. In essence, they weren't just managing money. They were managing emotion.

By 2023, robo-advisors had nearly $1.5 trillion under management globally. And while high-net-worth clients still prefer the handshake and eye contact of human advisors, for millions of younger investors, the interface is the experience. A swipe replaces a seminar.

It's not a revolution with fireworks. It's a quiet automation of wealth wisdom.

DeFi: Decentralized Dreams and Algorithmic Trust

If the old world of finance was built on marble columns and regulators in navy suits, DeFi—short for decentralized finance—is its punk rock sibling.

Born on the blockchain, DeFi apps promise a world without middlemen. No banks, no brokers, no wire transfer fees. Just code. Lending, borrowing, trading—done through smart contracts that execute without a single banker in sight.

By 2022, DeFi platforms such as Aave, Compound, and Uniswap were managing over $100 billion in cryptocurrency assets.

But freedom comes with fragility.

When Terra/Luna collapsed, it wiped out $40 billion in value, caused by an algorithmic stablecoin losing its peg. Elsewhere in the ecosystem, smart contract bugs led to multimillion-dollar exploits. The systems were transparent but unforgiving. Code was law. Until it broke.

Still, the idealism endures. Young developers in Berlin and Seoul stay up late coding to create decentralized futures where trust is shared, not assigned. Where wallets take the place of banks. Where governance is decided in DAOs (Decentralized Autonomous Organizations), not in boardrooms.

It's not yet a mainstream reality. But it's a mirror—reflecting what traditional finance often overlooks: the power of agency, access, and algorithmic trust.

What Connects Them All?

From fraud detection to robo-advisors to DeFi, one truth emerges: finance is no longer just about money—it's about information. Who controls it, Who analyzes it and who trusts whom.

And AI, in all its flavors—predictive models, reinforcement learners, blockchain oracles—is not just automating old roles. It's redrawing the boundaries of who gets to participate in wealth creation.

It's not just the rich getting richer. It's the smart getting smarter—and the systems getting faster than regulators can keep up.

And as history has shown, whether it's a printing press or an internet protocol, the story of technology isn't just about the tools. It's about the humans who use them.

The Brain of Wall Street: Aladdin, IndexGPT, and the Algorithmic Age

1. Aladdin

The $21 Trillion Operating System You've Never Heard Of: In a nondescript server farm nestled behind layers of encryption and regulation, a digital mind quietly watches over one of the world's largest concentrations of capital. It's not a hedge fund. It's not a bank. It's a piece of software.

Its name is Aladdin—short for Asset, Liability, Debt, and Derivative Investment Network. And it is the invisible nervous system of modern finance.

Built by BlackRock in the 1990s, Aladdin was never intended to become what it is today: a platform that analyzes over 21 trillion dollars in assets across pension funds, sovereign wealth funds, insurance portfolios, and even BlackRock's competitors.

Initially, it was a straightforward risk management tool—an internal compass to guide Larry Fink's bond strategies. But then something remarkable happened. It started getting smarter. More comprehensive. More predictive. More… indispensable.

By the 2010s, Aladdin wasn't just analyzing risk. It was forecasting stress events, simulating entire market crashes, optimizing global portfolios, and powering the guts of wealth management at scale. It processed millions of securities, ran tens of thousands of stress tests daily, and offered dashboards that made the chaos of global finance legible.

But Aladdin's magic isn't just computational power. It's trust.

That's what made central banks, Swiss insurance giants, and even Google's pension board sign up. Not because it was infallible. But because it allowed them to see around corners—to replace gut feeling with data-driven foresight.

Still, some critics argue that placing so much power into one centralized algorithmic brain introduces systemic risk. If too many firms rely on Aladdin to steer their ship, what happens when the compass errs?

It's a paradox of modern finance: the tool meant to reduce risk might, through ubiquity, become a source of it.

2. **IndexGPT: When JPMorgan Went Full Circle**

   In May 2023, JPMorgan Chase quietly filed a trademark for something called IndexGPT.

   To the untrained eye, it sounded like a gimmick. Another attempt to ride the coattails of ChatGPT. But insiders knew something deeper was unfolding.

   While BlackRock's Aladdin was designed to analyze portfolios, IndexGPT was designed to build them. From scratch. With AI.

   Imagine a wealth management client asking, "Can you build me a portfolio that avoids fossil fuels, invests in high-growth AI companies, and aligns with Catholic values?" A human advisor might need hours to compile research, debate ethics, and optimize exposure.

   IndexGPT could do it in seconds.

   At its core, IndexGPT was a fusion of large language models with financial data engines, trained not just on equities but on client behavior, market sentiment, risk appetite, and even regulatory compliance.

   Unlike traditional robo-advisors that stuck to ETFs and passive rebalancing, IndexGPT hinted at a future where portfolios were conversationally designed, dynamically updated, and individually tailored—at scale.

   Think of it as Spotify for wealth: not just playing your favorite songs, but creating a personalized playlist tailored to your past, mood, beliefs, and future goals.

   It wasn't science fiction. It was code.

3. **AI and the Philosopher's Portfolio**

   What connects Aladdin and IndexGPT isn't just that they're AI tools. It's that they're changing the philosophy of investing.

   Before, investing was about alpha, instinct, and edge. A legendary manager with a feel for markets. Now, it's about architecture—how you structure decisions, optimize across probabilities, and monitor signals humans can't see.

   Larry Fink once said, "The world is moving from judgment to analytics." But perhaps we're witnessing something subtler: a fusion. Human insight enhanced—not replaced—by artificial intelligence.

The paradox? The smarter the tools get, the more we must understand what questions to ask.

Because even the most advanced GPT model cannot decide whether your future should prioritize growth or stability, ethics or returns, conviction or caution.

Only you can do that.

Displacement in Retail Banking and the Rise of the Quant Class

1. **The Vanishing Smile at the Branch Counter**

   Once, a trip to the bank was a ritual. You'd walk into the local branch, greeted by a nameplate smile and a familiar nod. The teller—Mary or Raj, or Emilio—knew your children's names, your credit history, and that you preferred your cash in tens.

   In the U.S. alone, there were nearly 600,000 bank tellers in the year 2000. By 2023, that number had dropped by 30%, and the trajectory is clear. Branches are closing. ATMs and mobile apps are replacing the human handshake. In China, 80% of bank transactions are now conducted via mobile. In India, UPI systems outpace physical currency handling.

   It didn't start with AI. It started with automation. But AI is finishing the job.

   Today, virtual assistants like Erica (Bank of America) or Eno (Capital One) handle millions of queries—from balance checks to fraud alerts—without requiring a single human intervention.

   But it's not just the low-wage teller who's vulnerable. The very architecture of banking is being redefined.

2. **When the Spreadsheet Gave Way to the Algorithm**

   In a quiet basement office at a hedge fund in Connecticut, a 27-year-old PhD in theoretical physics isn't modeling particle collisions—he's pricing mortgage-backed securities with transformer models.

   This is the face of the new finance: the quant.

   Quantitative analysts aren't new. But their influence is exploding. As AI and machine learning fuse with high-frequency trading, credit modeling, risk analytics, and even customer behavior prediction, banks no longer just want MBAs—they want coders, physicists, and data scientists.

   At JPMorgan Chase, more than one-third of all hires into asset management are now quants. At Goldman Sachs, the Marcus platform was built not by bankers, but by software engineers. HSBC's quantum computing partnerships aim to simulate complex derivatives in a way that traditional computing can't match.

It's no longer about gut feeling or Wall Street bravado. It's about statistical edge, real-time optimization, and AI-assisted decisions made in milliseconds.

3. **Retail Displacement: Beyond the Counter**

   The impact goes far beyond tellers.

   Loan officers? Replaced by AI-powered credit models that don't just look at your FICO score, but at your digital footprint, cash flow patterns, and even linguistic sentiment from your emails (yes, really).

   Customer service reps? Being edged out by natural language processors that speak 20 languages and never go on break.

   Financial advisors? Facing competition from robo-advisors like Wealthfront and Betterment, whose models optimize portfolios in real time, with zero emotion and 0.25% management fees.

   Even collections and compliance are seeing automation. Machine learning detects money laundering patterns, flags insider trading signals, and optimizes debt recovery sequences—all without human intuition.

   And yet, the human story isn't gone.

4. **What Remains Human**

   What's left for humans in banking?

   The answer, paradoxically, may be the most human roles of all—those that require trust, empathy, complex judgment, and the ability to navigate ambiguity.

   Relationship managers who guide high-net-worth clients through life changes. Risk officers who weigh geopolitical uncertainty. Innovation leaders who imagine products that the algorithms haven't seen before.

   In an age of precision, the edge may lie in being imprecisely human.

5. **From Banks to "Bank-as-Code"**

   Retail banking is no longer a place—it's an API.

   The teller window becomes a voice assistant. The financial advisor becomes a dashboard. The checkbook becomes a blockchain wallet. Your entire banking experience fits inside a 6-inch glass rectangle.

   This is not the death of banking. It is its metamorphosis.

And in the code, there are still humans. But they no longer wear ties and sit behind plexiglass. They write Python. They design UX flows. They craft prompts.

They are the quants, the coders, the philosophers of finance—and they are building the future of money.

Retail Banking Jobs Then vs. Now — displaced vs. reimagined roles

1. **Bank Teller → Digital Concierge / Branch Relationship Specialist**

   Displaced By:

   ATMs and mobile banking apps quietly revolutionized transactions. Then came AI chatbots like Erica (Bank of America) and Eno (Capital One), which allowed users to check balances, pay bills, and even dispute charges with a few taps or a spoken sentence.

   Reimagined Persona:

   But even as automation swept the counters, the human need for trust and guidance remained. The Digital Concierge isn't just a greeter—they're a financial sherpa. Equipped with real-time dashboards and customer insights, they offer tailored advice, help with digital onboarding, and build enduring relationships. They don't just know your balance—they know your goals.

2. **Loan Officer → Credit Analyst for Edge Cases / Ethics Oversight**

   Displaced By:

   Firms like Zest AI and Upstart use thousands of variables (from job history to mobile data) to predict creditworthiness, outperforming legacy FICO models and slashing loan processing time from weeks to minutes.

   Reimagined Persona:

   Yet AI isn't perfect—it can entrench bias or fail in nuanced scenarios. The modern credit analyst doesn't rubber-stamp approvals. They audit edge cases, flag anomalies, and serve on ethics review panels. They bridge cold data with human warmth—advocating for fairness when machines miss the mark.

3. **Customer Service Rep → AI Escalation Specialist / Empathy Trainer**

   Displaced By:

   AI-powered voice response systems handle millions of queries a day. From checking balances to resetting passwords, bots never sleep—and they don't take breaks.

   Reimagined Persona:

   However, when emotions surge, bots falter. Enter the Escalation Specialist—the human that frustrated customers ultimately need. Trained in de-escalation and equipped with full customer context, they resolve what algorithms cannot. Some go further: they become Empathy Trainers, feeding conversation patterns back into AI systems to humanize future interactions.

4. **Financial Advisor → Hybrid Advisor (AI + Human Guidance)**

   Displaced By:

   Robo-advisors like Wealthfront and Betterment manage billions of dollars with sophisticated algorithms that rebalance portfolios, harvest tax losses, and optimize risk—all at lower fees than human advisors.

   Reimagined Persona:

   Still, algorithms don't necessarily hold hands in market crashes or understand the complexities of generational trauma surrounding money. The Hybrid Advisor utilizes robo-tools for data, while keeping the human element alive. They coach clients through fear, life transitions, and complex wealth transfers—combining logic with lived wisdom.

5. **Compliance Analyst → Ethical Compliance Strategist / Algorithm Auditor**

   Displaced By:

   AI models flag suspicious transactions in seconds, scanning for fraud, money laundering, or KYC violations across millions of datapoints. Regulatory reporting that took days is now automated.

   Reimagined Persona:

   But who watches the watchers? The Algorithm Auditor evaluates bias, fairness, and explainability in AI decisions. The Ethical Compliance Strategist helps write the very rules by which machines must play—ensuring that automated vigilance remains just and lawful.

6. **Portfolio Manager → AI-Enhanced Portfolio Architect**

   Displaced By:

   Quantitative models fueled by AI make lightning-fast market decisions. BlackRock's Aladdin analyzes trillions in assets using scenario modeling, predictive analytics, and macroeconomic forecasting.

   Reimagined Persona:

   The Portfolio Architect doesn't compete with machines — they orchestrate them. They create investment strategies that combine AI recommendations with geopolitical awareness, ESG insights, and client values. It's an art meeting an algorithm.

7. **Risk Assessor → Geopolitical & Scenario Risk Strategist**

   Displaced By:

   AI now detects patterns in real-time, including credit defaults, market volatility, and supply chain shocks. Risk modeling has evolved from a retrospective to a predictive approach.

   Reimagined Persona:

   The new risk specialist is part economist, part futurist. They simulate war games, forecast systemic shocks, and explore cascading risk in a multipolar world. Their toolkit includes AI—but their judgment comes from experience and intuition, not just computation.

8. **Collections Agent → Behavioral Economics Analyst / Digital Collector**

   Displaced By:

   Automated systems send reminders, negotiate payment plans, and even predict who will default based on subtle behavioral cues.

   Reimagined Persona:

   But true recovery lies in understanding why people don't pay—not just when. The modern collections expert employs behavioral nudges, designs compassionate repayment paths, and utilizes digital platforms to foster trust. They are part social scientist, part fintech strategist.

Chapter 6

Education — When the Teacher Becomes the Taught

There's a quiet revolution unfolding in classrooms, lecture halls, and learning platforms across the world—a revolution not declared with manifestos or megaphones, but one that emerges line by line, prompt by prompt, in the quiet hum of processors and the flicker of screens. The teacher is no longer the sole sage on the stage. Increasingly, they serve as a guide alongside intelligent machines that can now reason, coach, and even assess. Education, perhaps more than any other sector, is where the ancient meets the algorithm.

Let's begin, as we often must, with a story.

In 2023, Sal Khan, the visionary behind Khan Academy, stood on stage at TED and introduced the world to Khanmigo—an AI-powered tutor built on OpenAI's GPT platform. What made Khanmigo different wasn't its fluency or speed. It was its ability to pause and ask students why they reached an answer. It didn't give away the solution; it nudged understanding. And suddenly, AI wasn't just a homework helper. It became a Socratic mentor.

The Classroom is No Longer a Place—It's an Interface

Across New Delhi, São Paulo, and Detroit, kids who once lacked access to quality instruction are now learning math from AI tutors in their native languages. These digital teachers don't tire, don't shame, and are infinitely patient. They adapt to a learner's pace, mood, and mistakes.

Yet the story isn't all rosy.

Teachers, long overwhelmed by administrative overload, found in AI a promise: automated grading, personalized feedback, adaptive testing. But they also encountered fear. Would AI replace them? Would students cheat more easily? Would algorithms reinforce bias or kill creativity?

The Great Pedagogical Pivot

In some ways, this moment echoes the invention of the printing press. Just as Gutenberg democratized information, AI democratizes instruction. But it also requires a redefinition of what it means to teach.

At Arizona State University, professors now use ChatGPT as a co-instructor. It handles basic queries, offers practice problems, and even explains complex topics in multiple learning styles—visual, auditory, and narrative. The human professor? They double down on mentorship, critical thinking, and emotional intelligence. Teaching is no longer just about delivery. It's about cultivating wisdom in an age of infinite facts.

In Finland, a primary school teacher used an AI bot to translate Shakespeare into children's rhyme and code it into an interactive game. Suddenly, fifth graders were discussing Hamlet through a game interface—learning not only literature but also programming and ethics.

The machine wasn't replacing the teacher. It was reawakening the joy of teaching.

When Students Prompt and Professors Learn

A student at MIT used Claude to design an original neural net architecture for his thesis—guided not just by academic papers, but by dialogue with an AI that had read them all. Professors reviewing the work were stunned—not by plagiarism, but by innovation. The student hadn't copied. He had collaborated. The AI had become a lab partner.

Such moments hint at a future where the teacher-student relationship is no longer a one-way transmission, but a triangle: human + human + machine. The best learning happens when all three learn from each other.

The Risk of Algorithmic Tutors

But let's not be naïve. In the wrong hands, AI becomes surveillance. Some edtech platforms track eye movements and flag attention lapses. Others punish "non-standard" answers. Worse, when trained on biased datasets, AI tutors can misrepresent history, reinforce stereotypes, or gatekeep knowledge. The future of learning cannot be left solely to silicon.

The real challenge is not whether AI will teach. It's what values it will teach with.

Re-skilling the Educators

The best teachers of tomorrow are those learning today. Professional development must now include prompt engineering, AI ethics, platform fluency, and human-centered pedagogy. Some school districts have already begun training teachers to work with AI rather than against it—designing AI-infused lesson plans, co-creating projects, and understanding how to assess originality in a world where machines write prose and paint portraits.

Because in this new era, the question isn't "Will AI replace teachers?"

It's: "What kind of teacher can only a human be?"

A Quiet Closing

When the teacher becomes the taught, humility enters the system. That's not defeat. That's evolution.

Education is not about knowing more than your students. It's about kindling the courage to explore the unknown—together. And perhaps, in this age of intelligent machines, our greatest educators will be those who don't fear losing control, but who embrace the art of co-learning.

And in doing so, they'll pass on the most timeless lesson of all:

Learning never ends.

AI Tutors: When the Machine Learns to Teach

In the spring of 2023, when Khan Academy rolled out Khanmigo—an AI tutor powered by GPT-4—the moment felt uncannily familiar. Sal Khan, the MIT-educated educator who once transformed math lessons into YouTube videos, now stood at the threshold of another revolution. He wasn't just uploading explanations. He was building a digital companion—one that could explain, quiz, encourage, and, most remarkably, listen.

The concept of AI tutors had long been a staple in the realm of science fiction. But the reality unfolded first in classrooms across China with Squirrel AI. Unlike Khanmigo, which acted like a friendly, Socratic coach, Squirrel AI was a precision instrument. Founded by Derek Li, a Chinese entrepreneur who studied at Carnegie Mellon, Squirrel AI employs adaptive algorithms to dissect a student's knowledge map—identifying micro-concepts misunderstood, adjusting lesson plans in real-time, and predicting which learning path will optimize mastery. It was the Moneyball of education—turning learning into a sequence of probability models.

What made Khanmigo different wasn't just the technology. It was the ethos. Sal Khan didn't want to replace teachers. He wanted to empower them. In a TED Talk that went viral, he described AI as "a teaching assistant for every child—and a co-pilot for every teacher." It was an echo of Alan Kay's belief that technology should amplify human potential, not supplant it.

Khanmigo could engage in back-and-forth dialogue, simulate debates, and provide real-time feedback on essays. It was less like a drill sergeant and more like an educational conscience, nudging students toward reflection. In a pilot program across several schools in the U.S., children who were once reluctant to raise their hands found themselves typing away questions—unafraid of judgment. The AI was patient. Tireless. Nonjudgmental.

But beneath the optimism, serious questions simmered. Could these AI systems truly understand the emotional texture of learning? Could they notice the slumped shoulders of a child struggling silently? Could they encourage in moments of doubt or redirect when a student veered into unproductive tangents?

Squirrel AI responded with a different answer. Their platform integrated biometric data, such as facial expression tracking and eye-movement analysis, to detect disengagement. While impressive, it sparked debates about surveillance and privacy—particularly when applied to children. Were we nurturing curiosity—or engineering compliance?

As Isaac Asimov once noted, "The saddest aspect of life right now is that science gathers knowledge faster than society gathers wisdom." AI tutors sit at the intersection of that tension. Their promise is enormous: personalized learning at scale, democratized access to expertise, and 24/7 availability. However, the perils—data misuse, over-standardization, and erosion of the teacher-student connection—loom just as large.

And so we arrive at a paradox. In a world where AI can teach better than many humans, the role of the teacher becomes more vital, not less. As AI handles the mechanics of instruction, human educators are freed to do what only humans can—foster empathy, spark inspiration, and create the alchemy of connection.

In the classrooms of tomorrow, the best learning won't come from AI or humans alone—but from a new symbiosis where machines handle the routine and humans reclaim the sublime.

Redesigning the Curriculum: Rekindling the Flame of Curiosity

When Steve Jobs was a young man wandering the halls of Reed College, he audited a calligraphy course not because it would get him a job, but because the characters danced off the page. "It was beautiful," he later said. "Historical. Artistically subtle in a way that science can't capture." That class, useless by traditional metrics, would later shape the elegant typography of the Macintosh and revolutionize personal computing. Steve Jobs' life was a testimony to an often-forgotten truth: the fusion of creativity and critical thinking is where the magic happens.

In the age of AI, that truth is more vital than ever.

As algorithms now outperform humans in memory recall, logic puzzles, and even essay writing, a quiet crisis brews inside classrooms. The old curriculum—built to train humans to calculate, regurgitate, and comply—is rusting in place. Students still memorize facts that Siri can easily summon. They sit through lectures when learning could be an interactive experience. They answer multiple-choice questions while ChatGPT crafts poetry in perfect iambic pentameter.

The world has changed. The curriculum hasn't.

But in Finland, Singapore, Estonia, and experimental school districts across the U.S., a renaissance is underway. And at its heart is a provocative question: What does it mean to be human in the age of intelligent machines?

Curricula are being redesigned—not around subjects, but around skills that AI cannot replicate easily:

- Framing questions rather than just answering them
- Connecting ideas across disciplines
- Ethical reasoning
- Empathic storytelling
- The ability to sit with ambiguity
- The courage to challenge orthodoxy

In one redesigned middle school in Helsinki, students no longer study math in isolation. Instead, they explore "climate change" as a thematic inquiry—

drawing on statistics, biology, politics, and economics. They don't take tests; they build prototypes. In a pilot program in California, a history class doesn't end with a term paper but with students debating AI itself—its rise, risks, and the philosophical dilemmas it presents.

This is not a retreat from rigor. It is a recalibration.

Critical thinking, once reduced to logical syllogisms, is now taught as a living discipline: How do you evaluate the credibility of sources? How do you spot deepfakes? How do you hold two contradictory ideas in your mind and still move forward?

Creativity, once confined to the arts, is now embedded in science, technology, and even math. Students are given open-ended problems. They are asked not just to solve equations, but to invent the equations. Not just to analyze stories—but to write their own.

In place of standardized tests, portfolios emerge: curated bodies of work that reflect a student's curiosity, evolution, and voice. Assessment becomes narrative, not numeric.

And behind this redesign is a growing awareness: AI will never be curious for us. It will not take a walk in the woods and wonder why the leaves shimmer. It will not feel the pang of injustice or the thrill of creating something out of nothing. Only we can do that.

Education, at its best, was never about information. It was about transformation. And in the age of artificial intelligence, the most human classrooms may ultimately prove to be the most revolutionary.

The Last Human Touch: The Role of Educators in the Age of AI

If you want to understand the true purpose of an educator in the age of artificial intelligence, don't start in Silicon Valley. Start in a classroom.

Not the kind lined with Chromebooks and smart boards, but the kind where a teacher locks eyes with a restless student, recognizes the invisible weight they're carrying, and says something as simple—and seismic—as: "I believe in you."

That moment cannot be programmed.

It cannot be prompted.

And it cannot be replaced.

As AI becomes ubiquitous—writing essays, grading papers, generating lesson plans, even simulating Socratic dialogue—the question isn't whether teachers will be replaced. It's whether we will redefine what it means to teach.

In this new epoch, the role of educators is not to compete with machines. It is to champion what machines cannot do.

Educators become curators of curiosity, architects of empathy, and defenders of human nuance. They are no longer the sole transmitters of knowledge—that task has been delegated to algorithms that never sleep. But they are the translators of meaning, the ones who help students not just know the world, but understand their place within it.

When Khanmigo guides a student through algebra, it's the teacher who notices the deeper pattern—that the student has stopped believing they can succeed. When GPT-4 suggests a compelling thesis, it's the teacher who asks: "But do you agree with it?" And when an AI builds a simulation of climate change, it's the teacher who helps the class wrestle with the moral implications.

In many ways, the teacher becomes the Socrates to AI's Plato: always questioning, always pushing for something more human.

Across the globe, we are witnessing this shift materialize.

In Seoul, educators utilize AI to tailor instruction to individual learning styles—while they themselves become mentors, guiding students through the ethical and emotional complexities of AI-powered life.

In rural Kenya, AI chatbots assist in delivering multilingual education—but it's the community teacher who brings cultural context and compassion.

In Denmark, teachers are trained not only in pedagogy but also in algorithmic literacy—able to interrogate biases, explain model limitations, and spark classroom debates about what AI should and shouldn't do.

To teach in the age of AI is to be both a lighthouse and a mirror. A lighthouse, guiding students through the storm of information overload. A mirror, helping them see who they are beyond their digital reflections.

Yes, AI will answer the "what."

But educators must ask the "why."

And more importantly, the "who": Who are you becoming in this AI-shaped world?

Walter Isaacson once wrote that the best innovations occur at the intersection of the arts and the sciences—when Leonardo painted anatomy, when Einstein played the violin, and when Ada Lovelace imagined a machine that could write music.

Today, the classroom is that intersection.

And the educator is its conductor.

Chapter 7

Media, Journalism, and Entertainment: Truth and Deepfakes

In an unassuming newsroom in Brooklyn, a young editor hovers over her screen. The breaking news headline reads: "Explosion Rocks Downtown Houston." Within seconds, AI-generated images flood Twitter, some showing smoke plumes and shattered glass—except the event never happened. There was no explosion. The newsroom scrambles to verify, caught in a surreal dance between algorithm and accuracy. Welcome to journalism in the age of AI.

This chapter is not about dystopia. It is about decisions—how we tell stories, who gets to tell them, and what happens when the machines learn to craft compelling fiction dressed as fact.

When the Newsroom Meets the Neural Net

Journalism has always wrestled with two forces: speed and truth. With the advent of generative AI, speed has become almost instantaneous. Large Language Models can now summarize hearings, transcribe interviews, and even ghostwrite op-eds with an eerie level of fluency. Tools like BloombergGPT or NewsGPT.ai are transforming the backend of reporting—fact-checking, copyediting, and translation—into fully automated pipelines.

Yet with that velocity comes risk. When OpenAI's GPT-4.0 can generate a breaking-news draft in under 20 seconds, the journalistic value chain is disrupted. The question is no longer whether machines can write. It's should they—and under whose supervision?

Case in point: The Gannett Media Group had to pause its AI-generated sports recaps after readers spotted robotic, repetitive writing that failed to capture the human drama of a high school basketball game. It wasn't misinformation—it was missing emotion.

Deepfakes and the Death of Certainty

In April 2023, a video surfaced of Pope Francis wearing a Balenciaga puffer jacket. It was sharp, stylish, and utterly fake. Generated using Midjourney, the image was so convincing that it fooled millions. Welcome to the world of synthetic media—a world where what you see is no longer what happened.

This is not just a concern for celebrities and politicians. A deepfake of a local mayor promising a fake tax rebate nearly derailed a city election in Slovakia. In the entertainment industry, AI voice cloning has brought Elvis back to life—and raised concerns about consent, legacy, and ownership.

The Dual-Edged Lens in Entertainment

On the other hand, Hollywood is beginning to embrace AI—not as a threat, but as a co-creator. Marvel Studios used AI to storyboard action sequences in Avengers: Endgame. Netflix's recommendation engines, powered by deep learning, not only shape what you watch—they subtly shape what gets made.

AI is now scripting trailers, composing music, and even predicting audience sentiment before a film is released. In South Korea, Zae-In, a digital avatar powered by AI, has become a pop idol with a growing fan base—never aging, always singing, and never controversial.

This is not science fiction. This is the script being written right now, in studios and server farms across Los Angeles, Seoul, and Mumbai.

The Ethics of Truth in a Post-Truth World

To fight AI fakery, AI itself is being enlisted. Fact-checking engines like Full Fact and Logically AI utilize machine learning to identify disinformation more quickly than human moderators can. Blockchain startups are exploring ways to watermark authentic media at the point of creation—embedding proof of reality into every pixel and byte.

Still, the deeper issue is cultural. In an era when anyone with Stable Diffusion can generate an image of a war crime, the burden on audiences is no longer just to consume—but to question.

Isaac Asimov once said, "The saddest aspect of life right now is that science gathers knowledge faster than society gathers wisdom." That quote, ironically, has been misattributed by AI bots more times than one can count.

The Way Forward: Rebuilding Trust, Not Just Tools

The future of media will not be about choosing humans or machines. It will be about designing new collaborations, where humans wield AI with editorial judgment, and AI supports—not replaces—the sacred human duty to bear witness.

Journalists will need to be trained not only in ethics and storytelling, but also in prompt engineering, synthetic media detection, and data fluency. Think of them as hybrid archetypes: part reporter, part coder, part ethicist.

Like the printing press, radio, television, and the internet, AI is the next major medium changing how we tell stories. But as always, the story's integrity relies not on the medium but on the storyteller.

Key Takeaway

The AI revolution in media and entertainment demands not just innovation, but introspection. In an age of deepfakes and algorithmic news, the most radical act may be to tell the truth—with transparency, with humanity, and with the courage to stand against the tide of synthetic certainty.

Below is a Persona Grid showing the evolving roles in media, journalism, and entertainment, where human talent and AI intersect. This format highlights the transformation of traditional roles into hybrid, future-ready professions.

Persona Grid: Evolving Roles in the Age of AI Media

Let's now look at the evolving roles in media, journalism, and entertainment, where human talent and AI intersect. This format highlights the transformation of traditional roles into hybrid, future-ready professions.

Traditional Role	Reimagined Role	Description	AI Tools Involved	Skills Needed
📰 **Editor**	✍ **AI-Augmented Narrative Architect**	Oversees human-AI co-authored content, refines tone, ensures coherence, and adds nuance to machine-generated pieces.	ChatGPT, Claude, Jasper, GrammarlyGO	Editorial judgment, prompt engineering, narrative shaping, emotional tone calibration

Contd...

Traditional Role	Reimagined Role	Description	AI Tools Involved	Skills Needed
🔎 **Fact-Checker**	🛡 **Real-Time Verification Analyst**	Works with AI systems to validate facts, debunk deepfakes, and assess source credibility in real time.	Logically AI, FullFact AI, Microsoft Azure Content Safety	Data fluency, critical thinking, adversarial content detection
🎤 **Reporter**	🧠 **Multimodal Story Synthesist**	Combines audio, text, video, and AI-generated simulations to create immersive reporting experiences.	Synthesia, Descript, Midjourney, Runway	Investigative storytelling, ethical simulation, media literacy
? **Scriptwriter**	? **Narrative Co-Creation Engineer**	Uses generative AI to draft screenplays, dialogues, and scripts that are later human-edited and directed.	Sudowrite, Jasper, Sudowoodo	Genre intuition, character depth, multi-turn prompt crafting
🎬 **Director/ Producer**	🤖 **AI-Enhanced Visual Composer**	Incorporates AI into set design, CGI, casting, and storyboarding to enhance creative speed and output.	Runway, Adobe Firefly, ElevenLabs, Unreal Engine MetaHuman	Visual storytelling, human-AI coordination, digital rights awareness
🛡 **Legal & Compliance**	⚖ **AI Ethics & Provenance Officer**	Ensures content is labeled, sourced ethically, and meets emerging standards of synthetic	Blockchain watermarking tools, Truepic, AI content detectors	Legal acumen, media law, AI transparency protocols

Contd...

Traditional Role	Reimagined Role	Description	AI Tools Involved	Skills Needed
		media transparency.		
🎧 **Sound Designer**	▯ **Synthetic Audio Curator**	Designs personalized or emotion-aware soundscapes with generative audio models.	Suno.ai, ElevenLabs, Boomy	Audio editing, AI-tuned sound modulation, personalization
🧑‍🏫 **Educator/ Media Trainer**	🧒💻 **AI Literacy Coach**	Trains journalists, screenwriters, and creators in AI prompt engineering, bias detection, and verification.	Custom GPTs, Khan Academy AI, LMS platforms	Teaching, tech fluency, ethical storytelling practices

Observations:

- Every role is hybrid: Human + AI.
- Editorial judgment, ethics, and emotional intelligence are non-automatable.
- New skillsets include prompt design, deepfake detection, synthetic media ethics, and algorithm literacy.
- AI tools shift focus from mechanical tasks to creative and critical thinking.

GPT in Newsrooms: When the Algorithm Found a Byline

In 2023, a quiet revolution stirred inside a place once thought immune to automation: the newsroom. The smell of ink might still linger in memory, but today, news is a data stream—and now, machines speak it fluently.

At Bloomberg's bustling Manhattan headquarters, amid the flicker of a thousand terminals, a different kind of writer had emerged: BloombergGPT. Trained on a staggering corpus of financial documents, reports, filings, earnings calls, and market chatter, it wasn't just summarizing the news. It was understanding the markets—faster, deeper, and across dozens of languages.

Unlike consumer chatbots that stumbled over nuance, BloombergGPT was fine-tuned like a Stradivarius for financial language. It could parse complex derivatives announcements and regulatory statements, detect subtle shifts in tone during an earnings call, and draft readable, actionable insights in milliseconds. "It's not just summarizing data," one editor remarked. "It's rewriting how financial journalism is done."

But this wasn't the first time machines entered the newsroom. Years earlier, a startup from Chicago named Narrative Science had pioneered automated journalism, long before GPT was a household name. Their software, Quill, took raw data—sports scores, earnings reports, and public filings—and turned them into stories. Not fiction. Not poetry. Just clear, concise, data-driven news, built from rules and logic.

A baseball game ended? Quill had a summary ready before the last player left the field.

At first, these AI-generated articles appeared at the bottom of news websites, unsigned and unheralded. But over time, they crept up the hierarchy, trusted for speed and consistency. One editor at Forbes once quipped, "Quill never calls in sick, never files late, and doesn't get into office politics."

This transition—machine-generated content quietly replacing mundane reporting—wasn't a sudden coup. It was a creeping evolution, and one that sparked both admiration and anxiety.

Critics raised the obvious concerns: Could these systems distinguish truth from propaganda? Would data bias manipulate them? Could they understand human suffering, irony, or the politics between the lines?

The defenders replied with a pragmatic shrug: these systems were tools—extensions of the journalist's pen, not its replacement. By automating earnings reports and weather summaries, human reporters were freed to pursue deeper investigations, interviews, and analysis.

But the line between assistant and author was blurring. GPT-4, Claude, and their successors could now pitch headlines, write op-eds, and even simulate the tone of famous journalists. Some publications disclosed AI involvement, while others quietly integrated it into their workflows. Suddenly, a byline wasn't always a person—it was a process.

The newsroom had become a hybrid space: part writer's room, part algorithmic factory.

At the heart of it all is a fundamental shift: data is now narrative, and GPT-like systems are its interpreters. BloombergGPT doesn't just scan earnings reports—it narrates volatility. Narrative Science doesn't just automate summaries—it translates data into decisions.

The challenge now is not whether AI will write the news. It already does.

The question is: who controls the algorithm that shapes what billions read?

And that, as always, remains a human story.

The Algorithm Remixes the Muse — AI Music, AI Films, and the New Copyright Chaos

There's a moment in every artistic revolution when the brushstroke meets the algorithm. In the 2020s, that moment came when machines stopped merely organizing media—and began generating it.

Let's start with a small recording studio in someone's bedroom—no expensive instruments, no session musicians, no audio engineers. Just a laptop and a login to Boomy, an AI-powered music generator that allows anyone to create a full track in seconds. It asks you to choose a style—lo-fi beats, trap, EDM—and then… it composes. Not mixes. Not remixes. Composes.

You can tweak a melody here, adjust a tempo there, but the AI does the heavy lifting. In early 2023, Boomy claimed its users had already created over 15 million songs. That was more than 14% of the world's recorded music at the time. Not bad for a machine without ears.

Then came Runway, a tool for AI-generated video that took the idea of democratized creativity and injected it with cinematic ambition. Creators could write prompts like:

"A foggy forest at dawn, a girl walking alone, birds scattering,"

and watch as the model stitched together high-res, stylized scenes with eerie accuracy.

Hollywood took notice. Filmmakers worried that automation would replace animation and visual effects jobs, while independent creators, previously priced out of the industry, experienced newfound freedom. A new wave of directors was emerging—armed not with camera rigs, but with prompts.

The Copyright Catastrophe

But if art is creation, and creation is now shared with algorithms, who owns the output?

This is where the battle lines were drawn.

A copyright suit filed by Getty Images against Stability AI accused the AI firm of training models on copyrighted images without consent. Musicians, too, cried foul as AI systems mimicked the voices of Drake and The Weeknd with unsettling fidelity. These weren't covers. They were deepfakes in melodic disguise.

The legal world was left scrambling. U.S. copyright law, built in the analog age, struggled to answer questions that felt ripped from sci-fi:

- Can you copyright a song if no human composed it?
- Is a model trained on 1 million copyrighted tracks violating fair use?
- If I prompt an AI to mimic John Williams, is that plagiarism—or homage?

To date, U.S. Copyright Office rulings have stated that purely machine-generated content cannot be copyrighted. But that hasn't stopped the tidal wave of AI-generated IP from flooding platforms.

Human + Machine: The New Muse

And yet, for all the chaos, something profound was emerging.

Grammy-winning producer Taryn Southern began co-composing music with AI tools like Amper and AIVA. Visual artists used generative video to storyboard their films in minutes. Writers collaborated with GPT models to build narrative arcs and scripts, then rendered them in Runway.

This wasn't about machines replacing artists. It was about redefining authorship.

"AI is like jazz," one creative director at OpenAI quipped. "You riff with it. You don't control it."

The best creatives, it turned out, were not those who feared the machine—but those who adapted their vision to what the machine could amplify. The prompt became a brush. The interface, a new kind of canvas.

Echoes of Gutenberg

If there's one thing history teaches us—from Gutenberg's press to Photoshop—it's that disruption in art is always met with resistance, followed by reinvention.

Yes, there will be casualties: jobs lost in audio mastering, manual animation, or media production. But there will also be an explosion of creators—young, old, trained, and untrained—using AI as a co-creator, a partner, even a muse.

We stand at the edge of a new artistic epoch—where the creative act is no longer limited by skill, tools, or access. But with this comes an urgent need: to redraw the lines of copyright, consent, and credit in a world where anyone—or anything—can create.

In the next chapter, we'll journey into the legal labyrinth and the ethics maze AI has unleashed across media. But for now, pause. Play that Boomy track, rendered by a teenager in Nairobi, scored by code, and shared with the world.

Listen closely.

That's the sound of a new Renaissance.

Battling Misinformation in Real-Time

In a brightly lit room inside a modest office on the outskirts of Vilnius, Lithuania, a team of cyber-detectives—half coders, half journalists—works against the clock. Their mission: stop the spread of a lie before it metastasizes. This is the headquarters of DebunkEU.org, an organization dedicated to identifying, flagging, and neutralizing disinformation campaigns—often originating from state-sponsored troll farms—before they ripple across Europe.

It's not unlike trying to stop a virus mid-air.

The battle against misinformation is no longer about correction after the fact. It's about real-time containment, where AI-driven misinformation bots clash with AI-driven truth detection systems in a duel as old as civilization itself: belief vs. verification.

The Speed of Deceit

In the 20th century, misinformation traveled at the speed of the printed word. Now, in milliseconds, an AI-generated video can portray a politician declaring war, or a celebrity endorsing a dangerous drug—all before breakfast. Deepfakes powered by generative adversarial networks (GANs) have added a disturbing realism to digital lies.

By 2023, NewsGuard had found that AI-generated news websites—over 600 of them—were producing fabricated stories with robotic consistency. Entire narratives—built on fictional sources and pseudo-scientific claims—had the veneer of authenticity.

Misinformation isn't just fast. It's personalized. Microtargeted narratives are delivered to your feed based on your biases. AI knows what angers you, what affirms you, and what you'll click. In this ecosystem, truth becomes a casualty of convenience.

Rise of the AI Defenders

Enter the countermeasures.

At Google's Jigsaw division, machine learning models, such as the Perspective API, are being trained to detect toxicity and disinformation in comment threads. Facebook (now Meta) has deployed self-supervised learning models to scan billions of posts and spot harmful trends before they go viral.

And then there's Truth Goggles, a browser plug-in that highlights potentially dubious claims and offers sources in real time—like a fact-checking co-pilot whispering in your ear.

The hope is that AI can become a scalpel for discernment rather than a megaphone for deceit.

Real-Time Combat: The Ukraine Test Case

Nowhere was this battle more visible than in Ukraine.

In the early hours of Russia's 2022 invasion, doctored videos flooded Telegram and Twitter—Ukrainian officials surrendering, civilians turning on each other, NATO troops committing atrocities. But for the first time, digital sleuths armed with AI tools were ready.

OSINT (Open Source Intelligence) networks cross-verify locations, timestamps, and weather patterns to debunk fake information within minutes. Groups like Bellingcat—blending machine vision with journalistic rigor—showed what the future of information defense could look like.

Ethics at the Speed of Light

The deeper challenge lies in the ethics of automation. Who decides what's "misinformation"? Can we trust AI to be the arbiter of truth? What happens when governments use these same tools to suppress dissent, under the guise of fact-checking?

The specter of algorithmic authoritarianism looms.

In response, UNESCO has proposed global guidelines for AI in journalism, emphasizing transparency, human oversight, and the protection of dissenting voices. The future of truth must be more than technologically sound—it must be morally rooted.

The Human in the Loop

Despite the immense computational power, one thing remains clear: we still require human judgment.

Whether it's a teacher helping students recognize media bias, a journalist verifying sources, or a citizen taking a moment to pause before sharing, truth is not just coded into lines of Python. It is a shared civic responsibility.

The battle for truth in the age of AI is not just technological. It is philosophical. It is emotional. It is human.

And in that lies our greatest hope.

Chapter 8

Manufacturing and Supply Chains – The Smart Factory

It began, like many revolutions do, not with fanfare but with a quiet recalibration of code on a German assembly line. At Siemens' Amberg facility, a factory once manned by engineers carrying clipboards has evolved into a hive of interconnected sensors, predictive algorithms, and robotic arms that not only execute commands but also anticipate them.

This was not Henry Ford's factory. Nor even of Toyota's lean production system. This was the smart factory—the fusion of artificial intelligence, the Internet of Things (IoT), cloud computing, and cyber-physical systems. What electricity did for the Second Industrial Revolution, and automation did for the third, AI is doing for the fourth: injecting cognition into production.

The Digital Nervous System of the Factory

In this new paradigm, the factory floor is no longer dumb iron. AI stitches together a network where each machine, conveyor belt, and sensor becomes a node in a living nervous system. Real-time data from temperature, torque, pressure, and vibration is analyzed on the edge—close to the source—to flag anomalies before a failure occurs.

In a BMW plant, for instance, machine learning models detect minute changes in ultrasonic signals to predict welding defects. In a Tesla Gigafactory, AI algorithms orchestrate supply chain dynamics with the speed of a trading floor, adjusting material inflows as if playing a symphony with invisible hands.

These are not isolated anecdotes. According to McKinsey, AI could add between $1.2 trillion and $2 trillion in annual manufacturing productivity by 2030. But the transformation is not just about optimization—it's about adaptation.

Supply Chains That Think

When COVID-19 struck, it exposed the brittleness of global supply chains—just-in-time became just too late. In response, companies such as Unilever and Schneider Electric began deploying AI-powered control towers that offer end-to-end visibility, enabling them to simulate scenarios, rebalance inventory, and re-route logistics in real-time.

Amazon, for example, developed machine learning models that predict demand shifts not just at a national level, but at the neighborhood level. It was less about stockpiling, more about smartpiling. And it wasn't just the corporate giants—startups like Elementum and ClearMetal introduced supply chain AI as a service, democratizing resilience.

The Rise of Human-Machine Symbiosis

Inside the smart factory, workers are no longer merely operators. They are augmented analysts. Wearing AR headsets or working beside cobots (collaborative robots), they interact with AI not as a tool, but as a teammate. A technician at GE might consult a machine-learning-based diagnostic assistant, while an Airbus engineer uses an AI-powered visual inspection system to detect hairline cracks invisible to the human eye.

It's a shift not just in technology—but in identity.

The forklift operator now monitors logistics dashboards. The maintenance technician now interprets digital twins. The plant manager consults AI-generated what-if scenarios before reconfiguring lines. These are the new artisans of the Fourth Industrial Revolution.

Challenges at the Edge

But beneath the polished sheen of Industry 4.0 lies complexity. Security threats increase with connectivity. Algorithmic opacity can create black boxes in critical decision-making. And not all workers are thrilled by the change. A study by Capgemini found that while 60% of manufacturers believe AI will increase job satisfaction, only 23% of workers agreed.

There is also the question of digital divides—between high-tech factories and small or medium manufacturers, between developed and developing economies. China, Germany, and the U.S. lead the charge. But where does that leave Vietnam? Kenya? Argentina?

The race toward smart factories must not become a race that leaves others behind.

What's Next: Autonomous Production

Looking ahead, the vision extends beyond smart to autonomous. Factories that adjust production in real-time based on global news sentiment. Machines that learn from each other. Entire supply networks that operate like neural networks—self-healing, self-optimizing, self-directing.

Elon Musk famously tried to "automate everything" at Tesla and failed—at first. But that failure seeded the next wave of innovation. Today, Tesla's factories are learning organisms, with AI improving yield, reducing downtime, and shaping the blueprint for a manufacturing future that thinks.

Just as Babbage's analytical engine gave rise to the modern computer, today's intelligent production lines may become the birthplace of general industrial intelligence.

In the words of a production engineer at Siemens:

"We used to worry about whether the machine would run. Now we ask what the machine can teach us."

In the age of AI, the smart factory is not a place. It's a state of mind.

The Symphony of the Smart Factory : Predictive Maintenance, IoT and Human-Robot Collaboration

Every industrial revolution has had its virtuosos—engineers, machinists, and inventors who could hear the music of machines. In the Fourth Industrial Revolution, that music is becoming a symphony, orchestrated not by steam or steel, but by sensors, algorithms, and collaboration between humans and intelligent machines.

The Whispering Machines: Predictive Maintenance and the Art of Listening

In traditional manufacturing, the worst enemy was unpredictability. A machine could stop mid-shift, halting an entire assembly line and incurring millions of dollars in losses. Maintenance was reactive, and breakdowns were surprises—costly, frustrating, and often dangerous.

Enter predictive maintenance, the quiet revolution. With IoT sensors embedded deep within turbines, motors, and conveyor belts, today's machines no longer merely perform—they communicate. They emit data as regularly as a heartbeat: vibrations, temperature spikes, stress levels. Fed into machine learning algorithms, this data no longer just warns of failure. It foretells it.

Companies like Siemens and GE have turned factories into living organisms—nervous systems humming with alerts, dashboards pulsing with probabilities. Engineers are no longer just repairmen; they're diagnosticians, interpreting the language of machines long before a failure occurs.

The Neural Fabric: IoT + AI Integration

What powers this predictive capability is the convergence of IoT (Internet of Things) and AI—the sensors acting as sensory organs, the algorithms as the brain. Like the spinal cord of a sentient being, data travels from every cog and wheel to centralized or edge-based AI systems, which don't merely log information—they learn from it.

Amazon's fulfillment centers and Tesla's gigafactories are examples where thousands of sensors feed real-time data into systems that autonomously adjust speeds, reroute power, or fine-tune supply chains. In this environment, adaptability replaces rigidity, and foresight replaces reaction.

The Dance of Flesh and Steel: Human-Robot Collaboration

But perhaps the most fascinating transformation is not the replacement of humans, but the partnership being forged between people and intelligent machines. In old factories, robots were caged off—dangerous and unaware of the human workers beside them. In the smart factory, they move freely, equipped with vision, sensors, and AI-powered intent recognition.

Cobots—collaborative robots—work beside humans on the factory floor, lifting heavy parts, drilling with precision, or guiding the worker with visual cues. In BMW's plants, humans install car doors while cobots hold them in place. At Fanuc and ABB, robots learn from human demonstrations, adapting their movements in real-time.

This is not mere automation. This is augmentation. A symphony where the human brain, with its intuition and dexterity, partners with AI's relentless precision and stamina.

From Assembly Line to Neural Network

Henry Ford imagined an assembly line of interchangeable parts. The 21st-century vision is different: a living, learning ecosystem where machines anticipate, adapt, and collaborate.

The smart factory doesn't merely make things. It learns how to make better things tomorrow. And in doing so, it changes not just how we manufacture—but how we work, how we think, and how we coexist with the intelligence we've built.

Just as electricity once turned factories into engines of progress, AI and IoT are turning them into engines of foresight. And in this great transformation, we are all being taught a new language—one where silence is never empty, and every pulse of data is a line in an ever-evolving symphony.

BMW, Siemens and Foxconn: Precision, Partnership, and Productivity in the Age of AI

In the heart of Bavaria, where precision engineering has long been part of the national character, BMW quietly began transforming its automotive plants—not by adding more machinery, but by infusing intelligence into its existing systems. At the company's Regensburg facility, robots no longer move on preprogrammed tracks. Instead, guided by AI and computer vision, they adapt in real time to the manufacturing environment—identifying defects, self-correcting, and optimizing their routes. It is a dance of man and machine, choreographed not only by engineers but also by algorithms that learn from every movement.

BMW's journey into smart manufacturing was not a solitary one. It drew on partnerships—with Nvidia for AI computing, with Amazon Web Services for cloud architecture, and with a new generation of coders and data scientists who were as vital to the car's evolution as the designers once were. The "digital twin" of every vehicle allowed simulations of production before a single bolt was turned. This was not just about faster cars. It was about finding a faster way to learn—about creating a feedback loop where every assembly line action taught the system how to improve next time.

Siemens, meanwhile, wasn't just helping others build smart factories—it was building a philosophy. At Amberg, their electronics plant became a benchmark for AI-led precision manufacturing. Known as one of the most automated production facilities in the world, the plant uses AI to monitor and control every step of the PCB (printed circuit board) manufacturing process. What makes it stand out isn't just the automation—it's the harmonization of humans, data, and decisions. Engineers no longer just fix problems—they predict them. Algorithms scan data for anomalies before a machine fails, triggering maintenance before disruption. In essence, the factory thinks.

But Siemens didn't stop at internal transformation. It began offering these digital capabilities to partners across industries. Through its Xcelerator platform, Siemens transformed AI-powered manufacturing into a service—one that even small and mid-sized firms could afford to integrate. It was a democratization of German engineering. As if the centuries-old craft of Meisters had entered the age of machine learning.

On the other side of the globe, in Shenzhen, Foxconn —the company once synonymous with sheer scale —began to write a different kind of story. Known for assembling the world's iPhones, it turned its attention to AI not as an afterthought, but as the only way to remain viable in a world where labor costs rise, margins shrink, and customer demand shifts by the hour. Foxconn's "lights-out" factories—so named because they need no human illumination—became the symbol of a new frontier. Machines assembled machines, and vision systems tracked quality with a level of consistency that no human inspector could match.

But the real insight at Foxconn was this: AI wasn't just replacing labor. It was redefining it. Factory workers became drone pilots, quality auditors became data analysts. The company even retrained line supervisors to work with AI dashboards, interpreting predictive analytics to prevent breakdowns and bottlenecks. In short, human hands gave way to human judgment. It wasn't about fewer people. It was about smarter roles.

These three companies—BMW with its digital twins, Siemens with its self-aware systems, Foxconn with its autonomous lines—represent more than innovation. They embody a shift from industrial might to algorithmic agility. From throughput to thinking.

And like so many stories in the age of AI, theirs is not just about machines getting smarter. It's about people learning to lead with data, collaborate with code, and shape a new future of production—not just for profit, but for precision, purpose, and possibility.

Reskilling for the Age of Cobots: From Grit to Graphs

In the fluorescent hum of a midwestern parts assembly plant, Marvin Ramirez, 52, stands at a workstation next to a robot that doesn't quite look like a robot. It doesn't have the imposing bulk of an industrial arm or the whirring menace of a factory automaton. This one—sleek, shoulder-height, with soft rubber joints and a friendly LED face—is a collaborative robot, or cobot. It doesn't take Marvin's job. It works alongside him. And the story of how Marvin got here tells us everything we need to know about the real industrial revolution underway.

For decades, blue-collar work meant mastering repetition—tightening a bolt, welding a seam, checking a panel. The virtues were speed, consistency, and physical stamina. But cobots brought with them a new requirement: the ability to adapt, to interpret data, to communicate with machines not as tools, but as teammates. The line between laborer and operator blurred.

Reskilling, in this new world, didn't mean sending people back to school for years. It meant injecting just-in-time learning into the workflow—digitally, visually, tactically.

Marvin's factory partnered with a workforce development nonprofit, teaming up with a local community college and a tech start-up specializing in AR-based learning modules. He learned how to "train" his cobot using simple gestures, how to monitor sensor data on a tablet, how to troubleshoot faults by interpreting patterns—not wiring diagrams. It was no longer about welding skill; it was about pattern recognition, no longer about muscle memory, but about machine empathy.

In Stuttgart, Germany, Mercedes-Benz began introducing cobots across its body shop. But instead of reducing its workforce, it launched "Mechatronics Accelerators"—a fast-track reskilling program. Workers were upskilled to interface with AI-driven systems, using digital twin simulators to predict breakdowns and optimize workflows. The cobot became a partner, not a replacement, and those who once feared automation began designing with it.

In China's Pearl River Delta, Foxconn took it a step further. Each cobot deployment came with an AI dashboard and a mentorship pairing—a younger engineer with digital-native instincts was paired with an older worker steeped in mechanical intuition. It wasn't just reskilling—it was cross-generational fusion. The program was called "Human+." The philosophy: machines don't kill jobs; outdated mindsets do.

And so, the question isn't: Will cobots replace workers? The real question is: Are we equipping workers to collaborate with intelligence—both human and artificial?

At its core, this isn't a story of obsolescence. It's a story of transformation. Of retooling human capital for an era when adaptability beats automation. Where grit is fused with graphs. And where the factory floor, once an echo chamber of repetition, now hums with curiosity, collaboration, and co-creation.

The age of cobots may have started in labs. But its future lies in the hands of those like Marvin—who looked at a blinking robot, shrugged, and said: "I guess I'd better learn its language."

And he did.

Chapter 9

Retail and E-Commerce: The Age of Personalization

When Jeff Bezos launched Amazon from his garage in 1994, he wasn't simply trying to sell books. He was trying to understand customers at scale. "We start with the customer and work backward," he famously said. That philosophy—powered by data, feedback loops, and relentless experimentation—would become the DNA of the retail revolution.

But the next leap didn't come from warehouses or faster shipping. It came from intelligence. Not human, but artificial.

From Mass Consumption to Mass Customization

For over a century, the retail model was driven by economies of scale—piles of inventory, generic messaging, and location as king. Department stores thrived on uniformity. If you were lucky, the sales assistant remembered your name.

Today, AI remembers everything: what you browsed at 9:43 PM, the sandals you abandoned in your cart, your tendency to splurge after payday. From predictive algorithms that power Netflix recommendations to AI stylists that curate your fashion box, the retail experience is no longer transactional—it's psychological.

The New Merchants: Algorithms with Intuition

Consider Stitch Fix, the fashion startup that combines machine learning with human stylists. Customers fill out a questionnaire, and AI creates hundreds of outfit combinations based on data from similar shoppers. A stylist refines the final selection—but the algorithm has done the heavy lifting.

Then there's Shopify's Sidekick, an AI-powered assistant helping small e-commerce businesses make inventory decisions, create marketing copy, and even suggest discount strategies.

And don't forget Amazon's anticipatory shipping patents—algorithms so confident in your behavior that they prepare to ship items before you even click "Buy."

These are not just tools. They're new forms of retail intuition, crafted in code.

The Rise of the Algorithmic Aisle

In the physical store, the shelf was the battlefront. In the digital age, it's the feed.

Retailers like Walmart and Target are deploying real-time AI-driven demand forecasting. Cameras observe foot traffic patterns. Heat maps track which shelves convert best. Sensors know when your gaze lingers on a product.

AI knows when you're indecisive. And increasingly, it knows why.

Hyper-Personalization: Miracle or Manipulation?

AI's ability to tailor ads, discounts, and content to the individual shopper feels magical—until it doesn't.

When a teenage girl's pregnancy was predicted by Target's predictive analytics, long before she told her family, the headlines questioned not the accuracy, but the ethics. How much personalization is too much? What happens when AI knows us better than we know ourselves?

Isaac Asimov once warned, "Any technology sufficiently advanced is indistinguishable from magic." But in retail, that magic now walks a tightrope between delight and surveillance.

Virtual Try-Ons and Conversational Commerce

Step into the dressing room of the future. L'Oreal uses AI to let customers try on lipstick using augmented reality. IKEA's AR app lets you place furniture in your living room. AI is not just recommending—it's immersing.

Meanwhile, conversational commerce—shopping via AI chatbots or voice assistants—has experienced significant growth. You no longer click through categories. You say, "Find me a lightweight travel jacket under $100"—and the bot negotiates the digital mall for you.

Case Study: Alibaba's AI Empire

In China, Alibaba's City Brain doesn't just manage logistics—it manages entire ecosystems. Its AI predicts consumer surges, reroutes delivery drones, and even adjusts traffic lights to favor package vans during Singles 'Day sales.

Alibaba's FashionAI creates "smart mirrors" in stores that display outfit suggestions, drawing from both inventory and a customer's personal style history. The line between online and offline dissolves.

In the West, Amazon is the gold standard. In China, Alibaba is the future supermarket, urban planner, stylist, and checkout counter rolled into one.

Jobs Displaced˜ Jobs Reimagined

Yes, AI has automated routine tasks, including cashiering, stock management, and basic customer service. However, it has also given rise to new retail roles, including personalization analysts, chatbot scriptwriters, AI ethicists, and digital storefront designers.

The mall may be dying—but new marketplaces are being born in code.

The Path Forward: Trust˜ Transparency˜ and Experience

The future of retail isn't just about intelligence. It's about empathy encoded in design. Consumers will reward brands that use AI not merely to sell, but to understand, respect, and evolve with them.

Transparency—why a recommendation was made, how data is used—will become a differentiator. Privacy is not just a compliance issue. It's a brand value.

Think about it:" The true revolution is not that machines understand humans, but that humans learn to shape machines that reflect their better selves."

AI Production Recommendation Engines (Amazon, Shopify Magic)

In the history of commerce, few inflection points have been as quietly radical as the rise of algorithmic personalization. Where once the corner shopkeeper knew your name, your family, and your preferences, today's AI-powered recommendation engines have resurrected that intimacy—only now, at the scale of billions.

Let's start with Amazon. At first glance, its product suggestion bar—"Customers who bought this also bought..."—seems almost quaint. But behind that simple line is a thundering engine of data analytics, behavior tracking, and predictive modeling. Amazon doesn't just observe what you buy; it watches how long you hover, what you click, what you abandon in your cart, the time of day you shop, your reading habits, and even your scrolling speed. It feeds all of that into a massive neural network that outputs one thing: prediction. What are you likely to want before you even know you want it?

Jeff Bezos famously said, "We start with the customer and work backwards." AI has flipped that equation: now the machine starts with your past and works forward, anticipating your desires in real-time. The result? Its recommendation engine drives 35% of Amazon's revenue. It's not a sidebar. It's the core of the machine.

Then comes Shopify Magic, the upstart's answer to Amazon's behemoth. Shopify democratizes AI, offering small and medium retailers the same kind of power that Amazon has engineered in-house. A one-person t-shirt brand in Boise can now use GPT-powered product descriptions, auto-generated marketing emails, and real-time personalization tools that adapt to a user's behavior as fluidly as Netflix queues up your next show. Shopify Magic seamlessly integrates LLMs (like GPT-4), user behavior analytics, and tone-modulating copywriting into a unified backend. It's not just smart—it's empathetic. It adjusts its language, product prioritization, and recommendations based on how a user reacts in-session.

What's remarkable is the shift in how commerce understands people. Old-school segmentation was about demographic buckets—millennials, soccer moms, high-income Gen Xers. AI recommendation engines have obliterated that. Now, every person is their own segment. The new model is N = 1. You are the data point. You are the persona. You are the market.

This has created a paradox—a hyper-personalized scale. We are no longer mass-marketed to. We are individually marketed at scale.

But this shift also invites scrutiny. When algorithms decide what we see, they also decide what we don't. Personalization can become a filter bubble. Recommendations can become manipulation. The line between helpful suggestion and behavioral nudging blurs. If Amazon is the world's most successful recommender, it is also the world's most powerful persuader.

And in that tension lies the story of AI in commerce: the return of the shopkeeper's intuition—only now, it lives in the cloud, and it knows us better than we know ourselves.

Dynamic Pricing, Virtual Try-Ons, and Automated Fuflillment

In the winding narrative of commerce, some revolutions announce themselves with a bang. Others arrive with a ping.

Imagine opening your phone at 9:04 p.m. and seeing the price of the running shoes you'd been eyeing drop by $17.52. What caused that shift? Perhaps it was your browsing history. Or a sudden dip in regional demand. Or maybe a competitor, half a continent away, changed their offer by 3%, triggering a cascading recalibration across platforms. This is dynamic pricing, and it is no longer a tool reserved for airline tickets or Uber rides. It's woven into the DNA of modern commerce.

At Amazon, Walmart, and Alibaba, dynamic pricing algorithms don't just react—they predict. They consume trillions of data points, including weather, supply chain logistics, consumer sentiment, and even local events. A sudden rainstorm in Seattle might push up the price of umbrellas in real time. A TikTok video going viral about a skincare serum? Expect its price to surge by morning.

Behind it all are AI models constantly asking a single question: What is this shopper most willing to pay—right now?

But commerce isn't just numbers—it's experiences.

That's where virtual try-ons come in. Using AI-powered augmented reality, brands such as Warby Parker, L'Oréal, and Nike have transformed the mirror experience. A teenager in Jakarta can swipe through fifty lipstick shades and see them instantly rendered on her face. A dad in Munich can model six different frame styles, each automatically adjusted for lighting and facial geometry. The fitting room has become the algorithm.

This isn't mere gimmickry—it's a quiet revolution in confidence. When shoppers can see before they buy, they buy more—and return less. According to Shopify, retailers using virtual try-ons have seen up to a 94% increase in engagement and a 40% higher conversion rate.

Then there's the invisible ballet that unfolds after we click 'Buy'.

Welcome to automated fulfillment, where warehouse floors resemble a choreographed dance of robotic arms and autonomous shuttles. At Ocado, JD.com, and Zara, AI doesn't just power what gets sold—it orchestrates how it moves. Robots pick, sort, and pack. Predictive logistics determines the fastest route, not just to your city, but to your doorstep, optimizing based on traffic patterns and driver availability.

What once required armies of pickers and forklifts now unfolds in silence—guided by real-time demand signals and digital twins of every product, order, and pallet.

These aren't just efficiencies. They're philosophical shifts.

- Dynamic pricing reframes value as a conversation, not a sticker.
- Virtual try-ons collapse the boundary between self-image and shopping.
- Automated fulfillment dissolves the wait, turning desire into doorstep reality.

But here's the deeper story: In this new age, the moment of sale has stretched into a loop of prediction, interaction, and automation. The product is no longer the hero—the experience is. And AI? It is the unseen narrator of that story, shaping each scene before the customer even knows it's begun.

Human Touch vs. Machine Efficiency in Customer Experience

In the early 1990s, when Steve Jobs was asked what separated Apple from the rest, he didn't say "processing speed" or "RAM." He said, "We make tools for the mind that advance humankind."

It's a distinction that still matters in the age of AI—especially when machines can now anticipate your needs, your preferences, even your tone of voice.

But as algorithms become more adept at delivering convenience, we're left grappling with an increasingly urgent question:

What is the value of a human touch in a world optimized for machine efficiency?

The Rise of Frictionless Interactions

Walk into a Starbucks in Seoul or Seattle, and you may never speak to a barista. AI-powered kiosks remember your last five orders, recommend seasonal upgrades, and process payment—all within seconds.

At Amazon Go, you can walk in, grab your lunch, and walk out. No checkout. No cashier. No conversation.

Efficiency, yes. Elegance, perhaps. But does it feel… human?

The metrics are persuasive. According to McKinsey, customer service chatbots can resolve 80% of standard queries and reduce support costs by up to 30%. AI recommendation engines drive over 35% of Amazon's total revenue.

But here's the paradox: the more seamless the experience becomes, the more we notice what's missing.

When Empathy Becomes the Differentiator

In 2020, during the COVID-19 pandemic, JetBlue customer service reps were empowered to offer not just refunds—but reassurance. Some even called customers personally. It wasn't scalable. It wasn't automated. But it was remembered.

That's because humans don't just want answers—they want acknowledgment.

AI can recognize keywords in a complaint. A human recognizes the emotion behind it.

Consider the case of Zappos, the online retailer famous for its 10-hour customer service calls. No script. No bots. Just a human, listening. In a world of one-click returns, Zappos won loyalty through connection.

The Hybrid Future: Augmented Empathy

The real promise lies not in choosing between humans or machines, but in blending the two.

Imagine an airline agent whose screen, powered by sentiment analysis, alerts her: The customer is likely frustrated; speak gently. Or a physician, aided by AI, who knows exactly which patients are overdue for follow-up—but still sits down and says, "Tell me how you're doing."

Companies like Salesforce and Zendesk are already building AI copilots for service agents, combining speed with sensitivity.

Because machines can analyze feelings—but only humans can feel them.

A New Definition of Efficiency

In the industrial era, efficiency meant faster production. In the digital era, it meant faster transactions. But in the AI era, efficiency must evolve.

It must mean:

- Speed with empathy
- Accuracy with intuition
- Personalization with presence

Because in the end, it's not how fast you serve the customer—it's how deeply you understand them.

Think about it: If history teaches us anything—from Leonardo to Steve Jobs—it's that technology becomes transformative only when it amplifies our humanity, not replaces it.

AI can automate the transaction.

Humans can elevate it into a relationship.

And that, perhaps, is the greatest innovation of all.

Chapter 10

Transportation and Logistics – Steering the Autonomous Future

It began, as so many revolutions do, not with a bang, but with a data point.

Somewhere in a Waymo vehicle inching through the streets of Phoenix, a car hesitated at an unprotected left turn. A human driver might have darted forward. The AI, however, paused, calculated, and waited. Behind that pause were billions of parameters, a neural network trained on years of driving footage, edge cases, and accident simulations. That single decision—calculated in milliseconds—signaled something profound: the dawn of machine agency on the roads.

Transportation and logistics, once domains of gears, diesel, and manual schedules, are being reimagined by artificial intelligence into a choreography of data-driven decisions, sensor symphonies, and predictive precision. This isn't just about autonomous vehicles gliding silently along highways. It's about reshaping the entire flow of people and products, from warehouses to city streets.

The Algorithm That Drives

Tesla may have claimed the spotlight, but it was Google's sibling, Waymo, that quietly logged over 20 million autonomous miles before most of the world noticed. Meanwhile, in Shanghai, Baidu's Apollo Go launched driverless robotaxis across major business districts. In Europe, Volvo's autonomous trucking projects with Aurora are rerouting the very arteries of freight.

Each of these efforts underscores a new kind of mobility—where AI doesn't just assist the driver; it becomes the driver.

And it's not just road transport. In the skies, Zipline's autonomous drones deliver blood and medical supplies across Rwanda and Ghana. On the seas, autonomous cargo ships, such as the Yara Birkeland in Norway, navigate harbors with no crew on board. The transportation AI revolution is multimodal—and it's global.

The Invisible Intelligence of Logistics

Behind every package delivered in a day, every rerouted container at a port, or every restocked shelf at a retail store is a web of decisions driven by machine learning.

Amazon's fulfillment centers are legendary not just for their scale but for their machine-guided logistics. AI forecasts demand spikes, determines the optimal warehouse location, and guides robot arms that never tire. UPS's ORION system—short for On-Road Integrated Optimization and Navigation—saves the company over 100 million miles driven annually, thanks to AI that rethinks routes daily.

In logistics, success lies not only in speed but in foresight. And AI brings something rare: predictive clarity. When pandemic lockdowns disrupted global supply chains, companies that had invested in AI-based risk modeling, like DHL and Flexport, rebounded faster. Machines, it turned out, could see the ripple effects of a factory closure in Wuhan days before humans noticed.

The New Roadblocks

But the autonomous future isn't all smooth pavement.

There's the data dilemma: autonomous systems require vast amounts of training data—such as road conditions, pedestrian behavior, and traffic anomalies. Who owns it? Who regulates it?

There's the liability puzzle: if an AI truck crashes, is the manufacturer responsible? The coder? The company that deployed it?

And then there's the human cost. From long-haul truckers in the American Midwest to port workers in Asia, jobs built on muscle and memory face dislocation.

As with every industrial revolution, the key lies not just in the technology, but in the transition.

The Human at the Helm

Interestingly, even in this highly automated landscape, the human is far from obsolete.

Pilots still guide autonomous drones in the final mile. Remote operators monitor fleets of autonomous trucks. Dispatchers now act more like air traffic controllers, interpreting AI insights and making judgment calls.

The job isn't disappearing—it's being redefined.

New roles are emerging: mobility ethicists, AI safety trainers, simulation engineers, and autonomous system auditors. The autonomous era requires a hybrid workforce—humans who can trust, test, and team with machines.

The Road Ahead

Perhaps the most poignant symbol of this transformation comes not from Silicon Valley but from rural Arizona, where a visually impaired man took a ride in a Waymo without a driver. For the first time in his life, he traveled independently.

That's the paradox of the AI age. What seems like a machine revolution is, at its heart, a human one.

AI in transportation and logistics is not just about moving things—it's about moving people, capabilities, and aspirations. The roads we build with AI may be paved with algorithms, but they are driven by a very human hope: to get there faster, safer, and together.

AI in Self-Driving (Tesla, Waymo), Drones (Zipline), and Fleet Optimization

The Code that Learned to Drive

It began, not with a bang, but with a cautious, stuttering jolt—an awkward left turn on the streets of Mountain View. It was 2009, and a handful of Google engineers, fresh off their moonshot high, had decided to build something wild: a car that could drive itself. They called it Project Chauffeur. The world would come to know it as Waymo.

Meanwhile, halfway across the country, Elon Musk was reimagining cars not just as electric machines, but as software platforms on wheels. His company, Tesla, began feeding vast amounts of driver data into its AI systems—each mile driven became a line of code, a correction, a moment of learning.

Both were reaching for the same star: a car that didn't need a driver.

From Algorithms to Autonomy: A Tale of Two Approaches

Waymo took the academic route. With LIDAR sensors spinning atop their vehicles, high-definition maps, and tightly controlled environments, Waymo chased "Level 4" autonomy—where the car could handle almost all situations within a defined domain.

Tesla, characteristically, chose the edge. Eschewing LIDAR in favor of computer vision, it bet big on its neural networks, trained on billions of video frames from real drivers. Its Full Self-Driving (FSD) system is like a teenager learning by experience—awkward but relentlessly improving.

This isn't just a battle of AI philosophies. It's a redefinition of human-machine collaboration. When a Tesla updates overnight, it's not just a patch—it's the car getting smarter. It's the algorithm sleeping with one eye open.

Zipline: Drones That Save Lives

While cars were learning to drive, Zipline was learning to fly.

In 2016, the Rwandan government partnered with this Silicon Valley startup to solve a very human problem—getting blood to patients in remote areas quickly. Zipline's drones, powered by AI flight planning, were the answer.

They flew through valleys and monsoons, dropped packages using parachutes, and landed with precision honed by machine learning and physics.

Today, Zipline is expanding to Ghana, Nigeria, Japan, and the U.S., evolving from a humanitarian solution to a commercial logistics player. Each flight is autonomously planned, continuously optimized—an orchestra of wind patterns, demand prediction, and payload geometry. It's not just drones flying anymore. It's AI managing an aerial supply chain.

The Invisible Brain Behind Fleets

From Amazon vans to UPS trucks, fleet optimization is undergoing a silent revolution. AI doesn't just track packages—it predicts delays, reroutes in real time, and even advises on driver behavior to save fuel and time.

Startups like KeepTruckin and Nauto are leveraging vehicle data to gain behavioral insights. FedEx is using AI to predict what time you'll be home. Ryder is partnering with autonomous trucking firms, such as Embark and Aurora, to redefine long-haul freight.

This isn't the future of logistics. It's already here. When your online order arrives faster than expected, thank a convolutional neural network.

Where Roads Meet Ethics

The roads AI is steering us down are not without detours.

Who is responsible when an AI-driven car crashes? What happens when a drone delivers medication to the wrong house? How do you regulate algorithms that rewrite themselves faster than governments can legislate?

In 2022, a Waymo car was stuck in a construction zone and dialed support. In 2023, a Tesla with FSD mode nearly collided with a cyclist in San Francisco. These aren't bugs. They are signs that AI is still learning—and that we must guide that learning with human-centered values.

From Co-Drivers to Collaborators

Ultimately, AI will not replace us. It will be our co-driver.

A Tesla doesn't dream of freedom—it calculates it. A Waymo doesn't yearn for exploration—it maps it. But the human remains the storyteller, the navigator of meaning.

As AI gets better at driving trucks, flying drones, and optimizing fleets, the real question becomes: Can we steer its purpose as skillfully as it steers our machines?

That's not just a technical challenge. It's a human one.

Impact on Drivers, Pilots, and Logistics Managers

When the Wheel Steers Itself: Rewriting the Role of Humans in Motion

In 2025, a long-haul truck pulls out of a Dallas distribution hub bound for Chicago. There's no one in the cab. Instead, a logistics manager in Atlanta is monitoring its journey through a multi-screen dashboard, flanked by predictive analytics, weather alerts, and machine-learning forecasts. A human engineer in San Francisco wrote the AI routing algorithm. And a fleet supervisor in Austin just reassigned another autonomous rig on the fly to avoid congestion caused by a Taylor Swift concert.

The driver is no longer behind the wheel. But the human is still in the loop.

This is the paradox of autonomy: we remove the person from the cockpit, the cab, or the warehouse—but not from the equation.

The Driver: Displaced or Redeployed?

Truck drivers have long been icons of freedom and fatigue—hauling goods, sharing diner stops, and stitching the economy together mile by mile. Today, with companies like Aurora, Kodiak Robotics, and TuSimple accelerating Level 4 automation, we are witnessing what could be the most significant vocational shift since the advent of the assembly line.

And yet, while jobs at the wheel are being reduced, others are proliferating:

- Remote truck operators monitor AI rigs in real-time, stepping in when difficult weather or road anomalies arise.
- Fleet AI instructors train and refine driving algorithms based on edge-case feedback.
- Driver–technicians now partner with machines, becoming the new "ground crew" of mobility.

Instead of unemployment lines, we may see training lines—if we plan wisely.

The Pilot: Augmented Altitude

In aviation, commercial pilots already trust autopilot for 90% of flight time. But now AI co-pilots—like Airbus' Project DragonFly—handle taxiing, collision avoidance, and voice-activated assistance.

The role of the pilot is shifting from "operator" to supervisor of complex autonomy systems. Much like a conductor guiding an orchestra of machines, they remain vital—but their responsibilities are now strategic, not mechanical. Flight schools are beginning to teach:

- Human-AI interaction under stress scenarios
- Interpreting probabilistic AI recommendations
- Manual override protocols when trust fails the system

Here, trust is the ultimate altitude.

The Logistics Manager: From Dispatcher to Data Strategist

Few roles have undergone as quiet a transformation as logistics management. Once a discipline of clipboards and spreadsheets, it is now defined by:

- Real-time geospatial analytics
- Machine learning-driven forecasting
- Robotic warehouse orchestration

A manager at Maersk or DHL no longer thinks in terms of trucks and warehouses, but in terms of dynamic nodes, predictive delays, and supply chain twins. AI suggests when to reroute. Digital twins simulate outcomes before decisions are made.

The human manager's new value lies in judgment, escalation, ethics, and what-if thinking. They are now the "editors" of AI's predictions—contextualizing suggestions that machines can't fully understand.

The Deeper Question: What Is Work, Now?

What unites drivers, pilots, and logistics managers is not their displacement—but their transformation. Each must navigate a new frontier where machines are not just tools, but collaborators.

In that recalibration lies a deeper human journey—not one of obsolescence, but of adaptation. The wheel may steer itself, the autopilot may land the plane, and the warehouse may sort its own inventory—but in every node, a human is needed to ask:

"What if the unexpected happens?"

"Is this the right decision, or merely the efficient one?"

That, as always, remains a question only a human can answer.

Regulatory and Ethical Boundaries

Guardrails on the Autonomous Highway – Ethics and Regulation in AI-Powered Transport and Logistics

In the golden age of exploration, cartographers sketched dragons on the edges of maps to mark the unknown. Today, the boundaries of artificial intelligence in transportation and logistics are no less uncertain—and the dragons have returned, now embedded in lines of code.

At the heart of this revolution lies a tantalizing promise: self-driving trucks that never sleep, drone fleets that deliver life-saving medicine across impassable terrain, and algorithmic dispatch systems that orchestrate supply chains with balletic precision. But with each advance comes a nagging echo: Who is responsible when things go wrong?

The Autonomous Dilemma

When a human driver makes a mistake, the system—courts, laws, insurance—has a clear path. But when an autonomous delivery vehicle swerves into a cyclist, or a drone malfunctions over a crowded square, the calculus changes. Was it the algorithm? The data scientist? The company? The AI itself?

Regulators have struggled to catch up. In the United States, federal guidelines from the NHTSA (National Highway Traffic Safety Administration) offer suggestions rather than mandates, while states like California and Arizona have become testing grounds for robotaxis and delivery drones. The European Union, more cautious, has leaned on the EU AI Act to classify transportation AI systems as "high risk," subjecting them to rigorous oversight and human-in-the-loop safeguards.

But rules are inconsistent. A drone certified in Rwanda may be grounded in Chicago. An autonomous truck cleared for intercity hauling in Texas might be illegal just across the border in New Mexico. This patchwork regulation is both a breeding ground for innovation and a minefield for liability.

The Invisible Bias of the Algorithm

AI doesn't just automate—it optimizes. In logistics, optimization often involves determining who gets served first, prioritizing which routes, or assigning workers. These seemingly technical decisions can quietly encode bias.

If an AI routing algorithm consistently avoids "high-risk" neighborhoods, does it reinforce systemic neglect? If warehouse automation predicts productivity based on biometric data, does it penalize workers with disabilities or older employees?

The ethical lines are faint, but real. As companies adopt predictive maintenance, dynamic scheduling, and AI-powered inventory control, they must also address transparency, explainability, and fairness. Because when a machine denies a driver a shift—or a community access to services—the explanation matters.

Global Supply Chains, Local Laws

The globalization of logistics adds complexity. A single package might travel across multiple jurisdictions, each with different laws on privacy, labor, and airspace. A drone delivery that begins in Shenzhen and ends in San Francisco must navigate not just oceans and customs, but the regulatory philosophies of China and the United States.

Some governments, such as Singapore and South Korea, have adopted regulatory sandboxes—zones where companies can test autonomous logistics with reduced oversight. Others, like India and the EU, demand human accountability at every major decision point.

The challenge isn't just legal—it's philosophical. Can you regulate a system that is always learning? What happens when a self-optimizing fleet changes behavior mid-shipment? Who is liable if an update breaks the law?

Building the Ethical GPS

To navigate this landscape, leading firms are establishing AI ethics boards, conducting bias audits, and implementing "human-in-the-loop" protocols for all high-impact decisions. Some use "black box recorders" for AI—the digital equivalent of a flight data recorder—to understand decisions post-incident.

In the logistics space, companies like DHL and Maersk have launched ethical AI initiatives that attempt to align innovation with responsibility. Yet most ethical frameworks remain voluntary, and often, reactive.

The Human Driver Behind the Wheel

The fusion of human judgment and machine precision is very important. In transportation and logistics, that fusion is not optional—it is essential. Regulation should not stifle the autonomous future. It should choreograph it—ensuring that the dance between AI and humanity stays graceful, transparent, and just.

Because a delivery made faster is not progress if it endangers lives. A shipment optimized for cost is not efficient if it compromises dignity. The path forward is not paved by machines alone—it is built with ethical foresight, democratic oversight, and human wisdom.

Chapter 11

Legal, Governance, and Policy: Algorithmic Accountability

In the world of innovation, progress often outpaces regulation. From Gutenberg's printing press to Turing's machine, humanity has always created first and legislated later. But with artificial intelligence—especially the kind that makes decisions about lives, liberties, and livelihoods—we may no longer have the luxury of being late.

The invisible hand of the algorithm now shapes everything from parole decisions to healthcare diagnostics, from hiring outcomes to credit scoring. In transportation and logistics, it routes fleets; in finance, it trades billions in milliseconds. But it is important to remember, "What's invisible is often what matters most." And in this case, what's invisible must also be auditable.

The Birth of Black Box Law

When an algorithm denies a loan, sends a drone, or flags an anomaly, who is responsible? That is the defining question of algorithmic governance—the emerging discipline at the intersection of law, ethics, and software architecture.

In the courtroom, the traditional tools of justice—discovery, cross-examination, precedent—falter when the defendant is a neural network. Judges are not trained in gradient descent. Lawyers cannot subpoena witnesses or evidence. And yet, justice demands answers.

In 2022, the European Union introduced the AI Act, proposing classifications for risk and enforceable duties for developers. High-risk systems—those used in education, employment, credit, and justice—must meet strict transparency and human oversight standards. It was one of the first real attempts to regulate the algorithm, not just the outcome.

In the United States, progress has been more fragmented. While cities like New York have mandated algorithmic impact assessments, federal law still lags. Lawsuits are emerging—about biased hiring bots, predictive policing, and flawed facial recognition—but the legal system is reactive, not proactive.

When Policy becomes Product

At companies like OpenAI, Google DeepMind, and Microsoft, governance is no longer just legal—it is embedded in the engineering stack. Some firms now implement "constitutional AI," where systems are trained with ethical guardrails inspired by human rights frameworks. Others require "model cards" that disclose how an AI was trained, what data it ingested, and where it might fail.

These aren't just corporate social responsibility moves. They're attempts to pre-empt regulation by designing with responsibility in mind—what some call "policy as code."

As Steve Jobs once said, "Design is not just what it looks like and feels like. Design is how it works." In this era, ethical design is how AI behaves.

Transparency in a World of Trade Secrets

One of the most difficult issues is transparency. Many of the most powerful algorithms are proprietary—trade secrets protected from disclosure. A facial recognition company may impact your life but claim IP protection over how its system functions. A health risk score might influence treatment choices without revealing its formula.

This creates an epistemic imbalance: the algorithm knows you, but you cannot know the algorithm.

Some suggest solutions like algorithmic auditability, in which independent third parties review models, similar to financial auditors. Others advocate for AI version control—a digital record of every update, tweak, and modification to a decision-making system, much like how aviation tracks every revision to a jet engine's software.

Who Writes the Laws for Machines?

We're entering a world where code becomes law, and law must understand code.

Governments are establishing AI commissions, ethics councils, and national data regulators to ensure oversight, but staffing them with the right talent—people who can bridge the gap between law and machine learning—is still a challenge. Universities are launching tech policy dual degrees, preparing a new generation fluent in both Python and policy.

The stakes couldn't be higher. A biased algorithm can quietly scale injustice. A poorly governed model can disrupt elections or markets. But a well-governed one—clear in purpose, transparent in method, accountable in design—can amplify fairness and efficiency on an unprecedented scale.

Accountability in the Age of Diffusion

The hardest part is that AI decisions are often diffused across actors. A software engineer writes the code. A product manager chooses the objective function. A data scientist selects the training data. A company deploys the tool. A customer interprets the result.

Where does the responsibility lie?

The answer may not be a single person. It may be a chain of custody, a supply chain of accountability. Every node must be documented. Every hand-off must be clear. AI governance must become AI logistics—because only then can we track how a decision was made, and who shaped it.

Reflection Point:

The age of AI is not just about intelligence. It is about integrity.

Just as Franklin insisted on public libraries, Jefferson on transparency, and Ada Lovelace on the ethics of algorithms, today's innovators must ask: Can what we build stand the scrutiny of the societies we serve?

Algorithmic accountability is not just a legal necessity. It is a moral compass for the machine age.

AI in Legal Search and Contract Analysis

There was a time—not long ago—when an associate at a law firm would spend days hunched over towering stacks of casebooks, painstakingly scanning pages for precedent. In another corner of the office, a paralegal would squint at dense contractual language, searching for clauses that might unravel a deal. It was a process built on human memory, legal logic, and sleepless nights. That time is not yet gone, but it's fading—and AI is hastening its end.

Enter Harvey AI, an LLM-powered legal assistant co-developed with OpenAI and trained on mountains of legal documents. It doesn't just search keywords—it understands legal language, intent, and nuance. Instead of Boolean queries or linear sifting, Harvey returns context-rich answers, tailored summaries, and even full legal drafts—all in seconds. To old-guard attorneys, it feels like alchemy. But to a new generation, it's just Tuesday.

Harvey was born out of necessity. Law firms, burdened with rising client demands and thinning margins, were desperate for scale without compromise. What BloombergGPT did for financial reporting, Harvey aimed to do for the law: synthesize vast, ambiguous, highly sensitive information with precision, confidentiality, and speed.

On the contract side, platforms like Luminance, Kira, and Evisort brought similar intelligence to routine but mission-critical tasks. Instead of manually flagging a missing indemnity clause or an unusually aggressive termination condition, these systems learned from thousands of prior documents and surfaced anomalies instantly. They reduced days of work to minutes. And unlike human reviewers, they didn't grow tired.

Remember: technology alone doesn't transform professions—it's the fusion of man and machine that does. The best lawyers now act as strategic overseers, shaping prompts, validating output, and interpreting insights. Legal AI is not replacing judgment; it's augmenting it.

There's also a moral undercurrent to all this: transparency, bias, privacy. Can a client trust an LLM to interpret their intent? Will a model trained on Western law understand indigenous land rights? Should AI draft wills, defend clients, or litigate disputes? These are not technical questions—they are human ones.

As we stand at this digital jurisprudential frontier, one thing is clear: the future of law will not be just written in statutes and precedents. It will be trained, fine-tuned, queried, and—most of all—co-created by humans and machines, together.

Predictive Policing, Surveillance, and Bias

If history is a mirror, technology often reflects not only our progress but also our prejudices.

It began with promise. In precincts from Los Angeles to London, a new wave of software—armed with crime stats, weather patterns, and social signals—offered a tantalizing proposition: What if we could predict crime before it happened? Algorithms could identify hotspots. Officers could be redeployed proactively. Lives could be saved. Resources, optimized. It felt like the arrival of a clairvoyant cop—part mathematician, part detective.

A word of caution: every technological leap brings its moral dilemmas in tow.

Systems like PredPol didn't invent injustice—but they learned from it. Trained on historical crime data—data often riddled with racial disparities, over-policing, and social inequities—the models began echoing those same patterns back into the present. Neighborhoods already under scrutiny became perpetual "hot zones." Communities already distrusted by law enforcement found themselves more intensely surveilled, not because of new crimes, but because the system had learned to expect crime.

Bias, it turned out, was not just a human failing. It was now machine-learned and scalable.

Surveillance technologies followed close behind. CCTV evolved into facial recognition. Drone feeds were tagged with AI-powered object detection. Smart streetlights began to record not just light levels but conversations and license plates. In China, the surveillance state matured into a social credit system. In democracies, safeguards lagged behind.

The question wasn't just can we predict where the next crime might happen—but should we, and how do we know we're right?

Critics warned of algorithmic determinism: the idea that once flagged, a person or place might be treated as dangerous indefinitely. That pre-crime policing—once fiction in Minority Report—was tiptoeing into reality, but without the moral debates Hollywood demanded.

Think about it it: the heart of this story lies not in the software but in the humans who wield it. The programmers who define the labels. The officers who trust the outputs. The judges who weigh risk scores in sentencing. The citizens who are watched, tagged, and profiled—often without knowing.

And yet, there is potential. Predictive analytics can allocate social services before violence erupts. Real-time surveillance can protect vulnerable spaces. Transparency dashboards and algorithmic audits can check bias. But only if we design for equity, not just efficiency.

In the end, the algorithm is not the villain. It is the mirror. What it shows us—about power, race, justice, and fear—depends on who's asking the questions, and who is listening to the answers.

Regulatory Frameworks: Drawing the Line Around Intelligence (EU AI Act, White House Blueprint for an AI Bill of Rights)

In the long arc of technological revolutions—from the steam engine to the transistor—humanity has consistently learned that invention alone is not enough. Every major innovation demands its mirror: governance. Not a brake, but a steering wheel.

As artificial intelligence advances, integrating its neural networks into healthcare, finance, warfare, and the creative arts, policymakers worldwide are scrambling to answer a critical question: How do we ensure that this intelligence, powerful as it may be, remains aligned with human values?

The European Union's AI Act: A Constitution for Algorithms

In 2021, the European Commission made a bold move—it drafted what might be considered the Magna Carta of artificial intelligence. The EU AI Act, a sweeping legislation unlike any before, didn't aim to celebrate AI's potential. Rather, it sought to categorize and contain it.

Remember that Alan Turing once worried—not just about building intelligent machines—but about whether we would understand the consequences of doing so. The EU AI Act channels that same prudence.

The Act classifies AI applications into risk tiers:

- Unacceptable Risk: Banned outright—like social scoring à la Black Mirror.
- High-Risk: Subject to rigorous testing and documentation—think AI in hiring, credit scoring, or autonomous vehicles.
- Limited and Minimal Risk: Requiring transparency—such as chatbot disclosures or recommendation engines.

Its genius lies in this tiered nuance—not all AI is treated the same. Just as not all humans can be governed by one law alone.

The White House Blueprint: An AI Bill of Rights

Across the Atlantic, the United States took a more philosophical route. In 2022, the White House Office of Science and Technology Policy released its Blueprint for an AI Bill of Rights—a document as idealistic as it is urgent.

It doesn't legislate. It doesn't regulate. It inspires.

The blueprint offers five core protections:

1. Safe and Effective Systems
2. Algorithmic Discrimination Protections
3. Data Privacy
4. Notice and Explanation
5. Human Alternatives, Consideration, and Fallback

It echoes the Federalist Papers more than the EU's bureaucratic precision—a charter meant to stir ethical imagination as much as legal constraint.

Consider this contrast. Europe as Enlightenment realists. America as techno-romantic optimists. Both reaching into the same digital unknown with radically different gloves.

Between Control and Creativity

Both frameworks grapple with a deeper question: Can you regulate intelligence without stifling it?

We've seen this before. The creation of nuclear energy led to the development of non-proliferation treaties. Genetic engineering birthed bioethics councils. AI now demands the same laws that don't strangle innovation, but give it conscience.

In the coming decades, these early frameworks—the EU AI Act and the AI Bill of Rights—will be cited in the same way we cite the Geneva Conventions or the Kyoto Protocol. Not because they are perfect, but because they are first.

And, in the history of human progress, it is often the first attempt to draw boundaries around brilliance that defines how responsibly we evolve.

Global AI Regulations: A Timeline

Here's a timeline charting significant milestones in global AI regulation—from early ethical frameworks to groundbreaking laws:

- 2017: China unveils its Next Generation AI Development Plan
- 2018–2019: The EU issues its Ethics Guidelines for Trustworthy AI
- Apr 2021: The EU officially proposes the landmark AI Act

- Nov 2021: UNESCO publishes its Recommendations on AI ethics
- Mar 2023: The UK defines its "pro-innovation approach" to AI regulation
- Oct 2023: The UN forms an Advisory Body on Global AI Governance
- Feb 2024: The UK issues a formal AI Regulation White Paper
- Aug 2024: The EU AI Act officially enters into force
- Nov 2024: Global summit shifts language from AI Safety to AI Action

Why This Timeline Matters

This graphic serves as a snapshot of how AI regulation has matured—from aspirational guidelines to enforceable laws—and how it continues to evolve globally.

Key Highlights

- The EU's AI Act is the first comprehensive and binding regulation for AI, applying a risk-based approach and setting strong standards for high-risk applications.
- The UN Advisory Body marks a crucial shift toward international coordination on AI governance.
- The UK's dual path—between innovation encouragement and regulatory groundwork—illustrates a balancing act many democracies are grappling with

Chapter 12

Agriculture and Climate – From Soil to Satellite

In the annals of human progress, the great leaps have often come not from abandoning nature, but from better understanding it. This chapter tells the story of how artificial intelligence is doing just that—peering into the soil, scanning the skies, and reshaping agriculture and climate resilience from the ground up.

We begin, as all stories of cultivation do, with the farmer. But no longer is he merely reading the land by intuition or waiting for the weather to decide her fate. Today's farmer—whether in Iowa or Andhra Pradesh—carries a smartphone in his pocket, a satellite overhead, and an AI engine at her side. His plowshares are precision drones, predictive models forecast her irrigation, and sensors and machine learning monitor his soil health.

From the Plow to the Pixel

Agriculture was once humanity's first great algorithm: till, sow, water, harvest. Today, the cycle is being refined by a new intelligence—artificial, but astonishingly accurate. Companies like ClimateAI, Taranis, and Plantix have created tools that use satellite imagery, historical climate data, and neural networks to deliver insights with surgical precision. The goal is not just yield, but resilient yield—crops that survive droughts, pests, and shifting rain patterns in a warming world.

Business historians might draw a line from Leonardo da Vinci's botanical sketches to the modern agronomist running Python code on drone data. It is, at its core, the same pursuit: to know nature deeply enough to live in balance with it.

The Soil Whispers, and AI Listens

At the root of it all—literally—is soil. AI can now detect nutrient levels, moisture gradients, and microbial activity through sensors and remote sensing. Platforms like Agroscout and CropX help farmers target fertilizer application only where needed, minimizing environmental runoff and maximizing plant health.

This isn't just about precision; it's about ethics. With agriculture contributing roughly 25% of global greenhouse emissions, AI is being used to rethink supply chains, reduce overproduction, and minimize waste. Models that track carbon sequestration in regenerative farms are helping create markets for carbon credits tied to actual soil health, rather than vague promises.

From Satellites to Supply Chains

Consider SatSure, an India-based startup that combines AI, GIS, and satellite imagery to provide insights into crop performance, insurance risks, and creditworthiness. Or Descartes Labs, whose predictive algorithms help governments plan for food shortages before they occur.

This is AI not as a disruptor, but as a stabilizer—helping avert famine, manage water scarcity, and even predict locust swarms based on climatic shifts.

Climate, Collaboration, and the Cultivation of Hope

What emerges is a powerful feedback loop: AI-driven data enables better decisions, which lead to more sustainable practices, which in turn feed back into improved models. The farmer becomes part of a planetary system of feedback, resilience, and learning. It's an elegant symmetry—one Leonardo would admire.

In a world increasingly fractured, AI in agriculture and climate is a rare example of technology serving both profit and planet. It is the story of how we might feed 10 billion people—not by fighting nature, but by finally understanding her rhythms.

And that, perhaps, is the most human intelligence of all.

Invisible Roots, Visible Results: Charting AI's Evolution in Agriculture

1990s – The Seedlings of Precision

- Satellite Imagery & GIS: For the first time, farmers could see their fields from above, setting the stage for precision mapping and variable-rate soil analysis.

2010s – Digital Fields Take Shape

- Precision Agriculture Emerges: GPS-guided grid sampling, zone-based fertilization, and yield-monitoring sensors become foundational tools on farms.
- Hands Free Hectare Project (2016–17): The world's first fully autonomous cropping cycle was achieved at Harper Adams University, where drones and robotic tractors planted, managed, and harvested a field—without human presence.

Early 2020s – Crop Intelligence Blossoms

- Smart Greenhouse Success (2020): The Pinduoduo Smart Agriculture Competition AI teams outperformed traditional farmers in both nutrient yield and cost efficiency, marking a significant leap in indoor agtech applications.
- AI-Powered Weed Control: Innovative robotics, such as the LaserWeeder G2 (Carbon Robotics) and John Deere's "See & Spray" system, have begun precisely identifying and targeting weeds with lasers and AI, thereby minimizing chemical use.

Mid-2020s – Climate Meets Computation

- Norm, the AI Agronomic Advisor: Launched in 2023 by Farmers Business Network, Norm uses LLMs and proprietary data to answer farming queries about inputs, livestock, and crop protection—ushering in a conversational era of farm management.
- Soil Carbon Mapping for Climate Resilience: Companies like Perennial and Downforce Technologies, backed by significant public investment, began using machine learning and spectral probes to monitor soil carbon for regenerative agriculture and carbon markets.

The Future's Forecast: What Comes Next?

AI Expansion into IoT Weather Forecasting: Emerging frameworks (e.g., AI + IoT micro-weather stations) promise hyper-local, real-time weather prediction—enabling micro-adjustments in planting, irrigation, and harvest.

Why it Matters?

This timeline maps a profound shift: from an era when farming was guided by instinct and hindsight to one where AI provides insight, foresight, and adaptability.

While Leonardo sketched botanicals by hand, today's agronomists sketch them with code—layering intelligence onto cultivation. This synergy between soil and satellite defines the future of sustainable food systems.

Precision Agriculture: John Deere's See & Spray

When history looks back at how farming crossed the threshold into the digital age, it may not single out a Silicon Valley startup or a flashy moonshot. It may instead focus on a tractor—more specifically, a tractor that doesn't just plow and harvest, but sees.

In the annals of industrial ingenuity, John Deere is a name rooted in steel and soil, in the clang of iron and the rhythms of planting season. But in the last decade, this agricultural titan quietly reinvented itself—not as just a machinery company, but as a platform for artificial intelligence. At the heart of that metamorphosis lies See & Spray, a precision agriculture system that tells a deeper story about where intelligence, autonomy, and earth stewardship converge.

The principle is elegantly simple but technologically astonishing. Traditional farming sprays entire fields with herbicides, regardless of whether weeds are present. It's wasteful, expensive, and environmentally burdensome. See & Spray, however, uses computer vision and machine learning models mounted on the sprayer boom to distinguish weeds from crops in real time, down to the leaf. Every millisecond, high-resolution cameras scan the field. Algorithms trained on millions of images identify unwanted plants, and robotic nozzles respond instantly—spraying only what needs spraying, and leaving the rest untouched.

It's as if the tractor has developed a set of eyes and a conscience.

This isn't just automation—it's cognition. It's the moment when the analog rhythms of farming merge with the digital heartbeat of AI. And it's not merely about yield or efficiency; it's about rewriting the relationship between humans, technology, and nature.

The impact? Studies show a reduction of herbicide use by up to 77%. That's fewer chemicals in our ecosystems. That's lower cost for farmers. That's sustainability backed by silicon. In a time of climate crises, where every drop of water and every molecule of pesticide counts, this isn't just innovation—it's ethics in action.

But what makes See & Spray even more emblematic of this age is how it reframes the role of the farmer. No longer just a cultivator of land, the modern farmer becomes a data analyst, a systems thinker, an AI partner. Fields become datasets. Seasons become simulations. And farming—arguably humanity's oldest profession—becomes its newest frontier.

Much like Gutenberg's press democratized knowledge, Deere's green-and-yellow machines may help democratize sustainability—turning every acre into a laboratory, and every farmer into a technologist.

In the story of AI's expansion across sectors, See & Spray is a vivid chapter. Not just because it works, but because it shows that intelligence—when aligned with humility, purpose, and practicality—can quite literally make the earth greener.

AI for Climate Modeling and Disaster Response

In the sprawling, data-rich theater of Earth's climate, the stakes are existential and the timelines urgent. Weather patterns shift with alarming unpredictability, wildfires rage with newfound ferocity, and coastlines tremble under rising tides. For centuries, humans have looked to the skies, the soil, and the sea to divine the future. Now, they're looking to algorithms.

At the intersection of Earth science and artificial intelligence lies a quietly revolutionary idea: that silicon-based intelligence can help us understand—and perhaps even mitigate—carbon-based chaos. The climate, once modeled with gut instincts and paper charts, is now being simulated on quantum-inspired grids powered by GPUs and neural nets.

This is where AI doesn't just predict—it forewarns.

Take Climate Modeling, once the purview of massive mainframes and sluggish simulations. Today, tools like NVIDIA's Earth-2, Google DeepMind's GraphCast, and Microsoft's AI for Earth offer near-instantaneous, high-resolution models that learn from decades of weather data, satellite inputs, and atmospheric chemistry. These models don't just extrapolate—they adapt. They digest everything from ocean salinity to methane plumes and produce forecasts that are not only faster but far more granular. In this sense, AI doesn't replace the climatologist—it augments them, turning terabytes of static data into dynamic foresight.

But nowhere is the power of AI more urgent—or more visceral—than in disaster response.

Consider a hurricane forming off the Gulf Coast. Traditionally, responders had days to prepare, relying on projected storm paths that often changed by the hour. Now, AI systems like IBM's Weather Company, Descartes Labs, and the UN's AI for Disaster Risk Reduction integrate satellite imagery, real-time sensor data, social media signals, and historical precedent to anticipate where disaster will strike and who will be affected most.

It's not just about forecasting wind speeds. It's about triaging humanity.

AI helps emergency crews route supplies more efficiently. It predicts which roads will flood, which power grids will fail, and which hospitals will be overwhelmed. During the Australian bushfires, AI models mapped fire spread patterns and smoke density in real time, saving both human and animal lives. During earthquakes, drones powered by AI scanned rubble for survivors, listening for heat and heartbeat signatures.

As always, the story is not just about machines—it's about the humans behind them. The coders who translate urgency into code. The climatologists who train AI to distinguish signal from noise. And the first responders who, empowered with better information, can act not out of desperation, but precision.

Of course, ethical questions loom. Who owns the models? Who gets access to predictive insights? And how do we ensure that AI's foresight doesn't become a tool for geopolitical manipulation?

Still, the vision is unmistakably hopeful: a planet that watches itself more closely. A species that learns to act before reacting. And a technology that trades in the currency of seconds and saves in the currency of lives.

In the chronicle of artificial intelligence, AI's role in climate and disaster response is not just a subplot—it's a testament to our desire to understand the forces that shape us. And maybe, just maybe, to shape them in return.

The Ethics of Automating Life and Food

In the grand arc of innovation, few moments are as profound—or as perilous—as when machines begin to meddle with the essence of life itself.

We have long trusted technology to shape our tools, our homes, and our communication. But now, in an era where algorithms sow seeds and drones buzz over fields like pollinators of the future, we find ourselves asking: What happens when we automate not just labor—but the living fabric of existence?

This question, once confined to science fiction, now sits squarely in the furrows of our farmland and on the plates of our dining tables.

From Harvest to Hardware

Consider the modern smart farm, where AI systems determine which seeds to plant, when to water, how to treat for pests, and even when to harvest—often without human touch. Cameras, soil sensors, satellite imagery, and neural networks now play a crucial role in determining the fate of millions of crops. It's a ballet of precision and prediction. Efficiency, yes. But also a subtle erosion of the farmer's intuition.

And then there's lab-grown meat, where cell cultures are harvested like software updates. Or CRISPR-edited crops, which can resist drought, disease, and even time. We now have the power to reshape nature's playbook with the click of a cursor.

But who writes the rules?

The Algorithm vs. the Earth

Here lies the ethical rub. In automating food production—something so visceral, so elemental—what values are we encoding into our machines? If a recommendation engine prioritizes high-yield monoculture over biodiversity, is that an objective decision or a profit-driven one? If a proprietary AI controls seed optimization, does the farmer become merely a user of their own soil?

And then there is data ownership. The sensors on a tractor or drone collect petabytes of agronomic data, including moisture, nutrients, and yield per square meter. But does that data belong to the farmer, or the tech firm?

Life in the Loop

There's also a deeper, almost philosophical concern. As we automate more of the food chain—from genetics to logistics to nutrition delivery—do we risk commodifying life itself? Will future children learn how to grow food—or just how to program the system that does?

It's the same moral tension that accompanied the printing press, the steam engine, and the internet. But this time, it touches something more primal. Food is not just a product—it is culture, a ritual, and a memory. Automating it too fully may leave us with full stomachs but empty stories.

And yet, the alternative—doing nothing—poses its own dangers. A planet burdened by nine billion people will require every bit of ingenuity. AI can cut waste, feed the hungry, and respond to climate shocks with a speed no human alone can match.

Stewardship, Not Supremacy

The solution may lie not in resisting automation, but in redefining our relationship to it. We must design these systems not as overlords, but as partners. Ethics must be embedded—not as an afterthought, but as the operating system itself.

The farmers of tomorrow may not wear overalls, but they will need wisdom. The engineers developing agri-algorithms must understand the poetry of ecology. And policymakers must make sure that the benefits of automation are shared widely, not kept isolated.

Because in the story of humanity, food has always been more than fuel. It is where biology meets community. And if we automate that—which we already are—we must do so with reverence, humility, and the recognition that life, even when coded, must never be reduced to code alone.

In the age of AI, ethics will not be a footnote. It will be the first line of every script we write—especially when that script grows what we eat, sustains how we live, and ultimately, defines who we are.

Chapter 13

Defense and National Security — The New Arms Race

In every great technological leap—be it the telegraph, the jet engine, or the internet—military interests were never far behind. Innovation, after all, is not born in a vacuum. It is often birthed in the crucible of geopolitical urgency. And today, as artificial intelligence becomes the defining technology of our era, a new race is underway—not to the moon, but to the algorithm.

This is not your grandfather's Cold War.

This is a race fought not just with missiles and manpower, but with machine learning models, quantum encryption, and drone swarms. It is a silent battle—less about nuclear deterrence and more about data dominance. Less about who has more tanks, and more about who controls the flow of intelligence, prediction, and autonomous decision-making.

From Boots on the Ground to Bots in the Cloud

In 2020, when the Pentagon quietly released its Joint Artificial Intelligence Center (JAIC), it marked a turning point. The battlefield was no longer defined by topography, but by training data. Algorithms began combing through terabytes of surveillance feeds. Natural language processing began decoding chatter in multiple dialects. Pattern recognition predicted insurgent ambushes before boots hit the ground.

Meanwhile, DARPA-funded programs developed autonomous systems that could collaborate, adapt, and even deceive—not just mimic human soldiers, but outthink them in milliseconds. The so-called centaur warfare model—humans and machines working in tandem—emerged as a dominant paradigm.

But if the U.S. was racing ahead, it wasn't alone.

The Global Arena: Algorithms as Arsenal

China announced in 2017 its intention to become the world leader in AI by 2030, pouring billions into military-civil fusion initiatives. Surveillance technologies exported to dozens of countries were not just tools—they were Trojan horses, collecting data, training models, influencing regimes.

Russia, too, focused on AI-powered information warfare, leveraging bots and deepfakes not to win battles, but to shape narratives—undermining trust, fracturing democracies, and turning truth itself into a casualty of war.

Israel's Iron Dome now incorporates real-time AI filters to intercept missiles before the human brain can react. Turkey's drones, powered by onboard image-recognition algorithms, changed the course of the Nagorno-Karabakh war. And private firms—like Palantir, Anduril, and Helsing—blurred the lines between Silicon Valley and military command centers.

Ethical Firewalls in a Borderless War

But here's where the irony kicks in: the faster the machines became, the deeper the moral questions grew.

Who is accountable when an autonomous drone misidentifies a target? How do you program an algorithm with jus in bello—the ethics of war? What does "proportional response" mean to a neural network?

And what of the looming specter of AI-enabled cyberweapons—viruses that learn, adapt, and propagate faster than any firewall can defend? In the nuclear age, deterrence was based on mutual assured destruction. But with AI, the first strike might be undetectable—and the retaliation irrelevant.

The Arms Race of Intellect

This chapter, in many ways, echoes the arc of The Code Breaker, Steve Jobs, and Einstein—biographies of people who stood at the intersection of genius and responsibility. But here, the protagonists are not just individuals. They are nations, corporations, and machines—all locked in a co-evolutionary spiral.

Remember that technology is never neutral. It is shaped by the values of its creators, the ambition of its deployers, and the constraints of its era.

In the AI arms race, we are all creators now. And we must choose: will we train these models for control—or for conscience?

The Final Frontier

Defense will always be about preparation. But in the AI age, it must also be about principles. International treaties may not evolve as fast as algorithms. However, norms, alliances, and public pressure still hold significance.

The real question, then, isn't just who will win the AI arms race—but what kind of world will emerge if we do.

Because history has shown us something important: every new technology changes the way wars are fought—but also offers a chance to redefine what peace looks like.

Let us not lose that chance.

Think about it: "The best defense is not just building smarter machines, but wiser societies."

Lethal Autonomous Weapons (LAWS), AI in Cyberwarfare

The New Battlefield: Lethal Autonomy and Cyber Shadows

In the mythology of modern warfare, victory once belonged to the side with the largest bombs, the fastest jets, or the most extensive intelligence networks. But as we step into the third decade of the 21st century, a new kind of arms race unfolds—not of hardware, but of code, not of generals directing armies, but of algorithms selecting targets. This is the dawning age of Lethal Autonomous Weapons Systems (LAWS) and AI-driven cyberwarfare—a transformation so profound it echoes the invention of the longbow, the printing press, or the nuclear bomb.

And like every major pivot point in human history, it comes with both promise and peril.

Lethal Autonomy: Death at Machine Speed

Imagine a drone, small enough to fit in a backpack, programmed not just to find a target, but to decide whether it lives or dies—without human intervention. That is the defining feature of LAWS: the decision loop no longer includes a human finger on the trigger. The machine is the trigger.

Countries like the United States, Russia, Israel, China, South Korea, and Turkey have invested heavily in developing semi- and fully-autonomous weaponry. The Israeli Harpy loitering munition, the Russian Kalashnikov ZALA KYB, or Turkey's Kargu-2 drone, reportedly used autonomously in Libya, represent a future that has already arrived.

And yet, the most terrifying thing is not what they can do—it's what they might choose to do. A missile that chooses its target? A drone that weighs the civilian risk based on a confidence score?

This is not science fiction. It's battlefield math.

Remember that the same tension existed when Oppenheimer helped birth the bomb. Then, as now, it was not just a question of capability, but of conscience.

Code Red: AI in the Cyber Domain

Parallel to the physical battlefield is the digital one—an invisible, volatile theater where nations now engage in constant low-level warfare. Only here, the bullets are bots, and the attacks unfold not in weeks, but in microseconds.

AI has supercharged cyberwarfare.

Tools like deepfake propaganda, AI-generated phishing lures, and adaptive malware have evolved beyond static code to models that learn to evade detection in real-time. Just as GPT models can write convincing essays, AI adversarial networks can craft undetectable intrusion attempts—mutating as defenders respond.

Take Stuxnet, the joint U.S.–Israeli virus that sabotaged Iran's nuclear centrifuges. Now imagine its successor: self-replicating, self-rewriting, fully autonomous. Offensive AI doesn't just break systems—it breaks the rules of escalation. It's asymmetric, deniable, and near-instantaneous.

In 2021, U.S. cybersecurity leaders began experimenting with "zero trust" architectures powered by AI to detect anomalies and prevent breaches. But defending against AI requires… more AI. The battlefield is recursive, a chess game where each side plays a billion moves a second.

The Classic Dilemma: When Ethics Lags Behind Innovation

The lives of all great innovators, such as Steve Jobs, Leonardo da Vinci, and Jennifer Doudna, teach us—there's always a reckoning. Innovation without reflection risks unintended consequences.

With LAWS, the core ethical questions remain unresolved:

- Can machines understand proportionality or distinction under the Geneva Conventions?
- Who is accountable if an autonomous weapon commits a war crime?
- Should machines ever be allowed to make life-and-death decisions?

Even the naming—"lethal autonomous weapons systems"—feels sterile, like a euphemism for something deeply primal: the outsourcing of human judgment in killing.

Meanwhile, AI in cyberwarfare presents its own paradox. The more we automate defense, the greater the risk of autonomous attack becomes. The race becomes self-sustaining.

Between Control and Chaos

International organizations have debated bans or moratoriums on LAWS for years, but consensus remains elusive. Some argue it's better to regulate than to relinquish. Others warn that once the genie is out—once LAWS are cheap, fast, and global—no treaty can contain them.

And so, we stand again at a hinge of history.

The decision is not whether to build smarter machines. We already are. The decision is whether to remain wise enough to build ethical frameworks before the machines take command.

Because in this arms race, the victor may not be the one with the most AI. It may be the one who remembers to keep the human in the loop.

Think about it: "Technology is a tool, but it bends toward the values of those who wield it."

The future of warfare—and peace—will depend on what values we embed into the code.

The Ethical Red Lines and International Treaties

In every era of technological upheaval, humanity has paused—if only briefly—to ask a question that machines cannot: Just because we can, should we?

Drawing the Line in Silicon: Ethics, Treaties, and the Code of War

During the Manhattan Project, Oppenheimer remembered the words of the Bhagavad Gita. After creating CRISPR, Jennifer Doudna dreamed of Hitler. And today, as we usher in the age of autonomous weapons and algorithmic warfare, a new generation of engineers, ethicists, and diplomats is grappling with a similar reckoning. This time, the tools are not atomic but algorithmic. And the battlefield is not a desert test site but a cloud server.

The question remains: Where do we draw the red lines?

The Machine that Decides to Kill

For decades, international humanitarian law was built around the idea that a human would make the ultimate decision. Even in the fog of war, there was supposed to be someone—an officer, a pilot, a soldier—who weighed proportionality, distinction, and intent. But now, we are designing machines that detect patterns, assign probabilities, and pull the trigger—all before a human has blinked.

This is a defining moment, the kind where the tools we create begin to challenge the values we hold most sacred.

These aren't just military innovations. They're philosophical landmines.

The Campaign to Ban the Killer Robot

In 2013, a coalition of scientists, ethicists, and NGOs launched the Campaign to Stop Killer Robots, sounding an alarm about the emergence of fully autonomous weapons. Their argument wasn't Luddite—it was humanist. If a machine makes the kill decision, where lies accountability? If the algorithm is biased or flawed, who is held accountable?

The campaign gained momentum, with letters signed by figures like Elon Musk, Stephen Hawking, and Stuart Russell. Conferences at the UN in Geneva followed. Moratoriums were proposed. Drafts of legal frameworks floated. But consensus proved elusive.

Just as with nuclear arms in the 1940s, AI in warfare now pits innovation against restraint. And history tells us: restraint usually comes after disaster.

The EU AI Act: A Civilizational Blueprint

The European Union, often regarded as the conscience of the digital world, has stepped forward with the EU AI Act. This comprehensive legislative framework may become the GDPR of artificial intelligence.

Within its nearly 100 articles lies a powerful statement: AI must be used in a way that is human-centric, trustworthy, and rights-preserving. High-risk applications—like biometric surveillance, predictive policing, and autonomous weaponry—face strict limits or outright bans.

The Act doesn't ban AI. It seeks to domesticate it, embedding ethics not just into code, but into commerce and conduct.

You might compare it to Enlightenment-era constitutions: imperfect, yet aspirational—a framework upon which democracies strive to balance innovation and humanity.

The White House Blueprint: Guardrails, Not Chains

Across the Atlantic, the White House Blueprint for an AI Bill of Rights was released in 2022—not as a law, but as a statement of principle. Five core rights were outlined:

1. Safe and Effective Systems
2. Algorithmic Discrimination Protections
3. Data Privacy
4. Notice and Explanation
5. Human Alternatives and Fallbacks

It read like a cross between a civil liberties manifesto and a technologist's handbook. But the key phrase was in the title: Blueprint. Not a treaty. Not an act. A starting point.

This is more in line with the Jeffersonian tone—aspiring, idealistic, and open to amendment.

The Treaties That Might Be—And Might Not

Discussions at the Convention on Certain Conventional Weapons (CCW) have debated the potential for banning Lethal Autonomous Weapons Systems (LAWS), but have had limited traction. Powerful nations remain divided. Some argue a ban would stifle military innovation. Others warn of a digital Pandora's box.

Without binding agreements, the world risks sleepwalking into a new kind of arms race—one in which escalation could happen in milliseconds, and retribution could be coded in silence.

Remember, "Innovation is most powerful when tempered by ethics." History's greatest minds didn't just build—they wrestled with the implications of what they built.

What Would the Da Vinci Code?

If Leonardo were alive today, sketching drones and neural nets into his notebooks, he would likely ask not how to make a machine kill—but how to make it understand mercy. And that is the true challenge.

Because the most important lines in the AI age will not be drawn in code, or even in treaties.

They will be drawn in conscience.

As the lives of great innovators teach us:

Progress is not just about making smarter machines.

It's about making wiser humans.

Balancing on the Edge: Innovation and Control in the Age of AI

Progress has always walked a tightrope. On one side: the exhilarating promise of invention. On the other hand, the sobering necessity of restraint. From Prometheus stealing fire to Alan Turing unlocking machine logic, humanity's greatest leaps have arrived not with clear instruction manuals—but with questions that couldn't be answered by code alone.

Today, as artificial intelligence remakes industries, ideas, and institutions, we once again find ourselves straddling that line. And the balancing act has never been more delicate.

Innovation: The Relentless Force

AI systems now write poetry, diagnose disease, drive cars, and predict wars. They don't sleep. They don't forget. They don't flinch. In the hands of a visionary, they are tools of boundless creativity. In the wrong hands—or even just untested ones—they are forces of chaos wrapped in logic.

Take OpenAI's GPT, a marvel of linguistic mimicry. Or DeepMind's AlphaFold, which cracked a 50-year biological puzzle. These aren't just clever software; they are inflection points in how humans interact with knowledge itself.

But history tells us that the first wave of innovation is rarely the safest. The steam engine birthed both factories and war machines. Nuclear fission led to both power grids and mushroom clouds.

Remember, " Each invention creates its own moral gravity."

Control: The Invisible Art

Regulation is not the enemy of innovation—it is its co-architect. The brake is as important as the engine. The Constitution followed the Revolution. The FDA followed the pharmaceutical boom. Air traffic control followed aviation.

In AI, control isn't about pulling the plug. It's about embedding accountability, about building scaffolding for trust. That's what the EU AI Act and the White House AI Blueprint attempt to do—not stifle progress, but shape it into something responsible and resilient.

And it's not just policy. Engineers now bake explainability, fairness, and bias mitigation directly into their models. The coder becomes a custodian—not just of data, but of consequence.

The Dual Helix of Progress

Isaacson often speaks of "the dual helix" that defines great innovation: vision and values, intertwined. Leonardo had the imagination to design flying machines—and the wisdom to question whether humans were ready. Ada Lovelace anticipated not just computation, but the philosophical implications of it. And the inventors of the Internet realized too late that openness could also be exploited.

In today's AI landscape, the challenge is the same:

- How do we advance without overreaching?
- How do we unleash creativity while preserving humanity?
- How do we ensure that the machines we build serve our better angels—not our blind spots?

A Call to Principled Pioneering

The solution is not to choose between innovation and control. It is to marry them, continuously, iteratively, transparently. To build sandboxes before skyscrapers. To prioritize human-centered design before market dominance. To have philosophers at the table with programmers.

Because the future will not be written only by code, but by character.

Remember:

"Innovation without reflection is just acceleration.

Wisdom is knowing when to lift the foot off the gas."

Chapter 14

Startups, SMEs, and the Creator Economy — The Garage Reborn

In a quiet suburb of Austin, a teenager named Maya uploads her latest AI-generated artwork onto a decentralized creator platform. Meanwhile, a two-person startup in Nairobi utilizes a large language model to develop a supply chain recommendation tool in Swahili. A few miles away in a Brooklyn co-working space, an ex-ad agency executive uses generative AI to create custom video campaigns for Etsy shop owners. These are not just anecdotes—they are snapshots of a seismic shift. The same energy that once pulsed through the garages of Silicon Valley now hums in the cloud, encoded in lines of code and trained on terabytes of data.

This chapter traces how the fusion of artificial intelligence and creativity is empowering the underestimated and unscaled. It's a story of economic democratization—where intelligence, once the preserve of human cognition and later of elite institutions, becomes an accessible utility.

The Rise of the AI-Native Startup

In previous decades, startups had to worry about cloud storage, scaling infrastructure, and hiring costly engineers. Now, with API-accessible AI, even a solopreneur can deploy a personalized chatbot, a financial forecasting model, and a product recommendation engine in a matter of days. Tools like OpenAI's Codex or Google's Vertex AI have turned machine learning from a research discipline into a development toolkit.

Startups like Jasper, Synthesia, Copy.ai, and Runway emerged not as tech companies that use AI, but as companies built on AI. They are the new-age garages—lean, fast, and global from day one. They don't just disrupt industries; they rewire what it means to build a company.

The Creator Economy: AI as Co-Creator

When YouTube was born, it put a broadcast studio in every home. Now, tools like Midjourney, DALL·E, and ElevenLabs provide creators with a film studio, an animation lab, and a virtual voice actor all within their browser window. This is not merely a technological leap—it's a cultural one.

AI no longer powers the back office—it sings, writes, draws, edits, and narrates. And in doing so, it blurs the lines between human originality and machine collaboration. The solo creator becomes a polymath team.

Walter Cronkite once said Journalism is what we need to make democracy work. Today, creativity may be what we need to make democracy feel heard. The barriers between idea and expression have dropped. The only limits are taste, ethics, and imagination.

SMEs: Small Teams, Smart Engines

For small and medium enterprises (SMEs), AI is not just a cost-saving trick—it's an existential enabler. A corner shop can use AI to forecast foot traffic. A regional logistics provider can optimize routes using real-time predictive models. A local language school in Brazil can generate tailored learning modules powered by GPT-based tutors.

Companies like Zoho and Notion are embedding AI natively, empowering small teams to do big things. In this new economy, scale isn't about headcount—it's about headspace. AI augments the capabilities of a small team to deliver at an enterprise level.

Global Inclusion and the Cambrian Explosion of Entrepreneurship

From Bangalore to Buenos Aires, from Lagos to Lisbon, AI-native startups are skipping legacy stages and leapfrogging into new possibilities. Where once economic development followed a linear path—industrial to digital to intelligent—today it is exponential, borderless, and local at the same time.

Startups in rural India are now building precision agri-tech tools that utilize AI image recognition. Craftspeople in Indonesia launch AI-personalized e-commerce shops. Creators in Ghana remix global music with voice cloning and AI mastering. The long tail has teeth—and a voice.

The Creator-Startup-AI Feedback Loop

This is a loop of liberation. Creators build with AI. AI learns from creators. Startups scale those creations. And with every turn of the loop, the tools get smarter, cheaper, and more personal.

But with great amplification comes great responsibility: deepfakes, content pollution, misinformation, and questions of attribution demand new norms and possibly new laws. As we'll see in later chapters, the algorithmic age needs not only engineers, but ethicists, philosophers, and wise builders.

The Big Idea: The Return of the Garage

The story of Steve Jobs and Wozniak in a California garage is well-known. But today's garage is virtual. It's a browser tab. It's a Figma file. It's a Notion doc shared across time zones.

What remains unchanged is the spirit: curiosity, creativity, and courage.

If the 20th century gave us corporate giants and unicorn IPOs, the 21st may give us a world teeming with creator-led, AI-augmented micro-ventures—small in size, big in soul.

And that, perhaps, is the most revolutionary startup idea of all.

How Solopreneurs Use AI: A New Renaissance of One

In 1512, a solitary figure in Florence worked in oil and tempera, crafting The Mona Lisa with painstaking brushstrokes. In 2023, another solitary figure in Austin sits with a laptop, dragging prompts into Notion AI, refining slogans in Copy.ai, and rendering cover designs with Midjourney. The mediums have changed. The solitude has not. Nor has the spark of creation.

The modern solopreneur, much like the Renaissance polymath, embodies a confluence of skills—but today, those skills are increasingly augmented, not owned. What used to require a team of marketers, designers, copywriters, and coders can now be done by one person—armed with intuition and algorithms.

This is not merely about productivity. It is about a shift in what it means to create.

Thinking, Writing, and Planning with Notion AI

Before, the blank page haunted writers and planners alike. Now, Notion AI offers a gentle co-authoring feature—suggesting headlines, rewriting emails, synthesizing research, and even generating structured business plans.

For solopreneurs, this transforms the act of thinking out loud. Every bullet point expands into a blog post. Every note becomes a newsletter. It's not just faster—it's fluid. Like Da Vinci's notebooks, ideas no longer remain sketches—they iterate in real time with the machine.

One digital coach from Chicago described it best:

"Notion AI doesn't just speed up my process. It challenges it. It asks the questions I forgot to ask myself."

Branding and Design with Midjourney

In the age of visuals, your logo is your story—and now, storyboards no longer require Photoshop mastery. With a single prompt—"a minimalist logo for a climate tech startup, inspired by Bauhaus"—Midjourney paints possibilities in seconds.

Solopreneurs no longer wrestle with design paralysis. They dialogue with it. A photographer in Morocco utilized Midjourney to design packaging for her AI-printed coffee table books. A solo game developer in Croatia prototyped entire character arcs before writing a line of code.

Tools no longer bind the visual imagination of a company, but only by the poetry of its prompts.

Copywriting and Messaging with Copy.ai

Messaging used to be a bottleneck. Now, it's a faucet. Copy.ai gives solopreneurs instant access to taglines, email campaigns, product descriptions, and social copy. The magic lies not in replacing human voice—but in accelerating its emergence.

A wellness coach in Bangalore described the feeling:

"I used to spend hours writing Instagram captions. Now I spend minutes editing ones that sound like me—only better."

Copy.ai becomes less of a ghostwriter and more of a mirror—reflecting the brand's tone, audience, and purpose with sharper edges.

The Entrepreneur as Orchestra Conductor

Walter Isaacson has often portrayed innovation as symphonic: a Steve Jobs orchestrating designers, engineers, and marketers into harmony. But now, a solopreneur becomes that orchestra—with AI tools acting as instruments.

Notion AI is the strategist.

Midjourney is the visual artist.

Copy.ai is the speechwriter.

ChatGPT is the research assistant.

Canva is the stage designer.

Zapier is the operations manager.

One mind. Many extensions.

This is not efficiency. This is creative leverage—the kind that powered Franklin's printing press, Edison's lab, or Jobs's keynote stage.

From Freelancers to Founder-Creators

The greatest transformation AI brings to solopreneurs is a shift in identity. No longer just gig workers or freelancers, these individuals are founders—building products, communities, platforms, and brands. They are not scaling organizations—they are scaling selves.

And as AI continues to evolve, the archetype of the lone creator expands. She is not alone—she is augmented. She is not small—she is sovereign. In a world where intelligence is modular and creativity is iterative, the garage entrepreneur returns—not with a soldering iron, but with a prompt.

The Renaissance, it seems, has rebooted.

The Rise of Micro SaaS: Crafting Cathedrals from Code

In the grand narrative arc of innovation, there are moments when tectonic shifts don't announce themselves with explosions or IPOs. They begin quietly—in coffee shops, in dorm rooms, in the determined solitude of a developer's screen at 2 a.m. The rise of micro SaaS is one such moment: a story not of billion-dollar unicorns but of nimble, focused craftsmen reshaping the software economy one niche at a time.

Much like Steve Jobs tinkering in his garage, or Tim Berners-Lee envisioning the World Wide Web in the corridors of CERN, the builders of micro SaaS (Software as a Service) don't seek scale for its own sake. They seek elegance, precision, and a sense of purpose. They are the artisans of the digital age, targeting hyper-specific problems—an automated newsletter builder for Etsy sellers, a CRM tool tailored to yoga studios, a task manager for indie game designers.

And what sets them apart is not just what they build—but how they build it.

They leverage the democratizing power of AI tools like Notion AI, ChatGPT, Bubble, Webflow, Zapier, and Midjourney, orchestrating a lean workflow where one person does the work of ten. Design, copywriting, coding, marketing, customer support—it all lives in a fluid loop of automation and augmentation.

These founders are not chasing VC term sheets. They're chasing freedom. They craft tools that solve problems they understand intimately, often born out of personal frustration. The result? Products with soul. Interfaces with empathy. Business models with resilience.

Just as Benjamin Franklin wore many hats—printer, inventor, diplomat, and scientist—the modern micro SaaS founder is part coder, part designer, and part storyteller. They represent a new archetype of entrepreneur—sustainable, solo, and sovereign.

In a world often obsessed with blitzscaling, micro SaaS champions the power of calm growth and purposeful design. And in doing so, it revives a deeply human truth: sometimes, the most revolutionary innovation happens not in the boardroom—but in the focused mind of a single individual with a problem to solve and the tools to solve it.

Democratizing Innovation or Centralizing Power?

Throughout history, innovation has walked a tightrope between liberation and consolidation.

The Dual Helix of Technological Progress

When Johannes Gutenberg built his printing press in the 15th century, he did more than invent a machine—he unshackled ideas. Suddenly, knowledge could move beyond the cloisters of the elite and into the hands of the many. A similar pulse echoed centuries later when Tim Berners-Lee imagined the World Wide Web as a decentralized, open space where anyone, anywhere, could publish, create, and connect.

And now, as we stand on the precipice of an AI-powered world, we must ask: Are we democratizing innovation—or centralizing power under the guise of progress?

The story of this era is unfolding in paradoxes.

On one hand, AI tools like ChatGPT, Midjourney, and GitHub Copilot are leveling the playing field. A teenager in Nairobi can build an app, compose music, write a book, or launch a SaaS platform without needing capital or coding skills. The gatekeepers are being bypassed. Creativity is being unbundled from credentials. The spark of innovation is being lit in bedrooms, cafés, and rural classrooms—not just in Silicon Valley boardrooms.

On the other hand, the very models that enable this access are trained on oceans of proprietary data, controlled by a handful of tech giants. The compute resources needed to train next-generation models require capital and infrastructure that only the largest players—OpenAI, Google, Meta, and Amazon—can afford. The new oil isn't just data—it's GPUs, model weights, and distribution channels. Power, once again, risks becoming concentrated behind closed APIs.

It echoes the tension of the Enlightenment: the printing press gave rise to both revolutionary pamphlets and state propaganda. Radio and television amplified both civil rights leaders and demagogues. The internet gave birth to Wikipedia—and surveillance capitalism.

So the question we must grapple with is not whether technology empowers or oppresses, but who owns the means of augmentation.

Will we build systems that allow citizens to shape their own futures? Or will we hand the reins to a few who automate decisions too complex for scrutiny?

Benjamin Franklin—polymath, printer, rebel—once warned against letting power consolidate in the name of convenience. "Those who would give up essential Liberty, to purchase a little temporary Safety, deserve neither Liberty nor Safety," he wrote.

In today's world, the stakes are just as high.

Because when innovation is democratized, it becomes a tool for flourishing. But when it is centralized, it becomes an instrument of control—wrapped in sleek UX, guarded by algorithmic opacity.

We are writing the next chapter of human possibility. The pen is in our hands. But we must ask: Who holds the eraser?

PART III: HUMANS IN THE LOOP – PREPARING FOR AN AI-DRIVEN WORLD

Part III

Humans in the Loop

Preparing for an AI-Driven World

If the first chapters of this story were about the tools we built, the next are about the people who must wield them wisely.

History reminds us that every technological revolution, at its core, is a human story. The steam engine didn't just accelerate industry—it reshaped lives, from factory workers to railroad barons. The transistor didn't merely shrink electronics—it reframed how we think, communicate, and even govern.

And now, artificial intelligence is not only asking us what machines can do, but also what humans should become.

In the labs of Silicon Valley and Shenzhen, neural networks hum quietly, learning to recognize patterns, predict preferences, and mimic creativity. But behind every algorithm is a choice: What data to train it on. What outcomes to optimize for. What guardrails to erect. Machines do not make those decisions. We make them.

This part of the journey isn't about code. It's about conscience.

"Humans in the loop"—a phrase once used in engineering to signal oversight—is now a rallying cry for a future that is designed by humans, for humans. It serves as a reminder that empathy, ethics, and emotional intelligence are not outdated relics, but rather core competencies in the age of AI.

We'll meet the teachers learning to co-create with AI tutors, the doctors navigating diagnostics with machine-learning copilots, and the artists sketching side by side with generative tools. We'll explore how trust, transparency, and accountability must be embedded not just in systems, but in culture.

Because the defining question of our time is no longer whether AI will outperform us, but whether we will rise to the occasion of redefining ourselves.

In a world where machines can learn faster, reason deeper, and scale wider, our competitive edge is not speed—it's wisdom. Our greatest contribution will not be replicating intelligence, but reinventing responsibility.

As Leonardo da Vinci once observed, "Simplicity is the ultimate sophistication." In an age of complexity, that wisdom still holds. And so we turn the page—not just to a new era of technology, but to a new era of being more fully, wisely, human.

Welcome to Part III: Humans in the Loop.

Chapter 15

The New Skills Mandate – Rethinking Work and Worth

In every era of transformation—whether sparked by steam, electricity, or silicon—the rules of work have been rewritten. And yet, what we're experiencing now is not just a rewriting. It is a reevaluation of what it means to be skilled, valuable, and human in the labor equation.

In this chapter, we trace how the AI age is not merely automating tasks—it's reshaping the very architecture of employment.

From Rote to Resilience

Once, a job was defined by the repetition of what you already knew. Now, it's defined by how fast you can learn what you don't. In interviews across Germany's Mittelstand, American high schools, and rural Indian upskilling programs, a pattern emerges: curiosity, adaptability, collaboration—these are the new literacy.

We meet Maria, a manufacturing technician in Ohio, who used to work on the assembly line but now trains collaborative robots, or cobots, to work alongside humans. Her journey is less about "losing a job" and more about evolving her role.

We meet Kareem, a logistics planner in Dubai, who now works with predictive AI to optimize port traffic, not through command, but through conversation—prompting, querying, adjusting. His value lies not in managing freight, but in interpreting insights the machine itself cannot explain.

Upskilling vs. Right-skilling

The buzzwords are everywhere—reskilling, lifelong learning, microcredentials. But they miss a deeper truth. This isn't just about adding new skills. It's about rethinking which ones matter.

Once, we paid a premium for those who could calculate, remember, and repeat. Today, machines do that better and faster. What remains irreplaceable are the uniquely human abilities: empathy, moral judgment, contextual reasoning, and interdisciplinary synthesis.

As AI becomes our partner in decision-making, those who can ask better questions—not just find better answers—will emerge as leaders.

A New Toolkit of Worth

We visit schools teaching "prompt engineering" alongside algebra. We hear from mid-career nurses who are learning about AI triage assistants. We meet farmers receiving satellite-led precision advice via voice bots in their local dialect.

In Singapore, a program retrained airline stewards who were grounded during COVID to become healthtech concierges—with AI dashboards as co-pilots and compassion as currency.

The common thread? Every story reveals a shift in what society deems worthy.

Measuring What We Value

For too long, GDP and headcounts have defined productivity. But as we automate more, we must ask: How do we measure human flourishing in the age of machines?

Is a therapist who uses AI to surface deeper traumas more valuable? Is an artist collaborating with Midjourney less original?

As we blur the lines between tool and creator, between analyst and algorithm, we must expand our definitions—not just of skills, but of worth.

The Human Compass

In the final pages of this chapter, we return to the timeless: wisdom from Benjamin Franklin to Ada Lovelace. They remind us that while tools change, the true revolution lies in values.

Preparing for the AI age is not simply about programming machines better. It is to program ourselves—with deeper empathy, ethical foresight, and an expansive understanding of what it means to contribute.

Because the real question isn't whether AI will do our jobs, it's whether we will redesign work—and society—to ensure every person has a role worth doing, a skill worth learning, and a dignity worth defending.

WEF Future of Jobs 2025–2030

In the corridors of Davos, where snow-capped ambition meets systems thinking, the World Economic Forum (WEF) has long been a crystal ball for the future of work. Its Future of Jobs Report 2025–2030 reads not as prophecy, but as an urgent invitation: a call to rethink how societies allocate meaning to labor, value to contribution, and identity to occupation.

At the heart of the report lies a paradox that might have intrigued Leonardo da Vinci himself—an age that is both automating and humanizing simultaneously. Machines now draft legal contracts, detect disease, drive logistics, and design algorithms. Yet, it is emotional intelligence, creativity, resilience, and ethical judgment that are increasingly valued. In this see-saw of silicon and soul, it is not the replacement of humans that matters most—it is the reconfiguration of them.

The Great Rebalancing

You might frame this as a renaissance moment—not dissimilar to the invention of the printing press. Just as Gutenberg democratized knowledge, today's AI is democratizing capability. But with it comes disruption. The WEF report suggests that 44% of workers 'core skills will change in the next five years. By 2030, roles like data analysts, AI specialists, and sustainability officers will surge. Jobs in clerical support, accounting, and customer service, however, may fade like candlelight in an age of electricity.

Yet the story is not just about what disappears—it's about what reappears, reimagined.

The Rise of New Archetypes

Consider this as the emergence of new hybrids: the prompt engineer who merges art and logic; the algorithmic ethicist who straddles law and empathy; the mental health coach who deploys AI but delivers humanity. These are not mere jobs—they are frontiers.

The report forecasts that roles requiring analytical thinking, self-management, and lifelong learning will be paramount. In fact, resilience, flexibility, and curiosity top the list—soft skills with steel backbones. If the 20th century prized specialization, the 21st seems to reward synthesis.

From Reskilling to Reframing

What's radical here is not just the emergence of new jobs—it's the idea that humans must reframe their own worth. No longer tethered to static job titles, people must now adapt to portfolio lives—fluid, multifaceted, and iterative.

The WEF predicts that 50% of all employees will need reskilling by 2025. But Isaacson would urge us not to think of this as a burden. He would remind us of Benjamin Franklin, who was at once an inventor, printer, diplomat, and philosopher. In this new age, a worker is not merely what they do but what they can become.

Technology with a Human North Star

The report highlights a shift from automation that replaces workers to augmentation that enhances. AI will not just handle our tasks—it will challenge our judgment, support our decision-making, and boost our potential. However, this relies on governance, ethics, and a shared sense of purpose; without these, innovation risks becoming colonization.

It is perhaps appropriate to close this chapter with a reflection on values—perhaps reminding us of Ada Lovelace, who saw in machines not just calculation, but imagination. The future of work, as imagined by the WEF, is not a destination—it is a dance. Between man and machine. Between skill and soul.

And like all dances, it begins with listening.

The Future of Jobs (2025–2030): A Story of Reinvention and Resolve

In Davos, high in the Swiss Alps, where the world's power brokers gather under the snow-capped optimism of global cooperation, a quiet but profound transformation is unfolding—not in boardrooms, but in break rooms, classrooms, and coworking spaces across the globe.

The World Economic Forum's Future of Jobs Report doesn't shout headlines; it whispers a reality that many already feel in their bones: the very fabric of work is being rewoven. At the core is a question that echoes through every industry, every policy meeting, every kitchen table discussion: What will it mean to be employable in a world where machines learn faster than we do?

The Shift Is Not Coming. It's Here.

The data reads like a page-turner: by 2025, an estimated 85 million jobs may be displaced by automation, yet 97 million new roles could emerge—roles rooted in the symbiosis of humans and technology. This is not a doomsday narrative. It's a renaissance.

It's the cashier retraining as a robotic process controller, the graphic designer learning prompt engineering, the farmer becoming a precision agriculture technician. It's the coder who now also needs to understand empathy, and the nurse who now reads AI dashboards alongside patient charts.

Skills > Degrees

The WEF report underscores something Steve Jobs might have said: Don't hire for credentials, hire for curiosity. Skills like analytical thinking, creativity, and emotional intelligence rise to the top—surpassing even traditional technical expertise in importance.

The rise of reskilling and lifelong learning is not about getting ahead; it's about not being left behind. Companies are no longer just employers—they are becoming universities. IBM, Google, and Amazon no longer ask for diplomas. They ask: Can you adapt? Can you learn?

The Hybrid Human-AI Workforce

Imagine a factory floor in Shenzhen, a newsroom in New York, a design studio in Nairobi. In each, humans work not in competition with machines but in collaboration. AI does the data-crunching; the human draws meaning. AI drafts the layout; the human refines the emotion.

What the WEF calls the "augmentation era" is, ironically, a return to something very human: judgment, creativity, ethics, and collaboration.

Rising Roles

The fastest-growing roles aren't in the traditional domains—they're in data analysis, AI/ML specialists, sustainability analysts, and digital transformation managers. But equally important are care economy roles—mental health workers, care providers, education facilitators—those who can care for the humans in the loop.

It's not just about coding. It's about caring.

A Call to Action

You might frame it this way: Just as the printing press reshaped literacy, or the transistor reshaped computing, AI is reshaping human potential. But only if we seize it.

The report doesn't just warn—it challenges:

- Governments to invest not in subsidies but in skills.
- Businesses should build talent from within, rather than buy it.
- Individuals should become not just consumers of technology, but collaborators with it.

From Jobs to Journeys

In the end, the Future of Jobs is less a forecast and more a mirror. It reflects our anxiety, yes—but also our ambition. And like any good Isaacson biography, it reminds us that the future belongs not to the strongest or the smartest—but to those most willing to reinvent themselves.

Hybrid Skills: Where Empathy Meets Algorithms

In the early days of the digital revolution, the dominant skill was coding. The world lionized the lone genius—the hacker in a hoodie, building software that could scale across the globe. But as the second wave of AI washed ashore, something curious happened. The most successful innovators weren't just the best programmers. They were the best listeners.

Take the story of Aditi Rao, a UX designer turned AI conversational architect at a health tech startup in Bangalore. She wasn't the most technical person in the room, but she understood something essential: people. She could translate human anxieties into design prompts and patient frustration into machine-readable empathy. When her chatbot triaged mental health queries with warmth and responsiveness, it wasn't just because the model was smart; it was because she trained it to be kind.

That's the power of hybrid skill sets. We are entering an era where Emotional Intelligence (EQ) and AI Literacy must walk hand in hand.

The Rise of the Empathic Technologist

Emotional intelligence—the ability to read people, respond with empathy, and navigate social complexity—isn't new. From Lincoln's political acumen to Oprah's emotional resonance, history has always rewarded those who could connect. But AI changes the game. Today's tools can generate text, synthesize faces, and mimic tone—but they lack context. That's where humans step in.

At MIT's Media Lab, researchers are training students not just to build algorithms, but to question them. They ask, 'What is this system optimizing for?' Whose values are embedded in the code? The answers demand both technical fluency and moral clarity.

Why AI Literacy Needs a Human Heart

AI literacy encompasses more than understanding how ChatGPT works or building a neural network. It means understanding when not to use AI, how to identify bias in a dataset, and how to design systems that augment rather than replace human judgment.

And this is where EQ becomes the anchor. A teacher who understands her students' fears about being replaced by machines can introduce AI not as a threat, but as a partner. A manager who senses burnout in her team can deploy automation thoughtfully—removing drudgery, not purpose.

In the World Economic Forum's Future of Jobs report, "analytical thinking" and "empathy" top the charts—not in opposition, but in tandem. The hybrid future isn't soft skills versus hard skills. It's soft skills as the force multiplier of intelligent systems.

From Renaissance to Reinvention

When Leonardo da Vinci blended engineering with art, or when Steve Jobs fused liberal arts with computing, they modeled a truth that echoes louder today: innovation thrives at the intersection.

In tomorrow's workplace, the most prized professionals won't be pure technologists or pure humanists. They'll be translators. People who can bridge emotion and logic, ethics and execution, intuition and data. People who know that while AI might power the tools, it's human empathy that powers the trust.

And perhaps that is the greatest skill of all: knowing what it means to be human—even as we train the machines.

Hybrid Skill Sets: Emotional Intelligence + AI Literacy

In the late 20th century, companies valued IQ—raw intellect, logic, and mastery of subjects. By the early 21st century, Daniel Goleman helped redefine the landscape by spotlighting Emotional Intelligence (EQ)—the ability to read a room, resolve conflict, inspire loyalty, and navigate uncertainty. This wasn't just touchy-feely psychology—it became the differentiator in leadership, collaboration, and customer rapport.

Now, a new fusion is emerging. Call it "hybrid fluency," or what some recruiters describe as the T-shaped talent—a deep vertical of expertise, underpinned by broad lateral dexterity. And in today's AI-infused world, that lateral bar must include AI literacy.

This doesn't mean everyone must learn to code neural networks. Instead, it means understanding what AI can and cannot do. Recognizing data bias, prompt design, and model transparency. Being able to communicate with AI systems, not as black boxes, but as collaborative tools. The new fluency involves knowing how to ask the right questions—and recognizing when the answers might be flawed, incomplete, or even unethical.

Take a hospital administrator, for example. She may use AI to forecast patient loads or optimize schedules. However, when a model recommends cutting services to low-income communities, her EQ intervenes. She challenges the algorithm's assumptions, aware of its social consequences. Her human judgment becomes the last line of accountability.

Or consider a marketer using generative AI. He can spin hundreds of ad variations in seconds. But it takes empathy to gauge what tone resonates. It takes cultural awareness to avoid offense. The AI outputs content; the human curates meaning.

In these scenarios, it's no longer enough to be tech-savvy or emotionally attuned. The real leaders of the AI era are those who can do both.

This hybridization is not optional. As automation eats routine work and AI amplifies cognitive labor, the edge moves to those who combine data fluency with human nuance. These are the bridge-builders—those who connect silicon logic to human hearts.

In short:

The future does not belong to the algorithm or the empath alone.

It belongs to those who speak both languages—and translate between them.

The Rise of the T-Shaped Professional: Where Depth Meets Breadth

In the 15th century, Leonardo da Vinci sketched helicopters in his notebooks. But he was no mere engineer. He studied the flow of rivers, dissected human cadavers, and painted with a precision that still inspires awe. Leonardo was the original T-shaped mind—deep in anatomy and hydraulics, broad in art and observation. He wasn't a polymath by chance; he was a polymath by necessity.

Centuries later, in the swirling crosscurrents of the 21st century, we are rediscovering the need for T-shaped professionals —people who combine deep expertise in one field (the vertical stroke of the T) with a broad set of interdisciplinary skills (the horizontal bar). And nowhere is this shift more urgent than in the age of AI.

From Specialists to Synthesizers

For most of the 20th century, the labor market rewarded specialization. The best chemists worked in pharmaceutical labs, while the best coders worked in software firms. We lived in silos, and silos worked—until they didn't.

As machine learning began rewriting the rules across every field—from radiology to retail—the ability to speak across disciplines became more valuable than ever. Suddenly, a data scientist needed to understand behavioral psychology. A climate researcher needed to grasp machine vision. An economist needs to be aware of ethical considerations.

In this world, the vertical line of the T—your deep domain knowledge—is not enough. You also need the horizontal: the ability to connect, translate, and collaborate across fields.

The Airbnb Designer Who Could Code

Take Joe Gebbia, one of Airbnb's co-founders. He trained as an industrial designer. But what made him exceptional wasn't just his design depth—it was his fluency in engineering, business, and storytelling. He could sketch a UI mockup in the morning, debate venture funding terms at lunch, and pitch a brand ethos by dinner.

In Silicon Valley and beyond, this professional—the T-shaped bridge-builder—has become the model of modern talent. Agile teams don't want the deepest expert locked in a basement lab. They want the translator, the synthesizer, the collaborator who can wear multiple hats without losing their edge.

Why T-Shaped Beats I-Shaped in the Age of AI

As AI tools absorb and automate technical tasks, the value of being only a specialist diminishes. The coder who only knows Python is being outpaced by no-code tools. But the coder who also understands product strategy, UX design, and user psychology? She's irreplaceable.

According to the World Economic Forum's skills outlook, the top roles of the future require adaptability, systems thinking, and problem-solving across various domains. In short: T-shaped talent.

Think of a bioethics expert who understands neural networks, or a robotics engineer who grasps sociology. These aren't unicorns. They're the future of work.

The Horizontal Bar is a Muscle

The mistake people make is assuming breadth comes at the cost of depth. But in truth, the horizontal bar is a muscle—it grows by learning to speak other languages, working in teams, and seeing your narrow expertise in a broader canvas. It's not about being good at everything. It's about knowing just enough to ask better questions, build better bridges, and uncover patterns that others miss.

Just like da Vinci studied anatomy to draw better portraits, today's professionals must study other domains to build better futures.

From Renaissance to Reinvention

The rise of the T-shaped professional is not a fad. It is a return to an older idea—one that says knowledge is not a set of silos but a network of connections. As we stand at the edge of artificial intelligence, climate disruption, and economic transformation, the people who will lead us forward are those who can dive deep, reach wide, and pull insights from multiple worlds.

In a time when AI can mimic human skill, the truly human advantage is this: context, curiosity, and connection. That's the shape of the future. That's the T.

Chapter 16

Reskilling & Upskilling: Action Programs for the Current Workforce

In every technological revolution—be it the Gutenberg press, the steam engine, or the microprocessor—there comes a moment when society must recalibrate the skillsets of its people. Today, in the age of artificial intelligence, we stand at precisely such a moment. Algorithms now write news articles, diagnose diseases, design buildings, and optimize supply chains. And yet, the enduring truth is that humans are not being replaced—they are being repositioned.

This chapter tells the story of that repositioning.

The New Guilds of the Digital Renaissance

In the past, upskilling often meant moving from field to factory, or from typewriter to terminal. Now, it means blending the analog with the digital, the emotional with the computational. The carpenter learns to use AI-assisted design tools. The nurse learns to interpret outputs from predictive diagnostics. The marketing executive learns prompt engineering, not just storytelling.

Across industries, a new guild system is emerging—not based on traditional crafts, but on hybrid human-machine collaboration. Governments, corporations, and institutions are investing in this transformation—not out of charity, but necessity.

Take Singapore's SkillsFuture initiative: a national movement offering citizens credits to retrain in AI, robotics, and digital communication. Or AT&T's Future Ready program, which retrained nearly half of its workforce by forecasting which roles would be obsolete and which would be born anew. And then there's Amazon's $1.2B Upskilling 2025 pledge, equipping warehouse workers with data analytics and IT skills—training the people who once moved boxes to now manage the algorithms that decide what's in those boxes.

These aren't merely stories of corporate responsibility; they're blueprints for national resilience.

From Ladders to Lattices

One of the profound shifts in the AI era is the dismantling of linear career ladders. In their place: skill lattices—flexible, branching pathways where a data analyst can become a cybersecurity specialist, or a content writer can evolve into a conversational designer.

At the center of this new architecture is lifelong learning. Institutions like Coursera, Khan Academy, and edX are no longer just supplemental—they are central. Meanwhile, coding bootcamps, microcredentials, and stackable diplomas are enabling workers to reinvent themselves not over decades, but in months.

The AI age demands just-in-time education, customized and contextualized, much like the algorithms it seeks to master.

Humanity in the Loop

However, even as we develop AI literacy, we must not overlook the importance of emotional intelligence. The ability to listen, to collaborate, to make ethical decisions—these are not soft skills. They are core competencies in a world where AI can optimize but not empathize.

Thus, the most successful reskilling programs are not just about Python or SQL—they are about cognitive resilience, critical thinking, and human creativity. The World Economic Forum's Future of Jobs Report 2025–2030 projects that while 85 million jobs may be displaced, 97 million new ones will emerge—many of which will require precisely these human-AI hybrid skills.

The Quiet Heroes of Transformation

In this chapter, we meet people like:

- Maria, a textile worker in Mexico, retrained in robotic quality assurance through an NGO-public-private partnership.
- Kwame, a Ghanaian teacher now coaching students in AI ethics and data bias via an open-source curriculum.

- Anna, a mid-career HR manager turned digital skills evangelist within a European logistics company.

Each of them is a quiet hero in a broader transformation—a reminder that reinvention is not just possible but profoundly human.

The Final Lesson

What separates those who thrive from those who falter is not intelligence—it's adaptability. Reskilling is not just a workforce strategy; it is a societal imperative. It is how we preserve dignity in the face of disruption, and how we ensure that no one is left behind—not the mechanic in Detroit, the farmer in Punjab, or the call center worker in Manila.

The age of AI is not the end of work. It is the beginning of a new kind of craftsmanship—one where the tools are intelligent, but the vision remains deeply human.

Corporate Case Studies in Reskilling

From Assembly Lines to Algorithms: How Amazon and AT&T Rewrote the Corporate Learning Playbook

In the age of artificial intelligence and automation, companies aren't just competing on margins—they're racing against obsolescence. The most visionary among them understood that the battle for relevance would be fought not in factories or boardrooms, but in classrooms, coding labs, and micro-learning portals.

Amazon: The $700 Million Bet on Human Adaptability

In 2019, Amazon—a company long synonymous with logistics efficiency and cloud dominance—announced a bold move: a $700 million commitment to reskilling 100,000 employees by 2025. It wasn't just a corporate PR campaign. It was, in many ways, Jeff Bezos 'silent admission that the most valuable resource inside Amazon's warehouses and call centers wasn't the robotics infrastructure or AWS servers—but people.

Rather than fearing automation, Amazon opted to prepare its workforce to work in partnership with it. Programs like Machine Learning University empowered software engineers to deepen their expertise in AI. Meanwhile, fulfillment center employees were offered the Amazon Technical Academy, which guided them from picking and packing to programming.

One employee, originally hired to work night shifts in a Kentucky warehouse, shared in a town hall how she completed the AWS Cloud Practitioner certification in under six months. Within a year, she had joined a team supporting cloud migration projects—a transformation both personal and emblematic.

What made Amazon's initiative unique wasn't just the money—it was the modularity. Employees weren't expected to quit their jobs or enroll in MBAs. Instead, they were offered stackable credentials, on-demand video modules, and coaching—all integrated into their workflow.

"We're not just reskilling to fill jobs. We're reskilling to give people a stake in the future," said Beth Galetti, SVP of HR at Amazon.

In a company known for automation, it was a rare but deliberate investment in human optionality.

AT&T: From Telco Giant to Tech Pioneer

Flashback to 2013. AT&T executives saw the writing on the wall. As data replaced voice and apps replaced landlines, the traditional telco business model was in decline. Rather than panic, they embarked on an audacious project: reinventing themselves for a digital-first future.

The effort, dubbed Future Ready, was one of the largest corporate upskilling programs in American history. Led by then-CEO Randall Stephenson and Chief Learning Officer John Palmer, AT&T partnered with Coursera, Udacity, and Georgia Tech to build custom learning pathways.

AT&T didn't just encourage employees to take online courses—they mapped career progressions. Want to move from field technician to data analyst? There was a roadmap for that. From customer support agent to UX designer? Here's your playbook.

"If we don't reskill our people, we'll spend billions hiring people from the outside. Why not invest in the ones who already understand our culture?" Stephenson remarked in a CNBC interview.

The initiative wasn't without skeptics. Early participation lagged. Some employees resisted. But as internal success stories began to circulate, a culture shift took hold. By 2020, more than 60% of AT&T's workforce had completed at least one nanodegree or credential, with many migrating into entirely new roles.

And AT&T didn't just train—it redeployed. Rather than laying off network engineers, it retrained them in cloud architecture. Legacy teams were cross-pollinated with agile project managers and digital product leads.

What emerged was not just a more tech-savvy company—but a more resilient one. AT&T, once a dinosaur in the telecom industry, became a case study in corporate metamorphosis.

The Takeaway: Upskilling as Innovation Infrastructure

If the 20th century was about optimizing processes, the 21st is about upgrading people. Amazon and AT&T's journeys show that reskilling isn't a perk—it's the operating system of modern companies. Both organizations bet on learning agility as their competitive edge—not just hiring AI talent, but nurturing it from within.

What made these companies remarkable wasn't just their ability to build technologies—but their willingness to evolve the human beings who built them.

And in doing so, they didn't just future-proof their businesses. They restored something quietly radical: the idea that people can adapt, grow, and thrive alongside machines—if given the chance.

AI Bootcamps, MOOCs, and Nano-Degrees: A New Architecture of Learning

It used to be that the arc of education bent toward degrees, tenure, and traditional classrooms. But in the unfolding AI revolution, education is no longer a gated path; it's a rapidly evolving network of on-ramps. And the architects of this network are not always universities—but technologists, entrepreneurs, and self-learners, armed with cloud servers, machine learning models, and a deep belief in democratized access to opportunity.

Just as the printing press liberated knowledge from monasteries, today's digital learning platforms are liberating skills from the ivory tower.

Take AI bootcamps. These aren't your father's computer science courses—they are short, intense, and unapologetically applied. Companies like DeepLearning.AI, FourthBrain, and AI Planet are equipping learners not only with theory but also with deployable models and real-world projects. They teach students how to fine-tune a transformer, yes—but more importantly, how to ship something that works.

Then there are MOOCs—massive open online courses—which took root a decade ago but have since matured into global academies. Platforms like Coursera, edX, and Udacity now offer comprehensive learning journeys—often at no cost—that rival elite institutions in both content and quality. A young mother in Nairobi can now learn Python from MIT, AI ethics from Stanford, and prompt engineering from OpenAI—all before breakfast.

But the most radical innovation is the nano-degree: a micro-credential with macro implications. These are agile, stackable, and often employer-aligned. Udacity's nano-degrees in AI, data science, or autonomous systems are co-designed with Google, IBM, and Amazon. The curriculum evolves in real-time with industry needs, bypassing academic inertia.

What's happening here isn't just about teaching code or algorithms. It's about reimagining what it means to be educated.

Just as Steve Jobs once saw the personal computer as "a bicycle for the mind," these new models of learning are jetpacks for talent—turbo-charging careers, pivoting professions, and unlocking possibilities for millions who were never invited to the old game.

The gatekeepers are gone. The new gate is bandwidth, motivation, and curiosity.

And for the future workforce, the message is clear: you don't need to wait for permission to learn AI. You just need Wi-Fi.

Playbook: The 90-Day Reskilling Sprint for Managers

When the arc of innovation bends sharply—as it has with AI—it isn't just software engineers and data scientists who need to adapt. It's also the middle managers—the cultural glue, strategic eyes, and operational anchors of every organization. The 90-day reskilling sprint isn't about code or cloud. It's about mindset.

Day 1–30: From Control to Curiosity

The first month is a mindset detox. For decades, managers were rewarded for certainty—tight schedules, defined KPIs, and predictable outcomes. But the AI-infused world is probabilistic, not deterministic. The best managers now must unlearn rigidity and embrace uncertainty.

In companies like AT&T, this meant enrolling thousands of managers in AI literacy workshops—not to prompt engineers, but to make them question-askers. What can this algorithm do better? What should humans still own? What bias might be hiding in this dataset?

This phase is Socratic. It's about asking better questions before offering better solutions.

Day 31–60: Tooling Up and Trying Small

Once the mental blocks soften, the sprint moves to experimentation. Managers are equipped with foundational fluency in tools like Notion AI, ChatGPT Enterprise, and Power BI. But more importantly, they're asked to apply these tools to one real-world workflow: automating a repetitive report, streamlining a meeting summary, or co-drafting a customer email.

This isn't training for training's sake. At Amazon, this was referred to as "applied experimentation"—one of the key pillars of their $700 million reskilling fund. Their logic was clear: give a manager one AI win, and they'll never look back.

The emphasis here isn't perfection. It's speed. The objective is to move from theoretical comfort to operational confidence.

Day 61–90: Coaching, Scaling, and Storytelling

The final stretch is where reskilling becomes a cultural norm. Managers are encouraged to coach their teams through similar micro-experiments, turning one success into a playbook. They also document what worked and what didn't, feeding into the company's reskilling repository.

At Unilever, this reflective phase was designed around internal storytelling. Managers shared what they automated, how they communicated it to their team, and what emotional reactions surfaced—enthusiasm, fear, relief. These stories, collected like case studies, shaped company-wide adoption.

This phase transforms the manager from learner to change agent.

The Takeaway

The 90-day sprint isn't a silver bullet. But like Steve Jobs once said, "People with passion can change the world." Equip a manager with AI awareness, a sandbox for testing, and the confidence to teach others—and you haven't just reskilled one person. You've lit the fuse of cultural transformation.

In the age of artificial intelligence, the most important skill may be the ability to learn, unlearn, and relearn—quickly, curiously, and collectively.

Chapter 17

AI for Leaders — Strategic Imperatives for Executives and CXOs

In the great sweep of industrial history—from the steam engine to the silicon chip—leaders have always stood at the threshold of uncertainty and innovation. Chapter 17 is about the new frontier: the age of artificial intelligence. And the people holding the compass now aren't just engineers or coders—they are the CEOs, CMOs, CTOs, CHROs, and every other C-suite visionary responsible for steering companies through the murky waters of exponential change.

We are living in a moment where code is not just automating routines—it's authoring strategy, rewriting playbooks, and reshaping the very DNA of how businesses operate. This chapter explores how executives must evolve from operational overseers to algorithmic architects. The mandate is no longer merely to adopt AI, but to embed it deeply into the culture, strategy, and competitive core of their organizations.

The Strategic Shift: From Risk Mitigation to Opportunity Creation

For decades, leadership was about managing risk. But in the AI era, playing it safe is the biggest risk. Take Satya Nadella at Microsoft, who didn't just integrate AI into products—he reoriented the company's purpose around it. Or Arvind Krishna at IBM, who positioned Watson as a cognitive collaborator for enterprise decision-making. These are not tech moves; they're leadership moves.

AI demands a shift in mindset from control to collaboration with intelligent systems. The executives who thrive are those who ask:

- What new value chains can AI unlock?

- How does AI amplify human creativity and not replace it?
- Can we use AI not just to predict, but to prescribe and personalize experiences at scale?

From Vision to Execution: The Leadership AI Playbook

This chapter lays out a strategic blueprint for executives:

1. **Align AI with Business Outcomes**

   The North Star isn't the model or the algorithm—it's the problem being solved. Effective leaders ensure AI investments are outcome-driven, not tech-fueled experiments.

2. **Build AI Fluency Across the C-Suite**

   It's no longer acceptable for marketing, HR, or finance leaders to be AI-illiterate. This chapter describes how CXOs become "bilingual"—fluent in business and algorithms—much like Ruth Porat at Alphabet, who bridges financial strategy with AI-forward thinking.

3. **Champion Responsible AI Governance**

   Leaders must balance ambition with accountability. From bias audits to AI ethics boards, the book showcases how companies like Salesforce and Accenture built frameworks for trustworthy AI, not just performant AI.

4. **Reshape Org Structures for Agile AI**

   Hierarchies are out. Cross-functional pods combining data scientists, designers, and domain experts are in. The new CxO understands that AI is not a department—it's a horizontal capability.

5. **Create a Culture of Experimentation**

   AI is probabilistic, not deterministic. That means failure is part of the equation. The modern leader adopts a 'fail-fast, learn-faster' model. Case in point: how Spotify's leadership enables constant A/B testing of AI-generated playlists, empowering both creativity and accountability.

Thought Leadership, Not Just Technology Leadership

True AI transformation is about narrative leadership. The executives profiled in this chapter don't just build models—they craft visions that teams, shareholders, and customers can believe in. They become storytellers of the future, helping people imagine what's possible when humans and machines collaborate not out of fear, but out of mutual augmentation.

Just as Einstein reimagined space and time, today's great executives are reimagining work and value. The companies that will lead in the next decade will not be those with the most data—but those with leaders capable of translating intelligence into impact.

Creating an AI-Literate Boardroom

In every era of technological transformation, the boardroom has served as both a sanctuary and a battlefield. In the age of electricity, it was Edison and Westinghouse who sparked not only currents but corporate revolutions. In the age of the internet, it was Jobs, Gates, and Bezos who brought the network into the nucleus of executive decisions. And now, with artificial intelligence redefining every function of the enterprise, the boardroom is once again being tested—not by technology alone, but by its ability to understand it, steward it, and strategically govern it.

An AI-literate boardroom does not mean filling every seat with coders or data scientists. Rather, it involves retooling the mental models of decision-makers—shifting from quarterly earnings to long-horizon intelligence, from intuition-based choices to probabilistic reasoning, from static policies to adaptive governance frameworks. The goal is not fluency in Python but fluency in the implications of machine learning: bias, explainability, privacy, power.

Take the case of Satya Nadella's leadership at Microsoft. One of his earliest executive meetings featured not a slide deck, but a Socratic dialogue about the future of responsibility in autonomous systems. When a board truly understands AI, it no longer treats it as a "tool" relegated to IT—but as a strategic, ethical, and geopolitical force that permeates every line of business.

In recent years, firms like Accenture, Mastercard, and Unilever have begun mandating AI education for their senior leadership. They are partnering with universities, hosting internal AI bootcamps, and—most notably—appointing Chief AI Ethics Officers to report not just to the CTO, but directly to the board.

Yet the transformation is not just institutional—it is deeply human. A truly AI-literate boardroom asks better questions:

- What does it mean to optimize for efficiency in a world where transparency is equally vital?
- How do we balance automation with the dignity of human labor?
- Are we ready for the reputational fallout of an algorithmic misfire?

Just as boards once had to grapple with the regulatory complexities of Sarbanes-Oxley or the digital disruption of cloud computing, today they must confront the asymmetry of knowledge between technical teams and non-technical leaders. The best boards close that gap not by dumbing down the technology—but by raising their own bar of understanding.

In the end, an AI-literate boardroom is not defined by buzzwords or investments in AI startups. It is defined by courageous curiosity, structured foresight, and the willingness to ask second-order questions that reach beyond quarterly profit and into the fabric of society.

Because when the algorithm becomes the decision-maker, the board must become the conscience.

Data Ethics, Governance, and Responsible Deployment

In the grand arc of technological revolutions—from the steam engine to the semiconductor—every leap forward has ignited both boundless promise and profound peril. With artificial intelligence, that duality reaches its apex. At the core of this unfolding narrative lies not just algorithms or models, but something far more consequential: data. The raw material of the AI age.

And as with all powerful resources, how we collect, govern, and wield data will define the moral compass of this new era.

The New Oil, With New Risks

In the boardrooms of Silicon Valley and the policy corridors of Brussels, a new mantra emerged in the 2010s: "Data is the new oil." But while oil polluted the air, data—misused—can corrode the very fabric of trust.

Remember that the great inventors—from Benjamin Franklin to Ada Lovelace—were not just tinkerers of tech, but custodians of consequences. In the same vein, AI builders today must wrestle with how data is harvested, labeled, and repurposed.

Consider Amazon's delivery algorithms, trained on customer behavior. Or facial recognition systems fed millions of images scraped without consent. The tension isn't just technical—it's ethical. The choices made here have a ripple effect throughout society.

Governance is the New Innovation

Once, innovation was about speed. Now, it is equally about restraint.

Data governance—how data is accessed, shared, stored, and deleted—is becoming a strategic function, not just a compliance checkbox. Leaders from Microsoft to Tata Consultancy Services have begun appointing Chief Data Officers with authority equal to that of CFOs. In essence, every company is becoming a data company, and every leader a steward of digital trust.

The best organizations embed governance into their workflows—using federated data models, differential privacy, and algorithmic audits—not to stifle innovation, but to future-proof it.

Responsible Deployment Is Strategic Deployment

When AI models are deployed in hospitals, classrooms, or courts, the consequences are no longer abstract. They're human.

Consider this quote from Leonardo da Vinci—"Knowing is not enough; we must apply"—with the urgency of today's call for AI explainability, bias audits, and human-in-the-loop systems. It's not enough for an algorithm to be accurate. It must be accountable. Transparent. Contestable.

Take the case of credit scoring AI. If it denies a loan, the borrower deserves to know why—and have recourse. That's not a feature. It's a right.

The Future Demands an Ethical Compass

As the pace of AI accelerates, so does the need for ethical scaffolding.

From the EU's AI Act to the White House's Blueprint for an AI Bill of Rights, regulators are beginning to draw the contours of acceptable use. But the deeper responsibility lies not in legislation alone, but in leadership.

True innovation comes not just from what machines can do—but from what humans choose to do with them.

The CEO's Dilemma: Disruption vs. Legacy Protection

At the heart of every transformational era lies a crucible moment for leadership. For today's CEOs, that moment has arrived—and it's not binary, but paradoxical. The choice isn't simply between embracing disruption or protecting legacy. It's navigating both, often simultaneously. And no one understands paradox better than a CEO at the helm of an enterprise founded on yesterday's success, now being challenged by tomorrow's technology.

Think of Satya Nadella at Microsoft. He didn't tear down Windows or Office; he reimagined them through the lens of the cloud. He didn't dismiss the legacy—he evolved it. Or consider Andy Jassy's ascent at Amazon. He carries Jeff Bezos' innovative DNA but must now manage scale, regulation, and responsibility while pushing the envelope with AI and logistics automation.

The dilemma is existential: do you preserve the golden goose, or rewire it before someone else does?

Disruption Demands Courage

The new breed of disruptors doesn't knock politely—they arrive armed with algorithms and unencumbered by legacy infrastructure. They're lean, digitally native, and culturally agile. Whether it's fintech startups reimagining banking or AI-native firms rewriting marketing playbooks, they are not bound by history. This gives them the oxygen they need to move quickly.

For the CEO of a century-old conglomerate, that speed is threatening—and intoxicating. You want to be agile. However, your ERP system dates back to 2004, and your compliance playbook was written for a paper-based world.

Yet, disruption can't be ignored. Blackberry once scoffed at the iPhone. Kodak patented digital photography—and then buried it. Sears built catalog-based commerce before e-commerce existed. Their caution became their obituary.

Legacy is a Moat—Until It's Not

The reality is that legacy assets—brand trust, supply chains, customer relationships, regulatory know-how—are immense advantages if you can make them interoperable with innovation. The modern CEO must act less like a protector of turf and more like a conductor of transformation—knowing when to preserve, when to rewire, and when to burn the ships.

This is why boards are increasingly seeking AI literacy in the C-suite. Because today, the ability to understand model governance, ethical deployment, and platform strategy is no longer just the CTO's job—it's a CEO's imperative.

The CEO's Trilemma: Speed, Safety, Stewardship

In the age of AI, the CEO faces a trilemma:

- Speed: Move fast enough to compete with AI-native challengers.
- Safety: Protect customer trust, data privacy, and brand equity.
- Stewardship: Uplift employees, partners, and shareholders through transparent transformation.

Doing one or two is easy. Doing all three? That's leadership in the AI era.

Remeber that real innovation isn't just about inventing new things—it's about recombining old strengths in radically new ways. The legacy isn't what holds you back. It's what gives your leap credibility—if you're brave enough to jump.

Chapter 18

Students and the Next Generation – What to Study in the Age of AI?

In every age of upheaval, the greatest question faced by the young has been deceptively simple: What should I study to stay relevant? From the printing press to the steam engine, from the transistor to the internet, history has asked this of each generation. However, today's students face a new challenge: they must prepare for jobs that do not yet exist, using tools that are still being developed, in an economy being transformed by machines that learn.

What to do when knowledge is abundant but wisdom must be curated?

From Memorization to Mental Models

In a world where GPTs can summarize Shakespeare and solve equations in milliseconds, the value of rote learning diminishes. But understanding the "why" behind the "what" becomes paramount. Students must shift from being passive vessels of information to architects of inquiry, skilled in asking questions that matter. The future belongs to those who know how to think about thinking.

This is where the humanities re-enter the conversation.

Think about it: the great innovators weren't simply coders or chemists—they were curious polymaths. They combined scientific logic with artistic empathy. In the age of AI, this fusion is not optional. It is essential.

Coding Is the New Literacy—But Not the Only One

Yes, learning to code will remain useful. But far more important is computational thinking—how to break down problems, spot patterns, and design algorithms. Equally crucial is data literacy: understanding how to question data, where bias hides, and how machine learning models work.

But here's the nuance: just as not everyone needs to become a nuclear physicist, not every student must become an AI engineer. What they must all become, however, are AI-literate citizens.

They should understand what an algorithm is, how facial recognition systems can be biased, and why ethical guardrails are important. Whether they are future doctors, designers, entrepreneurs, or activists, they must speak the language of both the machine and the heart.

Skills for an Uncertain Future

- Learn to Learn: With knowledge half-lives shrinking, adaptability is more important than degrees.
- Interdisciplinary Fluency: The magic will happen at the intersections—biology + AI, ethics + engineering, art + neuroscience.
- Communication & Collaboration: Explaining complex ideas simply and working across cultures and disciplines will set leaders apart.
- Moral Imagination: In a world where machines make decisions, we need humans who can imagine their consequences.

The Rise of the "Portfolio Student"

Degrees will matter—but less than portfolios. A student's GitHub repository, YouTube channel, design prototypes, or climate activism track record will speak louder than transcripts. Platforms like GitHub, Kaggle, Substack, or Midjourney have become the new "résumé builders."

The wise student won't ask, What's the safest major? But instead, how can I become a thoughtful problem-solver who uses tech with purpose?

In Closing: The Da Vinci Within

In The Innovators, Isaacson highlighted how the digital revolution was powered by collaboration—by teams who blended technology with human insight. That's the roadmap for students now. Become not just good at one thing, but curious about many things. Be the kind of person who can hold paradoxes: logic and empathy, speed and reflection, code and conscience.

The next chapter of civilization will be written by those who are both tech-savvy and soul-wise.

From STEM to STEAM to STREAM: Weaving the Threads of a Human-Centered Future

When we trace the golden thread of innovation, it rarely runs in a straight line. It weaves through the curiosity of Galileo, the imagination of Da Vinci, the mathematical rigor of Ada Lovelace, and the poetry of Tagore. It is in this entanglement of disciplines — of logic and lyricism, code and creativity — that we begin to see the true story of how STEM became STEAM, and how STEAM evolved into STREAM.

In the early 2000s, the United States and much of the world began to rally around STEM — Science, Technology, Engineering, and Mathematics — as the engine of economic progress. This was the Sputnik echo reverberating through a digital age. The idea was clear: to compete globally, nations needed more engineers, coders, scientists, and data-savvy problem solvers.

And they were right — partially.

What they didn't see, at first, was what Steve Jobs once called "the poetry in the product." When he introduced the iPad, he said Apple lived "at the intersection of technology and the liberal arts." That intersection would become the bridge between STEM and STEAM, as artists, designers, and storytellers began playing a more vital role in how innovation was humanized and made beautiful, intuitive, and impactful.

STEAM added the "A" for the Arts, emphasizing creativity, aesthetics, and human empathy. It was no longer enough to build a machine — one had to design it for emotion, for ethics, for resonance. Think Pixar engineers collaborating with illustrators. Think MIT Media Lab merging computation with music. STEAM reminded us that humans are not just users of technology; we are narrators, dreamers, and meaning-makers.

But the story didn't stop there.

The next logical — and moral — progression came with STREAM, an acronym that added Reading (or Reasoning) and Ethics to the mix. Because in an age of AI, where algorithms decide loan approvals, parole decisions, and even battlefield targets, reasoning and ethics are no longer electives — they're prerequisites.

STREAM education prepares the next generation to ask better questions, not just code better solutions. It integrates critical thinking, digital literacy, emotional intelligence, and civic responsibility into the learning arc. It empowers a generation not just to use AI, but to guide it with wisdom.

Consider a high school in Finland where students use climate data to simulate urban planning. Or an Indian after-school program where young girls use generative art tools to tell stories rooted in their culture while learning Python. Or a U.S. classroom where kids build chatbots — but only after debating the implications of bias and misinformation.

We've entered a world where T-shaped talent — deep in one area, broad across many — is no longer idealistic but essential. A STREAM-ready learner can debate the ethics of deepfakes, sketch a UX wireframe, write a haiku, and still solve a quadratic equation — because they are not just learning to work — they're learning to be human in the loop.

From STEM to STEAM to STREAM, we are not just charting an educational framework. We are drafting a blueprint for human potential in a machine-augmented world. And like all the great revolutions before it — the Enlightenment, the Renaissance, the Digital Age — this one too is led not by machines, but by the minds that dare to connect the dots.

Learning to Learn, Curiosity as Capital

What separates humans from machines isn't just reasoning or speed. It's the boundless drive to ask, "Why?"

In the age of AI, where algorithms can memorize, categorize, and even summarize, the enduring human advantage lies in something beautifully chaotic: curiosity. Not the kind that skims headlines, but the sort that burrows deep—connecting unlikely dots, forming questions no one thought to ask, and relentlessly pursuing answers that aren't found on the first page of a search engine. If the 20th century celebrated expertise, the 21st rewards exploration.

Once, education was about what you knew. Today, it's about how quickly you can learn what you don't. That shift—from content to curiosity, from memorization to meta-learning—is quietly redefining success.

Jeff Bezos once said, "We are stubborn on vision, flexible on details." That's the mantra of curiosity-driven learning. You need a compass, not a map. The most successful thinkers—Leonardo da Vinci, Ada Lovelace, Steve Jobs—were polymaths, relentlessly curious, moving between disciplines with the ease of a jazz musician improvising across keys. They didn't just know more. They learned better.

In today's landscape, where ChatGPT can answer questions in seconds, the premium is on asking the right questions. Schools must now teach students not only to consume information, but also to evaluate and interrogate it critically. To design experiments, simulate outcomes, and reflect on the ethics of what they build.

This is the great pivot: learning how to learn. And at the heart of it sits curiosity—not as a soft skill, but as a capital asset. An engine for innovation. A hedge against irrelevance. And perhaps most critically, the one thing AI cannot replicate at scale.

In a world where change is the only constant, curiosity isn't a luxury. It's the new literacy.

Critical Thinking, Ethics, and Systems Design

If the first era of digital transformation was built on code, the next must be built on conscience.

At the dawn of the AI age, we stand not merely at the intersection of technology and humanity, but at a profound crossroads of choices. And the tools that will matter most—more than any programming language or machine learning framework—are those we often relegate to the liberal arts: critical thinking, ethical reasoning, and the art of systems design.

Critical Thinking is not simply skepticism. It is the ability to hold complexity without paralysis. It is what allowed Alan Turing to peer into the fog of war and envision the architecture of computation. It's what helped Steve Jobs fuse design with engineering, or Marie Curie pursue scientific truth amidst a field of naysayers. In an era of deepfakes, disinformation, and algorithmic opacity, critical thinking is less about what we know and more about how we know it.

Ethics, meanwhile, is not a checkbox—it is the operating system of our decisions. The Greeks taught it as a virtue. The Enlightenment saw it as reason. Today, it must be reimagined as a design principle. When we build AI to predict parole outcomes or optimize ICU beds, the real question is not whether the system works, but for whom it works—and who might be left behind. In every dataset is a set of values. In every algorithm, a worldview. The challenge is not to remove bias entirely—that may be impossible—but to be radically transparent about it.

And then there is Systems Design—the invisible scaffolding that shapes outcomes at scale. It's what separates apps from ecosystems, and hacks from human-centered innovation. To design systems in the 21st century is to choreograph feedback loops, incentives, and unintended consequences. It is both art and architecture. When done right, systems elevate. When left unchecked, they entrench. The gig economy, for instance, was a design choice. So is surveillance capitalism. But so, too, are regenerative agriculture, open-source platforms, and cooperative ownership models.

The true leaders of tomorrow will not simply be AI literate. They will be ethically fluent and systemically aware. They will move between disciplines—like da Vinci sketching flying machines and anatomical studies on the same page—not to show off, but because the future demands it.

And in that blend of logic and empathy, of design and responsibility, of silicon and soul—lies the next great human renaissance.

PART IV: ETHICS, EQUITY, AND THE HUMAN FUTURE

Part IV

Ethics, Equity, and the Human Future

In every era of human advancement, a moment arrives when our technological prowess outpaces our moral compass. The steam engine unlocked industrial might, but also child labor and soot-stained cities. The atom split in brilliance, but also cast shadows over Hiroshima. And now, in the age of artificial intelligence—a force that learns, evolves, and decides—we find ourselves again standing at a profound crossroads.

This section of the book is not about what AI can do, but what it should do. Here, the story shifts from code to conscience.

Part I laid the foundations of intelligence, and Part II charted its industrial applications. Part III explored its impact on the workforce, Part IV turns the lens inward—toward our values, our responsibilities, and our shared destiny. What does it mean to build machines that make decisions? Who gets to design these systems? And most importantly—who gets to benefit from them?

In interviews with ethicists, policymakers, technologists, and even students who will inherit this future, one theme emerged repeatedly: AI is not neutral. Every dataset reflects a past. Every algorithm encodes a worldview. Every automation impacts real lives. If we are not vigilant, the future could automate inequality, scale bias, and digitize exclusion.

But there is also hope.

We'll meet the thinkers drawing the red lines—around facial recognition, around surveillance capitalism, around lethal autonomous weapons. We'll explore the policy frameworks striving to balance innovation with protection—from the EU's AI Act to grassroots movements for data dignity. And we'll hear from a new generation of builders who believe that ethics is not a brake on progress, but its engine.

This is not just a philosophical exercise. It's a pragmatic reckoning because the real legacy of AI will not be its speed or scale—but whether it helped us build a more inclusive, just, and humane world.

Welcome to the moral frontier of intelligence. Welcome to the chapter where the story becomes ours to shape.

Chapter 19

Ethics by Design: Building Trustworthy AI

In the early days of computing, engineers obsessed over performance—how to make machines faster, leaner, more powerful. In the age of artificial intelligence, the frontier has shifted. The question is no longer just can we build it, but should we trust it?

This chapter begins in a design lab in Helsinki, where a team of ethicists sits not on the sidelines but beside engineers, sketching wireframes and writing model prompts. Their role? To make sure that empathy, fairness, and transparency aren't bolted on later—but embedded from the beginning. It's a scene that would have puzzled the early pioneers of computing. However, today it's becoming the new blueprint for building intelligent systems.

Welcome to the era of Ethics by Design.

Trust is not an abstract virtue in the world of AI. It is as tangible as a dataset, as measurable as a model's output, as fragile as a flawed recommendation. When an algorithm screens resumes, we must ask: Does it recognize potential or replicate past biases? When a chatbot dispenses health advice, do we know what sources it draws from? When a self-driving car must choose between a pedestrian and a passenger, whose values are encoded in that decision?

In conversations with thinkers like Timnit Gebru, who warned of the blind spots in large language models, and tech leaders at companies like Salesforce and IBM, who are pioneering AI governance protocols, one idea echoed: you don't audit ethics into a system—you design it in.

We explore frameworks such as Differential Privacy, Explainable AI, Model Cards, and Ethical Risk Assessments that are reshaping how engineers approach their work. We examine the emergence of EthicsOps, a new organizational layer akin to DevOps, which ensures real-time guardrails across the deployment lifecycle. We visit schools where "algorithmic accountability" is now taught alongside coding languages—because the next generation of builders must also be philosophers.

But perhaps most powerfully, we meet citizens: a mother in Boston fighting for facial recognition moratoriums, a student in Nairobi training AI to preserve endangered languages, and a disabled activist using open-source tools to ensure accessibility isn't an afterthought. Each reminds us that ethical design is not just a technical imperative. It's a human one.

In the end, trustworthy AI is not about perfection—it's about intention and iteration. It's about creating systems that can explain themselves, learn from mistakes, and serve humanity rather than obscure it.

Because as we code the future, the question isn't whether AI will mirror us. It already does.

The deeper question is: what parts of ourselves are we choosing to amplify?

Explainability, Fairness, and Non-Discrimination: Illuminating the Black Box

It's a scene that repeats itself across boardrooms and labs: someone asks, "But why did the algorithm make that decision?" And a data scientist, brilliant and well-meaning, shrugs slightly and says, "It's complicated."

That shrug is the silent tremor at the heart of the AI revolution.

In a world increasingly governed by machine decisions—decisions that determine who gets a loan, who gets hired, who is granted bail, or flagged for extra screening—explainability is no longer a luxury. It's the linchpin of trust.

Back in the 1960s, when Grace Hopper popularized the term "debugging," she believed computing should be understandable to its creators. Today, the challenge is larger: how to make AI understandable not just to engineers, but to regulators, judges, doctors, teachers, and to the people whose lives it shapes.

This is where explainable AI (XAI) comes in—a field that combines transparency, interpretability, and human-centered design. We meet developers at Google's building, creating "What-If" tools to explore how small changes in input lead to different outcomes, and researchers at MIT who train models not just for accuracy, but for legibility. Because what good is a model that's right if no one knows why?

But transparency alone isn't enough.

We turn next to fairness—a value easy to proclaim, harder to encode. At a startup in Atlanta, developers realize their facial recognition tool performs worse on darker skin tones. They pause the launch. They retrain on more inclusive data. They seek external audits. And in doing so, they remind us: bias is not just a glitch; it's a mirror. One that reflects the inequities of our world, unless we choose to intervene.

And so we arrive at non-discrimination—the ethical heartbeat of the AI age. Not just avoiding bias, but actively designing for inclusion. We explore frameworks like demographic parity, equalized odds, and counterfactual fairness. These aren't just mathematical constraints. They're moral commitments rendered in code.

In a conversation with Joy Buolamwini—whose work on algorithmic bias reshaped policy from San Francisco to the EU—she says, “You cannot solve what you cannot see.” That, in essence, is the call of this moment.

To shine light into the black boxes.

To ensure that when machines speak, we can ask, “Why?”—and get an answer that’s both intelligible and just.

To recognize that the true test of artificial intelligence isn’t how smart it is. It’s how fair, how accountable, and ultimately how human it allows us to be.

The Bias in the Training Data: Case Studies in Healthcare and Policing

In 2019, a quiet storm swept through the corridors of medical research when a study published in Science revealed something unsettling: an AI system used by major U.S. hospitals to allocate healthcare resources was biased. Not by design. But by data.

The algorithm in question, deployed across millions of patients, was supposed to predict who would benefit from enhanced care programs. But it relied on historical healthcare spending as a proxy for need. The result? Black patients were systematically underestimated—not because they were sicker, but because, historically, they had received less care. The machine hadn't learned to heal; it had learned to repeat injustice with mathematical precision.

This was not a story about rogue engineers or malicious intent. It was a lesson in how bias enters AI not through malice, but through history—smuggled in silently through the data we trust.

Travel east to the streets of London. In pilot programs, police departments began testing predictive policing algorithms. Feed in decades of crime data, and the system forecasts where officers should patrol. Sounds efficient. Even progressive.

But peel back the surface, and you discover a deeper flaw: the model wasn't predicting crime—it was predicting police presence. Neighborhoods historically over-policed showed up as hotspots. Meanwhile, white-collar crime, largely invisible in police logs, disappeared from the map entirely. The algorithm had inherited the biases of its teachers—old arrest records, neighborhood demographics, patterns shaped by decades of policy and prejudice.

The result? A digital feedback loop of discrimination.

In conversations with ethicists, data scientists, and even whistleblowers, a common refrain emerges: The data is not neutral. It is the residue of human systems—messy, unequal, sometimes unjust.

This realization is sparking a movement across disciplines. In healthcare, researchers are building fairness-aware models that adjust for access, not just outcomes. In law enforcement, activists are calling for algorithmic impact assessments, similar to environmental reviews, to be conducted before AI is deployed.

But the most powerful insight may be this: AI doesn't fix our flaws. It amplifies them—unless we teach it not to.

And that's the challenge of our era. Not just to make machines smart. But to make them wise. To train them not on the world as it was, but on the world as it ought to be.

Blueprints for the Moral Machine: Ethical Frameworks from MIT, OpenAI, and DeepMind

When Alan Turing first asked, "Can machines think?", he lit a fuse that would eventually lead us to a new, thornier question: Can machines act ethically?

As artificial intelligence escapes the lab and enters our lives—from recommendation engines to autonomous weapons—the need for a moral operating system has become urgent. And while governments have stumbled toward regulation, a trio of institutions—MIT, OpenAI, and DeepMind—have stepped into the breach, each with its own vision of how we should teach machines to do right by us.

MIT: The Philosopher-Engineer's Dilemma

At the Massachusetts Institute of Technology, ethics is not an afterthought—it's a core module.

MIT's Moral Machine project, launched in the late 2010s, became a global experiment in digital ethics. Millions of people across cultures were asked to make impossible choices—should a self-driving car save a child or an elderly person? A pedestrian or a passenger? The results revealed not just values, but value systems: different countries, different cultures, different instincts.

What MIT uncovered was that ethics isn't universal—but the conversation must be. This insight now underpins courses like "Ethics and the Law on Robotics." It informs a growing movement: embedding philosophers inside engineering teams, not just to audit decisions after the fact—but to shape them upstream.

It's ethics by design. And by debate.

OpenAI: Guardrails for General Intelligence

When the founders of OpenAI—including Elon Musk and Sam Altman—launched the lab, they did so with one conviction: AI must benefit all of humanity. That wasn't a tagline—it was a governance principle.

From its earliest days, OpenAI declared its intentions not just in papers, but in charter. Among its commitments: to avoid enabling uses of AI that harm humanity or unduly concentrate power. The organization would prioritize long-term safety over short-term gains and collaborate widely to democratize benefits.

Its structure reflected this philosophy: OpenAI was a capped-profit entity before it was a tech unicorn. Even its flagship systems—such as GPT—were released incrementally, with internal red-teaming and alignment research to mitigate the risks of misinformation, bias, or misuse.

At its heart is a delicate balance: How do you accelerate innovation while building brakes into the engine? OpenAI's answer lies in transparency, staged deployment, and a willingness to pause the race mid-stride to ask if we're heading in the right direction.

DeepMind: Ethics as a Scientific Discipline

Across the Atlantic, DeepMind—the London-based AI lab acquired by Google—approaches ethics not as a boundary, but as a frontier.

Their Ethics & Society unit operates like an internal think tank, recruiting ethicists, sociologists, and policy experts to anticipate the consequences of AI in health, governance, and climate. The team co-authored "The Ethics of AI in Health Care", a foundational text that doesn't shy from complexity: how do you train an AI on patient data while preserving dignity and consent? What happens when models outperform doctors but can't explain their reasoning?

DeepMind doesn't just publish code—it publishes ethical frameworks. It's one of the few institutions to release principled reviews alongside its technological breakthroughs, treating fairness, transparency, and non-maleficence with the same rigor as accuracy and latency.

Their ethos? That AI must not only be intelligent, but also aligned with human values—values that are themselves evolving.

Toward a Moral Compass, Not a Manual

These institutions—MIT, with its democratic dialogue; OpenAI, with its governance by charter; and DeepMind, with its ethical research—offer a spectrum of approaches. But they share one belief:

That ethics in AI cannot be patched in later. It must be coded from the start.

And in a world where machines make decisions once reserved for judges, doctors, and generals, that may be our greatest challenge. Not just to build intelligence—but to embed wisdom.

In the age of artificial intelligence, the most human thing we can do is ask: Should we?

Chapter 20

The Equity Divide – Will AI Widen the Gap?

In the early 20th century, when electricity began to illuminate the world, its promise was universal: brighter homes, safer streets, and increased productivity. But not everyone got it at once. Rural towns lagged behind cities. The affluent wired up quickly; the poor waited decades. Technology didn't invent inequality—but it often accelerated it.

Artificial Intelligence, many fear, may follow the same pattern. Or worse—amplify it.

As we stand at the cusp of a generational leap in capability—from GPTs that can write code to models that can analyze legal contracts or recommend cancer treatment—the question arises: Who gets to benefit? Who gets left behind?

Digital Aristocrats vs. Digital Underclass

In Silicon Valley boardrooms, AI is billed as a democratizing force—automating tasks, lowering barriers, unlocking productivity. But for a factory worker in Ohio, a gig driver in Jakarta, or a student in Lagos with no broadband, the reality can feel different.

The fear is not just job displacement—but dignity displacement.

AI can optimize hiring, but it can also embed bias. It can personalize learning, but it can also leave behind those without access to devices, data, or electricity. It can augment human capabilities—but only for those with the literacy and infrastructure to wield it.

As with the Industrial Revolution, the promise of prosperity risks being hoarded by the few—those with the capital, the compute power, the cloud credits.

The Global Imbalance

The divide isn't just within nations. It's between them.

While countries like the U.S., China, and the EU invest billions in foundational AI research, many nations in the Global South face a significant paradox: they are data-rich yet resource-poor. Their citizens generate health records, transaction logs, and mobility patterns that fuel global AI—but they see little return.

It's a form of digital colonialism—where data is harvested locally, but value is extracted globally.

And when language models are trained predominantly in English, when facial recognition fails on darker skin tones, when content moderation ignores cultural nuance—it's not just about fairness. It's about representation, respect, and rights.

Education: The First Great Wall

If AI becomes the new literacy, then unequal access to education is the first wall it builds.

In India, startups are using AI tutors to democratize learning—but only if a child has a smartphone. In the U.S., districts struggle to train teachers in digital tools, while private schools race ahead with AI-enhanced curricula. In rural Africa, kids still walk miles for chalkboards, not chatbots.

Unless we design AI for the bottom billion, the divide will deepen, not dissolve.

Policy, Not Pity

The solution isn't charity. It's the architecture of policy, infrastructure, and incentives.

We need what economists call inclusive innovation:

- Tax incentives for companies that create AI tools for underserved communities.
- Public-private partnerships to digitize rural schools and clinics.
- Global governance that mandates data equity, not just data security.

- Local language models that reflect every dialect, not just dominant tongues.

And above all, we need representation of diverse voices in the boardrooms and labs, building the next generation of AI.

Because fairness cannot be retrofitted, it must be built into the system from the outset.

AI Can Bridge the Divide—If We Let It

AI is neither inherently fair nor unfair. It is a mirror, reflecting the intentions of those who shape it. If designed thoughtfully, it can become a bridge—connecting marginalized voices to opportunities, enabling small farmers with predictive tools, empowering street vendors with access to markets, and giving refugees access to education and healthcare.

But only if we remember that technology alone does not level the playing field. People do. Policy does. Intent does.

As history teaches us, every great leap forward—electricity, the internet, the smartphone—has left someone behind. What defines our generation will be this:

Do we finally catch up to the divide? Or do we widen it again—only this time even faster?

In the era of artificial intelligence, equity is no longer a side issue. It is the central one.

Access to AI Tools and GPU Monopolies

When Steve Jobs built the original Macintosh, he knew the future of computing wasn't just about chips—it was about access. Democratizing power. Putting tools into the hands of artists, designers, and thinkers—not just engineers in labs.

Today, as we enter the age of Artificial Intelligence, that same question echoes again: Who gets to hold the paintbrush of the future?

Currently, it's primarily those with GPUs and financial capital.

Silicon Muscles: GPUs as the Steam Engines of AI

Every breakthrough in AI—from ChatGPT to autonomous drones—rides on a backbone of hardware: Graphics Processing Units, or GPUs. Originally designed to render video games, GPUs have become the workhorses of deep learning, capable of crunching trillions of calculations in seconds.

But here's the catch: they're not evenly distributed. Not even close.

One company, NVIDIA, controls over 80% of the high-performance GPU market. That's not just dominance; it's chokehold-level control over the tools that build the future.

If the industrial revolution had Carnegie's steel, the AI revolution has Jensen Huang's silicon.

The AI Oligopoly

Imagine a world where only a few empires—Microsoft, Google, Amazon, OpenAI, and Meta—can train frontier models, because only they can afford the necessary computing power. Renting an A100 GPU cluster for months can cost millions. Training a GPT-scale model? Tens of millions.

This is not just a hardware issue. It's an access issue. A power issue.

Startups, universities, independent researchers, and developing nations face an uphill battle—not for lack of ideas, but lack of access to the engines of modern intelligence.

The Global Compute Divide

While Silicon Valley's data centers hum with GPU-rich clusters, many nations lack sovereign access to high-end chips. Export restrictions, supply chain bottlenecks, and geopolitics around Taiwan's TSMC—all combine to make AI access a new geopolitical fault line.

Some refer to it as "AI nationalism." Others call it "compute protectionism."

Either way, the result is the same: the Global South risks becoming dependent on Northern algorithms.

Tools for the Few, or the Many?

In the early internet era, open-source software and falling hardware costs sparked a wave of bottom-up innovation. Blogs, Wikipedia, and YouTube—ideas flourished because the barriers were low.

AI is different. The models are massive. The compute costs are massive. And the companies that build them? They're getting bigger, not smaller.

Without intervention, we risk turning AI into a closed club—where only the rich can train, only the elite can fine-tune, and the rest can merely consume.

Building a More Equitable AI Ecosystem

If AI is to be a general-purpose technology like electricity or the internet, then we need public infrastructure, not just private platforms.

That means:

- National compute grids, like India's AIRAWAT and Europe's AI Factories.
- Subsidized AI access for researchers, educators, and creators.
- Open-weight models and shared datasets, so innovation doesn't get locked in corporate vaults.
- And regulations that prevent anti-competitive hoarding of foundational hardware.

The Choice Ahead

AI can empower a billion minds—or concentrate power in a billion-dollar vault. The technology is neutral. But how we distribute it is not.

The risk is not just financial monopolies, but also monopolies of intelligence.

Because in the end, the future won't just be built by those who think. It will be built by those who compute.

And if access to the GPU becomes the new access to the printing press, then ensuring equity is no longer a luxury. It's a democratic imperative.

Job Polarization, Income Inequality, and Regional Divides

When the personal computer emerged in the 1980s, it didn't just change how we worked—it changed where we worked, what we worked on, and who got ahead. Steve Jobs understood this when he told a room full of developers that the Macintosh was "for the rest of us."

Today, AI stands at a similar threshold. But this time, the revolution may not lift all boats. It might sink a few—and widen the gaps we've long tried to close.

The Great Split: What Job Polarization Looks Like

In theory, automation should free us from drudgery. But in practice, it's creating a split screen:

- On one side: high-skilled, high-paid knowledge workers—data scientists, engineers, designers—who use AI to amplify their creativity and productivity.
- On the other hand, low-skilled, low-paid workers in manual or service jobs—many of which are now vulnerable to automation or algorithmic control.

The middle? It's getting hollowed out.

Bank tellers, radiology technicians, paralegals, logistics clerks—the kinds of jobs that once promised upward mobility—are now under threat from smart systems that don't sleep, unionize, or take breaks.

This is job polarization in real-time: a disappearing middle class between the digital elite and the digitally displaced.

The Inequality Feedback Loop

Here's the twist: AI doesn't just automate tasks. It amplifies capital.

Those who own the data, the compute, and the algorithms see exponential returns. Those who rely on labor see their value diminishing. It's not unlike the Gilded Age, when railroads and oil rigs created titans of wealth—but this time, it's neural networks and platform economies.

We're seeing:

- Wage gaps widen, even within the same industry.
- Gig workers are managed by algorithms that they can't appeal.
- Productivity gains that no longer trickle down.

In other words, the economic pie is growing, but the slices are shrinking for most.

Geography of the Left-Behind

AI's benefits are clustering in a few key regions: Silicon Valley, Shenzhen, Bangalore, Tel Aviv, and London.

But what happens to Akron? To Flint? To mining towns in Appalachia or fishing villages in Kerala?

A child born in a data-rich, AI-enabled metro is not just born into a different economy—but into a different future. Access to jobs, education, and opportunity becomes increasingly tied to digital proximity, not just geographic location.

This is the new regional divide—not just urban vs. rural, but AI-enabled vs. AI-ignored.

Historical Echoes, Modern Consequences

We've seen this before. The Industrial Revolution displaced artisans. Globalization offshored manufacturing. The internet disrupted retail and media.

However, never has disruption occurred so rapidly, across so many sectors, with such little regulation or redistribution.

The question now is not whether AI will change the economy. It already has.

The question is: Who will it leave behind? And will we act before the divide becomes permanent?

Pathways Forward

To counter polarization, we need more than sympathy. We need systems.

- Reskilling and upskilling, not just for coders—but for caregivers, teachers, farmers, and frontline workers.

- Tax incentives for companies that hire human–AI teams instead of replacing workers wholesale.
- Digital infrastructure in underserved regions, from rural broadband to AI learning hubs.
- And crucially, policies that shift from GDP to GDI—Gross Digital Inclusion.

The Choice We Face

AI can either become the great equalizer or the great divider. It's not the algorithm that decides—it's us.

As we race to build faster, smarter systems, we must also pause to ask:

Are we designing a future for everyone, or only the few who already have a seat at the table?

If history teaches us anything, it's this: technological progress must be paired with moral progress, or we risk building castles in the cloud—and leaving far too many people outside the gates.

Global South vs. Global North: Uneven AI Futures

When Alan Turing laid the foundations for artificial intelligence during the chaos of World War II, his vision was mathematical, idealistic—and geographically agnostic. He wasn't coding for London or Lagos. He was unlocking the secret of thinking machines for humankind.

But today, as the AI revolution accelerates, the benefits aren't spreading evenly. We are witnessing a fault line—not in silicon, but in sovereignty and opportunity—between the Global North and Global South. And this divide may become one of the defining inequalities of our time.

Two Speeds, One World

The Global North—North America, Western Europe, parts of East Asia—is building AI ecosystems at breakneck speed. They possess:

- Capital for high-performance compute.
- Universities producing top AI talent.
- Corporations hoard massive datasets.
- Governments shaping frontier policy.

Meanwhile, much of the Global South is still catching up on the basics, including digital infrastructure, data protection laws, and electricity reliability.

It's like asking a sprinter in running shoes to race someone barefoot on a gravel road.

Data Colonialism: The New Resource Rush

In the 19th century, empires sailed across oceans to extract spices, oil, and minerals. In the 21st century, tech giants are reaching into the Global South to extract something just as valuable: data.

- Smartphones and internet access are spreading fast in Africa, Latin America, and Southeast Asia.
- But who owns the data generated by billions of clicks, swipes, and GPS pings?

- Often, it's not local governments or entrepreneurs. It's platforms headquartered thousands of miles away, repackaging those insights into models sold back to the world.

The irony is sharp: the Global South becomes the fuel for AI—but not the beneficiary.

Talent Drain vs. Brain Gain

AI talent in the Global South faces a paradox:

- The brightest minds—engineers in Nairobi, data scientists in Dhaka, policy scholars in São Paulo—are in high demand.
- However, the opportunities often lie elsewhere, such as Silicon Valley, Toronto, and Berlin.

This creates a digital brain drain, where the best are pulled away just as local ecosystems begin to take root. It's a tragic echo of colonial export models: raw talent out, refined products back in.

The Risk of AI Neo-Imperialism

Without intervention, the future could resemble a form of AI neo-imperialism:

- Rules made in Brussels, not Accra.
- Bias baked into models trained on Western norms.
- Automation decisions made in boardrooms with no understanding of cultural nuance.
- Security dependencies on foreign cloud infrastructure.

In such a world, the Global South doesn't just fall behind—it becomes dependent, locked into systems it did not design and cannot easily exit.

Signs of Hope: Sovereignty, Innovation, and South–South Collaboration

Yet, to view the Global South only as a passive recipient is to miss the plot.

- India's UPI system revolutionized digital payments without big tech.
- Rwanda became a global case study in drone logistics for healthcare (Zipline).

- Brazil is piloting AI-driven agricultural systems to improve food security.
- South Africa and Kenya are experimenting with AI for local language processing.

And more critically, countries are beginning to assert AI sovereignty:

- Data localization laws are being debated in Nigeria and Indonesia.
- AI ethics frameworks are emerging from African Union bodies and Latin American think tanks.
- South–South tech partnerships are slowly replacing North-bound dependencies.

This is the beginning of a new narrative—one where innovation is not just imported, but homegrown.

The Way Forward: Bridging the Divide

The goal is not to slow the Global North. It's to ensure that the Global South doesn't get left behind.

- Open-source AI models can lower barriers to entry.
- Decentralized cloud infrastructure can empower local innovation.
- Education platforms, MOOCs, and coding boot camps can cultivate next-generation talent.
- Policy collaboration, rather than paternalism, can establish truly global guardrails.

As the AI age unfolds, we have a choice:

Build a world of shared intelligence or drift into a digital version of the 20th-century world order—just faster, shinier, and even more unequal.

The Moral of the Machine

Isaac Newton once said he stood on the shoulders of giants.

In the AI era, let's ensure that no one is left behind.

The future of intelligence must be inclusive, or it risks becoming not just artificial, but also unjust.

Chapter 21

The Human Question — What Can't AI Do?

Throughout history, every revolutionary technology has forced us to ask not just what can it do, but what does it mean to be human?

The printing press democratized knowledge. The steam engine redefined labor. The internet connected minds across continents.

Now, artificial intelligence challenges us not only with its capabilities but also with its uncanny mimicry of human behavior.

It writes poetry, detects diseases, paints pictures, plays chess like a grandmaster, and composes symphonies that sound suspiciously like Mozart's ghost. But in this chapter, we must ask the deeper question: What can't AI do? And in doing so, we come closer to understanding what makes us—irreplaceably human.

Intelligence ≠ Understanding

AI can summarize a novel. But it doesn't feel the heartbreak in Anna Karenina.

It can scan thousands of CT scans in seconds. But it doesn't sense the trembling voice of a patient asking, "Is it serious?"

What's missing? Consciousness. Intent. Empathy.

The difference is more than technical—it's philosophical. Intelligence, as Turing showed us, can be mechanical.

But understanding, as Searle argued in his "Chinese Room" thought experiment, requires more than symbols—it requires meaning.

AI doesn't know what it knows.

The Spark of Creativity

A great deal has been made of AI-generated art, music, and writing. And yes, it can astound.

But even the most dazzling of these outputs is, fundamentally, derivative. Trained on oceans of existing human creation, they remix rather than originate.

Real creativity comes from:

- Lived experience
- Contradictions held in tension
- The leap beyond logic

When Einstein imagined riding alongside a beam of light, he wasn't prompted by data. He was driven by curiosity, wonder, and intuition. These are not mere functions—they are acts of the soul.

Moral Reasoning and Judgment

AI can simulate ethical choices, run utilitarian calculations, and even recognize patterns of injustice in training data.

But it cannot make moral judgments rooted in values.

A machine can be programmed to replicate what society has done in the past.

But should that always be the guide for what it ought to do in the future?

When Rosa Parks refused to give up her seat, she defied the rules of the day. Her decision wasn't statistically sound—it was morally right.

That's the paradox: AI learns from what was.

Humans are the ones who imagine what should be.

Relationships and Love

AI can simulate conversation. It can mirror tone. It can even respond with empathy scripts.

But it doesn't care.

Love, friendship, loyalty—these arise from vulnerability. From mutual recognition. From shared stories and the ineffable beauty of being known.

A chatbot might say, "I'm here for you."

But it will never truly be there—at a hospital bedside, at a funeral, at a wedding, tears in its eyes.

Machines can process language.

But only humans speak from the heart.

The Capacity for Meaning

AI is not burdened—or blessed—by mortality. It doesn't wonder what its purpose is. It doesn't ask why it exists.

Humans do.

We write poetry not just to communicate, but to connect. We build cathedrals not for utility, but for wonder.

We seek meaning—in faith, in science, in love—not because it's profitable, but because it's who we are.

This is what AI cannot replicate: the search for meaning. The ability to sit in mystery. To not know—and still press on.

The Mirror, Not the Soul

In the end, AI is a mirror—and a powerful one. It reflects our brilliance and our bias, our logic and our limitations.

But it is not the soul.

That remains our unique domain.

As we race forward into an era of synthetic intelligence, let us not forget the irreplaceable qualities of human life:

- To wonder.
- To suffer.
- To laugh.
- To love.
- To choose.

That is the essence of this final frontier—not what AI can do, but what it can't.

And what we must never outsource.

"The measure of intelligence," Einstein once said, "is the ability to change."

But perhaps the measure of humanity is the ability to care.

That, no algorithm can own. And in that space—in the human question—our truest answers still lie.

The Irreducible Human Spark: Empathy, Spirituality, Creativity, and the Unpredictable

Throughout history, it's not just logic that has propelled humanity forward—but something far more elusive.

An irreducible spark.

That spark isn't found in formulas or neural nets. It's the tremble in a poet's voice, the stillness in a prayer, the brushstroke that defies expectation.

It's what makes us laugh at absurdity, cry at beauty, or change our minds when the facts don't change—but we do.

AI, for all its brilliance, lives in the domain of patterns. But humans? We live in a paradox.

Empathy: The Shared Pulse of Being

Empathy is not data—it's a felt resonance.

When a nurse gently places a hand on a patient's shoulder or a friend listens through silence more than words, they tap into something AI cannot replicate: the embodied understanding of another's inner life.

Empathy doesn't scale. It dwells in the moment, not the model.

We don't empathize because it's efficient.

We do it because it's human.

Spirituality: The Search Beyond the Known

Steve Jobs once described the intersection of technology and the humanities as "where the magic happens."

But he also retreated to ashrams. Meditated. Searched.

Spirituality, whether religious or secular, is the longing to connect with something greater—call it God, the cosmos, or consciousness itself.

AI can simulate sermons.

But it cannot seek salvation.

It doesn't wonder why we suffer, or why the stars move us to silence.

It doesn't sit in awe at a child's first breath.

That, too, is ours alone.

Creativity: Leaps, Not Lines

Leonardo da Vinci once dissected corpses to gain a deeper understanding of anatomy. But he also imagined flying machines that were centuries ahead of their time, in terms of physics.

That's creativity: the ability to make leaps of association, to juxtapose the irrational with the rational and call it a masterpiece.

AI is trained on what has been.

But humans dream of what never was.

Creativity is messy, erratic, and often inefficient.

But it is the birthplace of everything truly original.

The Unpredictable: Serendipity, Error, and Grace

Alan Turing laid the foundations for machine intelligence. But he also knew its limits. He once mused:

"Instead of trying to produce a program to simulate the adult mind, why not rather try to produce one which simulates the child's?"

A child is unpredictable. So is genius. So is grace.

History's breakthroughs are rarely neat—they come from mistakes, misfits, misunderstood moments.

The Post-it note was a failed adhesive.

The pacemaker was a serendipitous short circuit.

Penicillin came from a dirty petri dish.

AI avoids error.

Humans turn it into insight.

The Final Frontier is Within

We can teach machines to imitate us. But can we teach them to feel awe? To grieve? To forgive?

Can they whisper words that heal, or choose courage over compliance?

The deeper question isn't "Will AI surpass us?"

It's "Will we remember what makes us us?"

As we engineer intelligence, we must also engineer humility—to know that our value lies not just in cognition, but in connection.

Empathy. Spirituality. Creativity. The unpredictable.

These are not system glitches.

They are the soul of the system.

"It is not the strongest who survive," Darwin wrote, "but those most responsive to change."

But perhaps the future will belong not just to the responsive—but to the empathetic, the creative, the spiritually awake.

In that, we are not coding a new machine.

We are remembering our oldest calling:

To be fully, gloriously, unpredictably human.

The Last Domains of the Soul: Artists, Caregivers, Monks, and Therapists

The Artist: Drawing from the Chaos

In a sunlit studio in Barcelona, a young digital painter named Lucía opens Midjourney to brainstorm color palettes. But the final brushstroke on her canvas comes not from AI's suggestions, but from a sudden surge of grief. Her mother, a flamenco dancer, had passed away the previous month—and now, Lucía paints with aching intention, every hue a hymn.

She doesn't want AI to finish her art.

"It can help me sketch. But only I know what this sadness feels like."

Art, she says, must bleed to breathe.

AI can replicate styles. It can compose symphonies in the voice of Beethoven or paint like van Gogh.

But it cannot feel heartbreak. Or redemption.

The Caregiver: The Ministry of Small Things

In a hospice center outside Chicago, Angela, a palliative care nurse, sits beside a nonverbal patient. The woman's breathing is shallow; her hands tremble slightly. Angela doesn't speak. She just holds her hand and hums a soft, off-key lullaby her mother once sang to her.

There is no data at the moment.

No biometrics. No optimization.

Just presence.

"Sometimes," Angela says, "the healing isn't in fixing. It's in being with."

Her hospital has implemented AI systems to monitor vital signs and recommend medication adjustments. But Angela believes care isn't just clinical—it's human attunement.

A machine can suggest a drug.

But it cannot wipe a tear with knowing eyes.

The Monk: Silence as Revolution

High in the Himalayas, in a monastery nestled in the clouds, a Buddhist monk named Tenzin recites verses from memory. No digital assistants. No transcripts. Just breath and awareness.

Tenzin once visited a tech summit in Singapore. He watched a robot mimic meditation poses.

"Stillness," he said with a smile, "is not a pose. It's a presence."

AI can simulate serenity. But true equanimity is born of inner discipline.

Monks are trained not to react—but to respond with wisdom. Their "algorithm" is ancient: compassion, clarity, and selflessness.

In Tenzin's world, knowledge isn't downloaded. It's lived.

The Therapist: Mapping the Inner Universe

In a Brooklyn clinic, Dr. Reema Patel, a trauma therapist, guides her patient through a childhood memory. The woman clenches her fists. Tears well. Words falter.

Reema doesn't rush. She listens between the words. She notices the slight change in breath. The long pause. The unspoken.

"There's no shortcut through pain," she says. "But there is accompaniment."

She's seen AI chatbots that offer cognitive behavioral therapy. They're good at triage. Excellent at scale.

But trauma, she believes, is not just data. It's a sacred unfolding.

AI can offer prompts.

But it cannot offer presence.

It cannot bear witness to shame without judgment.

It cannot hold space for healing.

What AI Can't Hold ?

These stories from the margins—an artist's grief, a nurse's hush, a monk's gaze, a therapist's stillness—reveal the terrain that machines may map but never inhabit.

AI works in precision.

But these lives move in poetry.

In ambiguity. In contradiction. In faith.

What artists, caregivers, monks, and therapists remind us is this: the future must not just be built on intelligence—but on wisdom, not just on speed—but on stillness.

They are keepers of what is ineffable.

And in a world seduced by the certainty of code, they remain faithful to mystery.

"The measure of progress is not just how fast we build machines—but how well we protect what makes us human."

And in that sacred space between logic and love, they lead the way.

Where we Draw the Line?

Throughout history, the most important moments of progress haven't just been about what we could do—but what we chose not to.

When the Manhattan Project's scientists unleashed the atom, some celebrated the possibility. Others trembled at the door they had opened. Oppenheimer, quoting the Bhagavad Gita, whispered:

"Now I have become death, the destroyer of worlds."

Even in the birth of modern computing, Alan Turing dreamed of machines that could think, but also feared what might happen if we let them act without conscience.

And now, in the age of artificial intelligence, we face a similar crossroads.

Capability vs. Conscience

AI can compose music, diagnose cancer, detect faces in a crowd, and command fleets of drones. It can score resumes. Predict recidivism. Simulate empathy.

But should it?

Should we let algorithms decide who gets hired or who goes to jail?

Should machines write lullabies without ever having felt heartbreak?

Should autonomous weapons be permitted to take a life without a human in the loop?

"The question is no longer 'Can AI do this?'

It is 'Should humanity allow it to?'"

The Pencil and the Boundary

One of Leonardo da Vinci's favorite tools was the pencil—not only because it let him sketch, but because it let him erase. That eraser, that power to undo, was as important as the graphite that created.

Drawing a line isn't always about restriction. It's about discernment. It's about values.

We draw lines not to hold back innovation, but to hold on to humanity.

The Lines We Must Draw

- In Privacy: We must draw the line before surveillance becomes omniscience. Before every movement, every purchase, and every emotion becomes monetized data.
- In Justice: We must draw the line where bias hides in code, cloaked in "objectivity," but trained on injustice.
- In Autonomy: We must draw the line where decision-making shifts from elected leaders to unaccountable algorithms.
- In Warfare: We must draw the line at autonomous lethality. Because war without remorse is not warfare—it's execution.

Our Greatest Invention Must Be Moral Imagination

As history has shown — from Franklin's diplomacy to Steve Jobs' design obsession—the magic isn't in the machine. It's in the human who shapes it.

This moment demands more than just coders. It demands philosophers.

It calls for policy architects as much as software ones, for ethicists in the boardroom and teachers in the loop.

Not because we distrust technology. But because we trust our human responsibility more.

In the end, progress is not measured by the speed of our machines, but by the care with which we use them."

And that care begins when we pause and ask:

Where do we draw the line?

Not out of fear. But out of wisdom.

Not to halt innovation. But to make it worthy of us.

PART V: THRIVING IN THE AI AGE

Part V

Thriving in the AI Age

When Alan Turing first proposed the idea of a machine that could simulate human intelligence, he posed not a technical challenge—but a philosophical one.

"Can machines think?" he asked, not as an engineer, but as a student of logic, language, and humanity.

Today, that question no longer lives in theoretical journals. It permeates boardrooms, classrooms, hospital wards, and the dim-lit rooms of coders training large language models that speak with eerily human cadence.

The question has evolved—from can they think?

To what does it mean for us to think alongside them?

From Calculation to Cognition

We are entering a world where thinking is no longer the sole domain of the human mind.

AI doesn't just automate tasks; it begins to mediate cognition. It filters what we see, anticipates what we want, and, increasingly, guides how we make decisions.

- Students co-write with AI tutors.
- Scientists partner with algorithms to decode protein folding.
- Judges review algorithmic risk assessments.
- Patients ask chatbots if they should worry about their symptoms.

We are no longer at the center of a solitary thinking process. We are part of a network of thinkers.

And with that comes a profound shift:

We must now think about how we think.

Thinking, Rewired

As Isacson rightly observed, greatness is not found in singular genius—but in the interface between disciplines:

- Leonardo da Vinci blended anatomy and art.
- Benjamin Franklin fused politics and printing.
- Ada Lovelace imagined poetic logic.
- Steve Jobs married calligraphy with code.

Today, we are called to a similar synthesis.

To navigate this AI-infused world, our thinking must become multimodal:

- Logical, yet empathetic.
- Creative, yet structured.
- Data-driven, but ethically anchored.
- Rooted in curiosity, fluent in code, and fearless in ambiguity.

What this Part Explores ?

In this final part of the book, we journey beyond policies, jobs, and technologies—and into the evolution of the human mind itself.

We examine:

- The new cognitive habits AI invites and demands.
- The hybrid literacies of the 21st century: data, empathy, systems, ethics.
- The redefinition of expertise, where knowing is less about memory and more about meaning-making.
- And the mental models that help us distinguish noise from wisdom in an algorithmically curated world.

Why this Matters?

Because in the end, the age of AI won't just be about better tools.

It will be about better thinkers.

It will be about citizens who ask better questions, leaders who integrate better perspectives, and students who grow up fluent in both logic and love, both systems and soul.

Think About It:

" What made the Renaissance wasn't the invention of the printing press.

It was that people learned to think differently because of it."

And so too, with AI.

Let this not be the age where we outsource our minds, but rather the age where we expand them.

Let this be the era where we didn't just teach machines to think—but learned anew how to think as humans.

Chapter 22

AI x Human Synergy: Building a New Social Contract

Every technological revolution forces us to redraw the lines—between labor and capital, between rights and responsibilities, and, perhaps most fundamentally, between man and machine.

From the spinning jenny to the steam engine, from the assembly line to the microchip, each leap reshaped what society expected of its people—and what people could expect in return. The social contract, that unwritten pact between citizens, governments, and institutions, has always been a moving target.

But with the rise of artificial intelligence, we are witnessing a rupture, not just a revision.

This chapter explores the new terrain we must now chart:

A social contract for an AI-augmented civilization.

From Replacement to Relationship

AI is not just replacing jobs—it's redefining the nature of contribution itself.

- A nurse consults an AI triage assistant.
- A journalist co-writes with a text generator.
- A teacher personalizes learning through predictive analytics.
- A factory worker manages robotic colleagues—not just tools.

In each case, the power lies not in AI alone, but in the synergy between human and machine.

And yet, that synergy is not automatic.

It must be designed. Negotiated. Protected.

Rethinking the Rights and Responsibilities

What does it mean to be "employed" when algorithms amplify your cognitive labor?

What are the new rights we need?

The right to meaningful work, not just any work.

- The right to algorithmic transparency, so people understand how decisions are made.
- The right to reskill, not just to survive but to thrive in a shifting world.
- The right to dignity, in a world where surveillance and optimization too often cross the line.

What are the responsibilities we must accept?

- To engage, not disengage, with new tools.
- To question outcomes, not blindly trust them.
- To uphold the human values, machines cannot.

Institutions at a Crossroads

Just as Roosevelt's New Deal recalibrated America for the industrial age, we now need a Civic AI Deal. In this framework, education, employment, equity, and ethics are reimagined in a post-automation economy.

- Governments must guarantee inclusion, not just innovation.
- Companies must invest in their people, not just in productivity.
- Schools must teach adaptability, not just algebra.

The playing field has changed. So must the rules.

Humans Are Not Redundant—They Are Relational

What defines great minds—like Leonardo, Franklin, and Steve Jobs? It wasn't their technical skill alone, but their deep humanism. Their ability to see across domains, to connect dots, to imagine better futures.

AI can process. But it cannot care.

AI can optimize. But it cannot hope.

AI can predict. But it cannot aspire.

In this synergy, humans are not the error-prone sidekick.

They are the moral compass. The creative spark. The conscience of the system.

Toward a Renewed Contract

In this final chapter of Part V, we explore:

- Case studies of collaborative intelligence in hospitals, classrooms, and creative studios.
- Policy proposals for universal access to upskilling and digital inclusion.
- Ethical frameworks that elevate human agency—not diminish it.
- Visions of a co-created future, where AI and humanity don't compete—but complete one another.

Because the most important output of artificial intelligence

…must be a more intelligent society.

A society where progress is not just measured in compute cycles or parameter count, but in compassion, curiosity, and connection.

This is the new social contract.

Not written by code.

But by conscience.

Augmentation Over Automation

In every technological revolution, a choice emerges.

We can automate—turning humans into overseers of machines.

Or we can augment—elevating human potential through the use of machines.

It is a choice between efficiency and enhancement, between replacement and reinvention. And as we stand at the dawn of the AI age, this choice has never been more consequential.

From Automation to Augmentation: A Historical Rhythm

In the 15th century, Gutenberg's press didn't replace scribes. It augmented literacy.

In the 19th century, the telephone didn't eliminate human contact—it expanded its reach.

In the 20th century, calculators didn't make mathematicians obsolete—they freed them for higher-order thinking.

And today, artificial intelligence offers us a similar pivot.

We can build systems to replace judgment, skill, and intuition.

Or we can build systems to amplify them.

The New Augmented Worker

Picture a radiologist scanning through hundreds of images.

AI flags anomalies—patterns too subtle for the human eye.

But it doesn't make the diagnosis. The doctor does.

Picture a teacher, facing a classroom of 30 different learners.

AI suggests personalized content and learning paths.

But it doesn't inspire the student. The teacher does.

Picture a writer with an idea, struggling with phrasing.

AI proposes variations, tones, and even structures.

But it doesn't choose the story. The author does.

In each case, AI doesn't take over. It lifts.

Human-in-the-Loop

The promise of AI is not to replace humans with machines—it's to place humans at the center of smarter systems.

This is known as the "human-in-the-loop" model, which can be compared to a jazz ensemble:

- The AI offers a baseline.
- The human improvises.
- Together, they create something neither could do alone.

Augmentation is not subservience—it's synergy.

Why Augmentation Matters

Automation sees humans as the bottleneck.

Augmentation sees humans as the breakthrough.

Automation strips context.

Augmentation invites creativity, compassion, judgment.

Automation narrows the focus to what can be done faster.

Augmentation expands the vision to what can be imagined better.

The Business Case for Augmentation

Companies that adopt augmentation-first models don't just protect jobs—they unlock new forms of value:

- Increased productivity without sacrificing morale.
- Higher customer trust, because decisions are explainable.
- Deeper innovation, because humans remain involved in problem framing—not just problem-solving.

Remember: the soul of invention lies not in the algorithm, but in the artisan.

The Moral Imperative

In an era of deep fakes and algorithmic opacity, keeping humans in the loop isn't just efficient—it's ethical.

Augmentation respects:

- Human agency
- Human dignity
- Human accountability

Because machines can optimize outcomes, but only people can understand consequences.

The Future is Collaborative

In the end, the AI revolution should not be about making humans more like machines.

It should be about making machines more attuned to what makes us human.

The future belongs to those who can combine the precision of AI with the imagination of the human spirit.

In the story of progress, the most powerful chapters are not those written by machines alone—but those co-authored by mind and machine.

Humans as Curators, Coaches, and Conscience: The Roles AI Can't Replace

When humanity stands at the edge of profound technological shifts, the roles that endure are not the ones that dominate through brute force or even computational prowess. They are the roles that resonate with judgment, compassion, nuance, and soul.

In the age of artificial intelligence, as algorithms proliferate and machines master cognition at dazzling speeds, we are reminded once again of what makes us human. Not simply our ability to process information, but our ability to shape it meaningfully. To inspire. To discern. To guide. In this emerging world, three deeply human archetypes emerge: the curator, the coach, and the conscience.

The Curator: Meaning in a World of Overload

In an era flooded by infinite content—text, images, data, voices—the need for curation becomes critical. While AI can generate a thousand options, it takes a human to know which one matters.

The curator isn't just a filter. They are the ones who bring cultural memory, aesthetic sensibility, emotional tone, and ethical insight to the table. Whether selecting which story goes on the homepage, which voice to amplify, or which idea to pursue, the curator asks not just "What's trending?" but "What's true?"

Jobs once considered niche—such as editors, museum curators, and brand strategists—are now central. In AI-assisted workflows, the human becomes the narrative architect. We're not just ingesting AI output; we're composing meaning from it.

The Coach: Empathy Over Optimization

AI can simulate knowledge, but it cannot substitute the emotional resonance of human mentorship. That's where the coach comes in.

Whether it's an executive helping a team navigate change, a therapist supporting someone in crisis, or a teacher guiding a student through doubt, the coach's strength lies in connection. Empathy, encouragement, knowing when to push and when to pause—these are not formulaic.

AI can train. But it can't inspire in the same breath. And as the workplace becomes increasingly dynamic and AI-infused, the human coach will serve as the guide—helping others develop resilience, confidence, and a sense of worth beyond performance metrics.

The Conscience: The Moral Compass of the Machine Age

Perhaps the most essential—and irreplaceable—role of the human in the loop is that of conscience.

As algorithms make decisions about credit, justice, medicine, and war, we will need people who ask: "Should we?" not just "Can we?" These are ethicists, watchdogs, activists, spiritual leaders, and policy shapers—people who serve as society's gut check.

We may use AI to detect bias. But only a human can say, "This isn't fair." We may use AI to forecast crime. But only a human can ask, "What kind of society do we become if we rely on that?"

It is the human conscience that will hold the line between augmentation and abdication. Between using technology to uplift and using it to control.

Reclaiming the Irreplaceable

As we build AI that can do, we must elevate human roles that can discern, feel, and guide. These are not fallback positions—they are frontiers of meaning. The future isn't a contest between humans and machines. It's a collaboration, where the human plays an elevated role—not in speed or precision, but in wisdom, care, and vision.

In the symphony of this new era, let the machines handle the percussion. But let the humans compose the music.

Co-Pilots, Not Replacements: The Future of Human-AI Collaboration

Throughout history, our greatest innovations have not eliminated the human spirit—they have elevated it.

When Gutenberg introduced movable type, he didn't render scribes obsolete. He democratized knowledge. When the steam engine powered the Industrial Age, it didn't remove the role of human labor—it redefined it. And today, as artificial intelligence becomes our newest and most potent invention, we are at a similar inflection point. The question is not whether AI will work for us—but whether it will work with us.

The answer lies in the metaphor of the co-pilot.

Why the Cockpit Matters?

Pilots don't fly alone. In every modern aircraft, the captain is supported by a co-pilot—alert, responsive, and deeply trained. They monitor instruments, run checklists, and flag anomalies. But when a storm rolls in or something unexpected unfolds, it's the human instinct, the judgment, the feel of flight that takes control.

In this new age, AI should play a similar role. Not the captain of the ship—but the co-pilot beside us. Not an autonomous overlord, but an augmented companion.

The Power of Human-AI Synergy

A radiologist, with the aid of an AI model, detects anomalies with higher precision than either could alone. A coder, assisted by a generative AI like GitHub Copilot, can draft functions in seconds—freeing her time to architect systems rather than wrangle syntax. A teacher, using an AI tutor, tailors learning to each student's pace and struggle, while still nurturing curiosity and confidence.

In these moments, AI becomes not a replacement, but a force multiplier.

Just as a composer uses a piano to bring melody to life, or an astronaut relies on telemetry to guide a re-entry, the human remains at the helm—steering, interpreting, deciding.

When We Confuse Tools with Masters

But there's a danger in forgetting this balance. In offloading too much to the algorithm, we risk losing something essential—accountability, creativity, and above all, purpose.

Autopilot may fly the plane. But when the unexpected hits, it's the pilot's hands—and mind—that matter. In the workplace, too, the best outcomes won't come from surrendering judgment to machines, but from intertwining intuition with computation.

We must resist the allure of complete automation and instead embrace collaborative intelligence—a relationship in which both partners elevate each other.

The Role of the Human: Still Critical

In a world of AI copilots, humans are not obsolete—they are more important than ever. We are the ones who:

- Define the destination
- Make the judgment calls
- Handle the gray areas
- And bear the responsibility when the unexpected strikes

AI can write poetry. But it can't feel heartbreak. It can predict trends. But it can't feel urgency. It can optimize performance. But it can't inspire greatness. These remain—irrevocably—human domains.

From Automation to Amplification

In the age of intelligent machines, the goal is not to hand over the wheel, but to build copilots that sharpen our vision, lighten our load, and help us fly farther than we ever could alone.

Like all great inventions, AI should not diminish us. It should amplify us.

It's not here to replace the pilot.

It's here to make us fly better.

Chapter 23

A Call to Action — Policy, Purpose, and Participation

When history reaches an inflection point, it rarely announces itself with fanfare. It is instead glimpsed in the silent shifts—the glimmer of a new tool, a ripple in the labor force, or the quiet hum of a machine outthinking its creator. This chapter stands at one such precipice. AI is not just a tool or a trend—it is a tectonic force reshaping what it means to participate in a modern democracy, to govern wisely, and to live with intention.

Just as the steam engine demanded new labor laws and electricity gave rise to urban policy reform, artificial intelligence now calls for a reimagining of the social contract itself. And, as always, the choices we make now—individually, collectively, and politically—will determine whether AI becomes a force for inclusive growth or deepened inequality.

The Policy Imperative: Regulation at the Speed of Innovation

The great inventions—like the transistor or the internet—thrived when paired with forward-thinking governance. In that tradition, this chapter profiles the White House AI Bill of Rights, the EU's AI Act, and UNESCO's guidelines—not as bureaucratic jargon, but as humanity's early attempts at placing moral scaffolding around machine intelligence.

We meet the policymakers in backroom meetings, trying to craft language that can evolve as fast as the technology. These are not perfect documents—but they are beginnings. They reflect a deeper truth: that in a democracy, governance is not about control but about stewardship.

The Purpose Principle: Why We Build Matters

From the earliest days of Leonardo sketching mechanical wings, the question has not just been can we build it, but why? Through interviews with AI ethicists, open-source advocates, and purpose-driven startups, we explore a shift from profit-maximizing algorithms to mission-aligned models.

These stories echo a deeper narrative: that the future must be rooted not just in code, but in compassion. The chapter revisits the words of Ada Lovelace, who foresaw the machine as a partner in creativity—not just calculation. AI's purpose must mirror our highest aspirations, not our narrowest interests.

The Participation Imperative: Democracy in the Age of Algorithms

Perhaps the most stirring section of the chapter is its meditation on participation. In a world where decisions about surveillance, automation, and algorithmic justice affect every citizen, who gets a seat at the table? This chapter tells the story of communities—from Nairobi to Appalachia—where citizens, not just coders, are engaging in "algorithmic audits" and "civic hackathons."

This is the future of AI governance: not cloistered in corporate boardrooms or elite institutions, but crowdsourced, localized, and deeply democratic. In this world, participation is protection.

Closing Reflection

"The measure of our intelligence," a voice recalls, "will not be how smart we make our machines, but how wisely we use them to make ourselves more human."

This is not just a call to regulate. It is a call to imagine, to engage, and to build—with purpose, policy, and participation at the core.

National AI Strategies: USA, India, EU, China

Great technological leaps—whether it be the printing press, electricity, or the internet—have always demanded not just visionaries, but also national strategies. The advent of Artificial Intelligence is no different. In this chapter, we step into war rooms, policy labs, and innovation hubs across Washington, Brussels, Beijing, and New Delhi to witness how nations are not just reacting to AI—but actively sculpting the future.

Each country's approach, like its cultural DNA, reflects a deeper story about its values, fears, and ambitions.

United States: Innovation First, Guardrails Later

The American story of AI is quintessentially Silicon Valley. From Stanford dorm rooms to DARPA-funded think tanks, the U.S. approach to AI is shaped by a culture that prizes speed, disruption, and private sector leadership.

Picture this: In the offices of OpenAI, where developers debate the societal impact of AGI between Red Bull-fueled coding sprints, or the halls of Congress, where senators grapple with regulating an industry they barely understand.

In 2022, the White House AI Bill of Rights marked a shift—from unchecked innovation to responsible deployment. The U.S. now balances two competing imperatives: maintain its lead in AI while safeguarding civil liberties. It's an awkward, often contradictory dance—but it's dancing nonetheless.

"The U.S. doesn't just build tools," one policymaker says, "We build the values behind them."

European Union: Human-Centric, Rights-Driven

Across the Atlantic, in the grand buildings of Brussels, the EU has taken a more cautious path. While American companies race ahead, the EU is deliberate. You might compare it to the drafting of the Magna Carta—a sweeping attempt to enshrine rights before the power grows too great.

The EU AI Act, passed in 2024, does not just categorize AI systems by risk—it frames AI as a human dignity issue. Facial recognition in public spaces? Banned. Emotion recognition in schools? High-risk.

The continent that once built cathedrals over centuries now builds AI ethics frameworks with similar ambition and care.

"We regulate not to slow down," says an EU commissioner, "but to ensure everyone arrives at the future together."

China: Centralized Power, Strategic Scale

If the U.S. leads with innovation and the EU with regulation, China leads with orchestration. Beijing's AI strategy is less of a white paper and more of a grand symphony—state, academia, and enterprise playing in harmony toward national goals.

Since the 2017 Next Generation AI Plan, China has integrated AI into its geopolitical strategy. Smart cities, surveillance systems, and facial recognition—all fueled by massive state-backed datasets and a vision of technological supremacy by 2030.

A Chinese entrepreneur may be telling "We don't ask what AI can do. We ask what the Party needs it to do."

India: Inclusive AI for 1.4 Billion Minds

India's approach is something else entirely. It is not the fastest, nor the most centralized. But it is perhaps the most human-scaled.

With the National Strategy for AI (NITI Aayog) and platforms like IndiaAI.gov.in, the country is positioning AI not just for tech exports, but also for addressing deeply local challenges—such as crop forecasting, rural health diagnostics, and multilingual education.

Imagine visiting a remote clinic in Tamil Nadu where a nurse uses an AI-enabled tablet to detect early-stage TB, or a classroom in Uttar Pradesh where speech-to-text tools assist visually impaired children.

India's AI is frugal, plural, and democratic—a public utility, not just a private luxury.

"We don't need AI to impress the world," a young developer says, "We need it to uplift our people."

Four Strategies, One Future

We might not crown one of these strategies superior. Instead, let's weave their contrasts into a shared human story—of innovation with responsibility, progress with reflection, and ambition with empathy.

"In the end, how each nation wields AI will say less about their machines, and more about their humanity."

The Importance of Interdisciplinary Education

In the Renaissance courts of Florence, a young artist named Leonardo da Vinci sketched the muscles of a horse one moment and sketched the flight of birds the next. What made him extraordinary wasn't just his art or his science—it was the bridge he built between the two. Leonardo didn't just paint anatomy; he understood it. He didn't just dream of flight; he studied wind, mechanics, and the structure of wings. He was, in every sense, an interdisciplinary thinker.

Today, in the age of artificial intelligence, quantum computing, and CRISPR, we are once again at an inflection point that demands this Renaissance mindset.

The myth that education must be siloed—that an engineer should stick to coding, a philosopher to metaphysics, and a biologist to petri dishes—is fast eroding. The world's most pressing challenges—climate change, pandemic resilience, misinformation—do not fit neatly into departmental boxes. Solving them requires teams that can blend logic with ethics, systems thinking with empathy, and data science with storytelling.

At MIT, students of computer science now study moral philosophy. At Stanford, design thinking merges art with engineering. Companies like Google hire not just coders, but anthropologists who can interpret human behavior. In India, the National Education Policy is promoting flexibility, allowing students to combine physics with political science, or AI with Sanskrit.

This isn't fluff—it's survival. The machines we build will reflect the limitations of our own thinking unless we broaden our perspective. A neural network can spot tumors, but only a doctor trained in human dignity can decide how to break the news. AI can write a symphony, but only a human being can know when it moves the soul.

Interdisciplinary education doesn't just create better workers. It creates better citizens. It reminds us that truth is often found at the boundaries of disciplines, and progress comes when those boundaries dissolve.

In a world increasingly run by algorithms, we need more da Vincis—those who can connect the dots between science and soul, between silicon and conscience.

The most vital skill we can teach the next generation is not how to specialize, but how to synthesize.

Responsible Citizenship in a Digital World

When Benjamin Franklin walked the cobbled streets of Philadelphia, he carried with him not just a printing press and a lightning rod, but a deep belief in civic virtue—the idea that a society is only as strong as the character of its citizens.

Today, we no longer gather at town squares. We log into platforms. We don't pass pamphlets down cobblestone lanes; we retweet across fiber-optic cables. The marketplace of ideas has gone digital, but the responsibility that comes with citizenship has not vanished—it has only grown more complex and more urgent.

In the age of AI, social media, and deepfakes, citizenship is no longer just about voting or paying taxes. It's about the choices we make each day in a hyperconnected world:

Do we fact-check before we share?

Do we know how our data is being used?

Do we pause before engaging in outrage that algorithms amplify?

Do we understand the biases embedded in the code that shapes our reality?

Being a responsible citizen now means becoming digitally literate—not just knowing how to use technology, but also knowing how to question it critically. It means understanding that every click trains a model, every upload writes a history, and every online interaction leaves a footprint on a global commons.

It also means holding our institutions and tech leaders accountable. Just as previous generations fought for environmental protections or civil rights, this one must demand algorithmic transparency, data privacy, and equitable access to the tools of the future. Democracy, after all, cannot function if its citizens are misinformed, manipulated, or left behind.

But responsibility is not only defensive. It's generative. It's about using these tools not to retreat into filter bubbles, but to build bridges. Not to inflame division, but to amplify decency. Franklin wrote, "Well done is better than well said." In today's context, well-coded, well-shared, and well-governed must join that pantheon of civic action.

We are all, now, publishers, broadcasters, and participants in a digital experiment that spans borders and generations. The question is: will we shape it with integrity, or will it shape us by its inertia?

The future doesn't just need tech-savvy citizens.

It needs wise ones.

Chapter 24

Epilogue –"The Mirror of the Mind"

In the final pages of any great transformation—be it Da Vinci sketching flying machines in a Florentine notebook, or Steve Jobs unveiling the iPhone with a Zen-like swipe—we are often reminded that the most profound revolutions are not just technological. They are internal.

This chapter is not about a new model of AI, a new milestone in machine learning, or the next wave of exponential computing power. It is about reflection. About turning the lens inward.

"The Mirror of the Mind" is both a metaphor and a manifesto.

For centuries, humanity has peered outward—into space, into code, into matter. But now, we stand at a juncture where the tools we've built begin to look back. AI systems learn from our behaviors, mirror our patterns, and echo our biases. The question is no longer "What can machines do?" but "What do they reveal about us?"

When we teach an algorithm to write, we're not just automating prose. We're encoding style, perspective, and priority. When we train an AI to recognize faces or detect emotion, we are embedding our assumptions—often unconsciously. The mirror does not lie, but it reflects what we give it.

And sometimes, what we see is unsettling.

We see the unequal access to technology that threatens to widen the gap between the privileged and the marginalized. We see the temptation to chase efficiency at the cost of empathy. We see the urge to outsource decisions rather than deepen discernment. And yet, within the same mirror, we see potential: of tools that can assist the blind, predict pandemics, teach a child in a remote village, or compose symphonies of staggering beauty.

This moment demands more than engineering skill. It calls for ethical imagination. For humility. For a revival of humanistic thinking in tandem with digital innovation.

We must not only teach machines how to think.

We must remind ourselves why we think.

In the end, the most transformative impact of AI may not be in what it builds, automates, or predicts—but in how it forces us to confront who we are, and who we wish to become.

As with the telescope or the microscope, AI enlarges our field of view. But the final image, as always, remains human.

The mirror is here.

We can turn away.

Or we can gaze in—and grow.

What we Build Reflects Who we Are

Throughout history, the tools we've crafted have been more than just functional. They've been mirrors. When Gutenberg assembled his printing press, he wasn't merely mechanizing the written word—he was democratizing knowledge, broadcasting curiosity, and igniting revolutions. When Ada Lovelace imagined machines composing music or weaving patterns, she wasn't just programming numbers. She was projecting a deeply human impulse: to create, to express, to connect.

The same is true of artificial intelligence.

AI doesn't arise in a vacuum. It is shaped by our values, our questions, our blind spots. The datasets we feed it contain the residue of our histories—who we've included, who we've ignored, what we've celebrated, what we've feared. Every algorithm, in some form, is a crystallization of human priorities. Every model, a snapshot of our moment.

And that is both a risk and a responsibility.

If we build with haste, the systems we create will reflect our short-sightedness. If we build with exclusion, they will inherit our inequities. If we build with arrogance, we will be surprised when they amplify our mistakes.

But if we build with thoughtfulness—if we infuse our technology with empathy, transparency, and integrity—then AI becomes more than just a mirror. It becomes a canvas. A place to imagine not only what machines can do, but what humanity ought to do.

We often speak of artificial intelligence as a leap forward. But in truth, it is also a loop back—to the fundamental question: Who are we?

Because in the end, what we build reveals more than our capabilities.

It reveals our character.

And that is the greatest innovation of all.

Will AI Inherit Our Flaws or Magnify Our Wisdom?

Every great leap in human progress—from the compass to the computer—has carried with it the DNA of its creators. And now, in the age of artificial intelligence, we stand once more at that inflection point. The question isn't just whether machines will become more powerful. It's whether they will become more human—and which parts of our humanity they will carry forward.

AI, after all, learns from us. It absorbs our language, our decisions, our histories. It mimics our preferences and reproduces our logic. But embedded in that inheritance is a paradox: We are a species capable of both remarkable wisdom and tragic error. We've decoded the genome and also built atomic bombs. We've crafted symphonies and written propaganda. We are, simultaneously, our highest aspirations and our lowest impulses.

And so the question becomes: What will AI reflect to us?

If we train it on biased data, it will inherit our blind spots. If we prioritize profit over principle, it will become an agent of acceleration, not reflection. It will automate injustice with breathtaking efficiency.

But there is another path.

If we imbue it with ethical guardrails, with diverse perspectives, with a commitment to truth and transparency, then AI can become more than an echo. It can become a clarifier—a system that helps us see ourselves more clearly, act more justly, and think more expansively.

The choice, then, is not about the intelligence of the machine.

It's about the intention of the maker.

Will AI inherit our flaws? Undoubtedly—if we're careless.

But can it also magnify our wisdom? Absolutely—if we are deliberate.

Ultimately, AI won't just be a measure of our technical prowess.

It will be a measure of our moral imagination.

And the legacy we encode today may well define the humanity we become tomorrow.

A Closing Reflection: With Hope and Humility

We stand at the threshold of a profound transformation—one not driven solely by algorithms or quantum processors, but by the enduring question of what it means to be human in an age of machines.

History teaches us that every technological revolution is also a moral reckoning. The printing press democratized knowledge—but also spread propaganda. The steam engine shrank distances—but widened empires. The internet connected the world—but fractured our attention.

Now, artificial intelligence offers another promise—and another test.

Will we wield it to elevate humanity or merely to amplify convenience? Will we design systems that reflect our better angels or our baser instincts? Will we build a world that is more equitable, creative, and wise—or one that is merely faster and more automated?

The answers will not come from machines. They will come from us.

And that is where hope lives.

Hope lives in the teacher reimagining her classroom with AI tutors—not to replace her, but to reach more children.

Hope lives in the young coder in Nairobi or Hyderabad, using open-source tools to solve problems once thought unsolvable.

Hope lives in the ethicist who sits beside the engineer, asking not just can we, but should we.

But let us also carry humility.

Humility in knowing that intelligence—no matter how artificial—is not the same as wisdom.

Humility in remembering that data is not destiny.

And humility in accepting that no model, no matter how large, can ever fully model the mysteries of the human heart.

If we move forward with both—hope as our compass, humility as our ballast—then we can navigate this new era not with fear, but with purpose.

Let this be our guiding creed in the age of AI:

That we build not only what we can,
But what we must—
To leave behind not just smarter machines,
But a wiser, more compassionate world.

APPENDICES

Appendix A

AI Literacy Toolkit

Essential Terms, Concepts, and Tools Everyone Should Know

When Leonardo da Vinci sketched the first mechanical knight, he wasn't just imagining a machine—he was exploring the boundaries of possibility. In much the same way, today's AI pioneers are mapping the new frontiers of intelligence. But to truly participate in this journey, each of us—whether a policymaker, teacher, designer, or parent—needs a compass. This appendix is that compass.

This AI Literacy Toolkit is less about turning everyone into data scientists and more about giving everyone the fluency to speak the language of tomorrow. Because understanding AI is no longer optional—it's the new grammar of the 21st century.

1. **Core Concepts: Foundations of AI**
   - Artificial Intelligence (AI): The science of building machines that simulate human intelligence—from learning to problem-solving.
   - Machine Learning (ML): Algorithms that learn patterns from data rather than being explicitly programmed.
   - Deep Learning: A subset of ML using neural networks with many layers to detect complex patterns—powering image recognition, voice assistants, and more.
   - Natural Language Processing (NLP): Teaching machines to understand and generate human language.
   - These aren't just buzzwords—they're the gears inside the machine.
2. **Essential Tools & Platforms**
   - Python: The lingua franca of AI programming.

- TensorFlow / PyTorch: Open-source libraries for building machine learning models.
- ChatGPT, Claude, Bard, Gemini: Examples of large language models (LLMs) transforming how we search, write, and interact.
- AutoML / No-Code AI Tools: Democratizing AI building for non-engineers.

Like Gutenberg's press or Ford's assembly line, these tools are turning specialists into creators.

3. **Key Metrics & Terms**
   - Training Data: The historical examples used to "teach" the AI.
   - Bias: Systematic errors embedded in training data that skew outputs.
   - Accuracy / Precision / Recall: Measures of how well a model performs.
   - Overfitting / Underfitting: Pitfalls when models are either too tailored or too vague.

   These are the dials and gauges we must watch to steer AI responsibly.
4. **Governance & Ethics**
   - Explainability: Can we understand why an AI made a decision?
   - Fairness: Are outcomes equitable across race, gender, geography?
   - Privacy: How is personal data collected, used, and protected?
   - AI Alignment: Does the system's goal match human values?

   The Renaissance was characterized by ethics embedded in its art. Therefore, AI must be infused with human-centered values.
5. **Everyday Applications**
   - Healthcare Diagnostics (AI-powered scans and triage bots)
   - Transportation (autonomous driving, route optimization)
   - Finance (fraud detection, robo-advisors)
   - Education (personalized tutoring, AI feedback)
   - Marketing & Media (customer segmentation, content generation)

   Understanding AI means seeing how it's already shaping your world.
6. **Curiosity Toolkit: Learn More**
   - MOOCs (e.g., Coursera's AI for Everyone by Andrew Ng)

- Newsletters & Podcasts (e.g., MIT Technology Review, Lex Fridman)
- Books (e.g., Weapons of Math Destruction, Human Compatible, The Age of AI)
- Regulatory Briefs (EU AI Act, U.S. Blueprint for AI Bill of Rights)

Because, like Franklin and Jefferson, today's most valuable citizen is an informed one.

This appendix is your Rosetta Stone for decoding the world of artificial intelligence. In an age where the boundary between human and machine blurs, fluency in AI is not just a technical skill—it's civic literacy. This toolkit doesn't give you all the answers, but it empowers you to ask better questions. And that's where the future begins.

Appendix B

Top 50 Reskilling Platforms and Programs

Where the Future Learns to Work

In every era of transformation, some institutions prepare people not just to survive the shift—but to lead it. In the Renaissance, it was the guild. In the Industrial Revolution, it was the factory school. Today, it is the reskilling platform—part digital workshop, part modern library of Alexandria—where coders, creatives, caregivers, and CEOs alike learn to adapt to the age of artificial intelligence.

This appendix is more than a directory. It's a landscape of learning, charting where workers, leaders, students, and dreamers are rewiring their capabilities for the future of work.

The Big Players: Scalable, Global, Accessible

These platforms are shaping millions of careers with AI-powered personalization, industry partnerships, and recognized credentials.

- Coursera – From AI to data science to soft skills, backed by Stanford, Google, and Meta.
- edX (by 2U) – University-level learning, featuring MITx, HarvardX, and MicroMasters.
- Udemy – Peer-to-peer powered skill marketplace, constantly updated with trending technologies.
- LinkedIn Learning – Career-oriented content with built-in networking and certification.
- Khan Academy – Free, accessible, and expanding into AI and financial literacy.

"What libraries were to Gutenberg's era, platforms like Coursera and edX are to ours."

Nano-Degree & Bootcamp Innovators

Rapid, focused, and job-ready—these programs are the accelerators of skill transformation.

- Udacity – AI, autonomous systems, cloud engineering with Google, Amazon, and IBM.
- Springboard – Career track programs with mentorship and job guarantees.
- General Assembly – Bootcamps for coding, UX, and data—now with DEI focus.
- Lambda School / BloomTech – Income-share models for learning software engineering.
- Ironhack / Le Wagon – Global coding bootcamps with immersive tech stacks.

Workforce + Industry-Led Initiatives

Where government, corporate, and nonprofit sectors align to reskill at the national and organizational scale.

- Amazon Career Choice – $700M investment to retrain 100,000 workers for cloud, IT, and healthcare.
- AT&T Future Ready – A blueprint for company-wide upskilling in data, design, and decision-making.
- IBM SkillsBuild – Free learning pathways for marginalized groups in AI and cybersecurity.
- Google Career Certificates – High-demand jobs without a college degree.
- Microsoft Skills for Jobs – Global partnerships to teach digital fundamentals to 25M+ people.

MOOCs & Open Access Champions

Knowledge made borderless—education without barriers.

- MIT OpenCourseWare – MIT's brain trust open to the world.
- FutureLearn (UK) – Government-endorsed, future-focused programs.
- Swayam (India) – India's digital university platform, scalable for millions.
- OpenLearn (The Open University) – Humanities and tech, together.
- Canvas Network – Open learning for educators and lifelong learners.

Soft Skills, EQ & Human-Centric Reskilling

Because the age of machines requires deeply human strengths.

- BetterUp – Coaching and leadership development for emotional resilience.
- Mindvalley – Personal growth, productivity, and purpose reimagined.
- LifeLabs Learning – Managerial and interpersonal upskilling with neuroscience-backed techniques.
- Rung for Women – Free career services focused on dignity, equity, and impact.
- IDEO U – Creativity, design thinking, and human-centered innovation.

Next-Gen Learning Startups: AI-Native and Immersive

They don't just teach AI—they use it to teach.

- Quantic School of Business & Technology – Mobile-first MBA.
- Replit AI Bootcamps – Coding in real time with AI co-pilots.
- Labster – Virtual labs for science, biotech, and engineering.
- Crehana / Platzi (LatAm) – Creator economy and digital skills in Spanish-speaking markets.
- Skill-Lync (India) – Engineering and job-linked courses, AI-powered matching.

Government, Nonprofit & Multilateral Programs

Reskilling at the scale of society.

- UNESCO Global Skills Academy
- Skill India / National Skill Development Corporation (NSDC)
- European Digital Skills & Jobs Platform
- Singapore's SkillsFuture
- African Union's 1 Million Next-Level Initiative

How to Use This Toolkit

Each entry includes:

- Focus Areas (e.g., AI, Data, Design, Healthcare)

- Delivery Model (Self-paced, Instructor-led, Mentorship-based)
- Credential Offered (Certificate, Degree, Badges)
- Price Range (Free to Premium)
- Best For (Beginners, Mid-career transitions, Corporate L&D)

In an age of relentless change, the most critical infrastructure is not just broadband or batteries—but brains on fire with possibility. These platforms are on-ramps to reinvention, highways of hope. Because in the end, the most powerful algorithm is a human being who keeps learning.

Appendix C

Industry-Wise Job Transformation Map

Tracing the Ripple Effects of AI Across the Economic Landscape

Throughout history, technology has reshaped the labor force—one sector at a time. The spinning jenny revolutionized textiles. The assembly line redefined manufacturing. The microchip rewrote the rules of knowledge work. And now, in the age of artificial intelligence, every industry is in flux—each one a canvas upon which the future of work is being redrawn.

This is not just a snapshot of disruption. It is a dynamic chart of adaptation—an atlas of where old roles are fading, new roles are emerging, and hybrid roles are evolving at the intersection of human insight and machine intelligence.

Healthcare

- **Declining**: Manual medical transcriptionists, radiology image taggers
- **Transforming**: Primary care physicians → augmented with diagnostic AI
- **Emerging**: AI clinical workflow architects, empathic AI trainers, virtual care coordinators

"The stethoscope once symbolized the clinician. Now, it's joined by data dashboards and diagnostic algorithms."

Education

- **Declining**: Rote-based instruction, curriculum standardizers
- **Transforming**: Teachers → AI-integrated facilitators of learning journeys
- **Emerging**: Prompt-savvy educators, learning experience designers, AI ethicists in pedagogy

"The best teachers won't be replaced—they'll be amplified by intelligent tools that help unlock each learner's potential."

Finance

- **Declining**: Repetitive auditing, entry-level compliance roles
- **Transforming**: Wealth advisors → AI-assisted financial planners
- **Emerging**: Algorithmic risk managers, AI ethics auditors, decentralized finance (DeFi) analysts

"Spreadsheets and instincts now share the table with predictive models and real-time data."

Manufacturing

- **Declining**: Traditional assembly line roles
- **Transforming**: Process engineers → co-working with intelligent robotics
- **Emerging**: Smart factory supervisors, digital twin engineers, machine-learning safety officers

"Automation didn't end the factory—it evolved it into an intelligent organism."

Retail & E-Commerce

- **Declining**: Cashiers, warehouse pickers
- **Transforming**: Store managers → omni-channel, data-driven decision-makers
- **Emerging**: AI personalization designers, virtual shelf curators, fulfillment optimization leads

"Customer experience has moved from the checkout lane to the algorithm."

Media & Creative Industries

- **Declining**: Traditional content sorting, manual editing
- **Transforming**: Writers and designers → co-creators with generative tools
- **Emerging**: AI prompt engineers, digital brand storytellers, synthetic media ethicists

"The blank page is no longer blank—it listens, learns, and suggests."

Agriculture

- **Declining**: Manual crop monitoring
- **Transforming**: Farmers → tech-enabled, satellite-informed agri-managers
- **Emerging**: Precision agri-technologists, drone operators, climate resilience advisors

"From soil to satellite, AI is cultivating more than crops—it's seeding sustainability."

Transportation & Logistics

- **Declining**: Dispatch clerks, manual schedulers
- **Transforming**: Fleet managers → data-driven route optimizers
- **Emerging**: Autonomous operations supervisors, last-mile AI planners, EV fleet strategists

"It's not just about where goods move—it's about how intelligently they get there."

Public Sector & Law

- **Declining**: Routine legal review, document discovery
- **Transforming**: Lawyers → AI-enhanced case strategists
- **Emerging**: Digital policy advisors, algorithmic justice advocates, civic tech leaders

"Justice must be blind, but AI must not be—hence the rise of legal tech watchdogs."

Technology

- **Declining**: Rule-based coders
- **Transforming**: Developers → prompt engineers and AI product designers
- **Emerging**: Multi-modal AI architects, responsible AI leads, data visualization strategists

"The future coder speaks both in Python and in questions—good prompts are new code."

A Note of Perspective

As with any map, this one isn't the territory—it's a narrative of change. What matters most is not where the arrows point, but how we move. And in that movement, there lies opportunity, reinvention, and the enduring human spirit to adapt.

Appendix D

Recommended Reading and AI Watchlist

"To see where we are headed, we must first understand where we've been—and who is leading the charge."

In the rapidly evolving world of artificial intelligence, knowledge is not a luxury—it's a compass. Appendix D offers a curated, thoughtful map for lifelong learners, professionals, policymakers, and students to navigate the layered complexity of AI through a library of seminal works, contemporary thought leaders, and real-time digital sources.

Curated Booklist: Where Thought Meets Technology

The books selected are not just technical manuals or futurist predictions—they are reflections on the philosophical, societal, and ethical dimensions of intelligence, both natural and artificial.

"Life 3.0" by Max Tegmark

A sweeping overview of what AI might become—and the values we must imbue it with.

"Superintelligence" by Nick Bostrom

A chilling but necessary read on the existential risks of unregulated AI power.

"AI 2041" by Kai-Fu Lee & Chen Qiufan

Where fiction and nonfiction blend to show how AI may transform lives globally.

"The Age of AI" by Henry Kissinger, Eric Schmidt, and Daniel Huttenlocher

A statesman's vision of diplomacy in the digital age.

"Atlas of AI" by Kate Crawford

A deeply humanistic investigation into the labor, geopolitics, and ethics behind AI systems.

"Architects of Intelligence" by Martin Ford

First-person perspectives from leaders like Demis Hassabis, Ray Kurzweil, and Fei-Fei Li.

Podcasts and Documentaries: Thought in Motion

To keep the conversation alive beyond pages:

Podcasts

- Lex Fridman Podcast – Longform interviews with AI thinkers, engineers, and philosophers.
- Hard Fork (NYT) – Weekly, digestible takes on AI's cultural and tech impact.
- Eye on AI – Analytical deep dives on real-world AI deployments and controversies.

Documentaries

- The Social Dilemma – The algorithmic roots of modern society's dilemmas.
- iHuman – A stark look into surveillance, control, and AI-driven futures.
- Coded Bias – Unveils the Embedded Prejudices within AI Systems.

Real-Time Watchlist: Who to Follow, What to Track

Stay current with the voices shaping tomorrow's decisions:

People to Follow

- Fei-Fei Li (Human-centered AI)
- Timnit Gebru (Ethics and bias)
- Yann LeCun, Geoffrey Hinton, Yoshua Bengio (The "Godfathers of AI")
- Kate Crawford (AI sociology and justice)
- Andrew Ng (AI education, AI for all)

Platforms

- Stanford HAI (Human-Centered AI initiatives)
- Partnership on AI
- MIT Technology Review – AI Section
- OECD.AI Observatory
- World Economic Forum AI & Jobs Tracker
- AI Index Report – Stanford University

In the end, this appendix serves as a launchpad—not into a single future, but into many possible ones. Remember: "The great leap forward in human history has always involved the marriage of art and science, ethics and engineering. These works help us think not just with code, but with conscience."

Appendix E

Voices of the Future

"Progress is not a monologue. It's a conversation—between scientist and citizen, coder and caregiver, algorithm and ethicist."

In every era of transformation, the story is not just told through code or policy papers—it's etched in voices. This appendix gathers a chorus of perspectives from across the AI spectrum, including the builders, regulators, and real-world users. Together, their insights form a living dialogue—one filled with hope, concern, and a call to responsible imagination.

The Architects: Vision from the Inside

These are the minds shaping the architecture of intelligence.

"The key question is not if machines can think, but whether we are thinking deeply enough about what we want them to do."

- *— Fei-Fei Li, Professor, Stanford HAI*

"AI doesn't replace jobs. It replaces tasks—and frees us to focus on the deeply human ones."

- *— Andrew Ng, AI educator, co-founder of Coursera*

"We must ensure that AI reflects not just human intelligence, but human values."

- *— Demis Hassabis, CEO, DeepMind*

The Policymakers: Framing the Future

In the halls of policy, AI is not just a tool—it's a terrain.

"Our challenge is not only to regulate AI—but to do so without choking innovation. We must be agile, ethical, and inclusive."

- *— Margrethe Vestager, Executive VP, European Commission*

"The AI Act is not about banning progress. It's about defining the boundaries that protect our humanity."

- *— Dragoș Tudorache, Co-Rapporteur, EU AI Act*

"Technology moves fast. Democracy must learn to move wisely."

- *— Gina Raimondo, U.S. Secretary of Commerce*

The Frontline Workers: Where Algorithms Meet Reality

These voices remind us that AI is not just theoretical—it's tactile, tangible, and sometimes fraught.

"When the algorithm changed my warehouse schedule, it didn't ask if I had a child to pick up. That's the problem."

- *— Sonia Alvarez, logistics worker, Amazon fulfillment center*

" AI helped me triage faster. But it can't look a patient in the eye and calm their fear."

- *— Dr. Naima Patel, ER Physician, London*

"I use ChatGPT to plan lessons for my students—but my job is still to inspire, not just inform."

- *— Joseph Kim, High School Teacher, Seoul*

The Takeaway:

These quotes are not footnotes to the AI story—they are its heartbeat. As Walter Isaacson might write:

"When innovation becomes destiny, it is our voices, not our wires, that determine what kind of world we build."

Bibliography: The Trail of Thought that Led Us Here

Behind every revelation is a reference. Behind every insight, a lineage of ideas. The bibliography in this book isn't just a list—it's a trail of breadcrumbs tracing the intellectual and ethical journey humanity is undertaking as we stand at the precipice of the AI age.

Here, you'll find the foundational papers that birthed modern machine learning and deep learning, from Backpropagation to Transformer models. You'll encounter essays by ethicists and philosophers grappling with the soul of machines, alongside economic treatises predicting the tectonic shifts in labor markets. There are policy briefs from Brussels and Beijing, code repositories from open-source pioneers, and ethnographic accounts from gig workers and caregivers as they adapt to a new world.

We include works by:

- imnit Gebru, Kate Crawford, and Ruha Benjamin, who challenge us to see the hidden biases in data and design.
- Fei-Fei Li, Geoffrey Hinton, and Yann LeCun, who helped give birth to intelligent machines.
- Shoshana Zuboff, Nick Bostrom, and Yuval Noah Harari, who ask not just what we can build, but what we should.
- The World Economic Forum, OECD, and UNDP, whose reports provide context for policy and global impact.
- Startups like OpenAI, DeepMind, and Anthropic, whose white papers and blog posts offer a glimpse into the labs of the future.
- MIT Media Lab, Stanford's Human-Centered AI Institute, and the Alan Turing Institute, whose interdisciplinary scholarship inspires balance between innovation and responsibility.

Each citation is an invitation to explore further, to question deeper, and to join the conversation.

Because if AI is rewriting the rules of human potential, then the bibliography is the ledger of how we got here.

And knowing where we've been might just help us decide where we want to go.

Bibliography

Academic and Technical Foundations

1. Hinton, G., Osindero, S., & Teh, Y. W. (2006). "A Fast Learning Algorithm for Deep Belief Nets." Neural Computation, 18(7), 1527-1554.
2. LeCun, Y., Bengio, Y., & Hinton, G. (2015). "Deep Learning." Nature, 521(7553), 436-444.
3. Vaswani, A., et al. (2017). "Attention Is All You Need." Advances in Neural Information Processing Systems, 30.
4. Silver, D., et al. (2016). "Mastering the Game of Go with Deep Neural Networks and Tree Search." Nature, 529(7587), 484-489.
5. OpenAI. (2023). "GPT-4 Technical Report."
6. Chollet, F. (2019). Deep Learning with Python. Manning Publications.

Ethics and Governance

7. Bostrom, N. (2014). Superintelligence: Paths, Dangers, Strategies. Oxford University Press.
8. O'Neil, C. (2016). Weapons of Math Destruction: How Big Data Increases Inequality and Threatens Democracy. Crown Publishing.
9. Zuboff, S. (2019). The Age of Surveillance Capitalism. PublicAffairs.
10. Benjamin, R. (2019). Race After Technology: Abolitionist Tools for the New Jim Code. Polity Press.
11. Crawford, K. (2021). Atlas of AI. Yale University Press.
12. Whittlestone, J., et al. (2019). "The Role and Limits of Principles in AI Ethics: Towards a Focus on Tensions." Proceedings of the AAAI/ACM Conference on AI, Ethics, and Society.
13. MIT Media Lab. (2021). "Moral Machine Project."

Economic and Labor Impacts

14. World Economic Forum. (2023). Future of Jobs Report.
15. Brynjolfsson, E., & McAfee, A. (2014). The Second Machine Age. W. W. Norton & Company.
16. Acemoglu, D., & Restrepo, P. (2019). "Artificial Intelligence, Automation and Work." NBER Working Paper No. 24196.
17. Chui, M., Manyika, J., & Miremadi, M. (2016). "Where Machines Could Replace Humans—and Where They Can't (Yet)." McKinsey Global Institute.
18. OECD. (2022). AI and the Future of Skills: Insights from a Global Observatory.

Education and Reskilling

19. MIT Task Force on the Work of the Future. (2020). Building Better Jobs in an Age of Intelligent Machines.
20. World Bank. (2021). The Changing Nature of Work.
21. Khan Academy, Coursera, Udacity, edX. (2020-2023). MOOC Curricula on AI and Data Literacy.
22. Schmidt Futures. (2022). AI and Learning Ecosystems: Equitable Futures for All.

Policy and Global Strategy

23. European Commission. (2021). Artificial Intelligence Act: Proposal for a Regulation.
24. White House Office of Science and Technology Policy. (2022). Blueprint for an AI Bill of Rights.
25. India NITI Aayog. (2020). Responsible AI for All: National Strategy for Artificial Intelligence.
26. China State Council. (2017). New Generation Artificial Intelligence Development Plan.
27. UNESCO. (2021). Recommendation on the Ethics of Artificial Intelligence.
28. OECD. (2019). Principles on Artificial Intelligence.
29. Global Partnership on AI (GPAI). (2023). Annual Progress Report.

Culture, Society, and Human Experience

30. Harari, Y. N. (2018). 21 Lessons for the 21st Century. Spiegel & Grau.
31. Dignum, V. (2019). Responsible Artificial Intelligence: How to Develop and Use AI in a Responsible Way. Springer.
32. Tegmark, M. (2017). Life 3.0: Being Human in the Age of Artificial Intelligence. Penguin Books.
33. Kelly, K. (2016). The Inevitable: Understanding the 12 Technological Forces That Will Shape Our Future. Viking Press.
34. Turkle, S. (2011). Alone Together: Why We Expect More from Technology and Less from Each Other. Basic Books.
35. Susskind, R. & Susskind, D. (2015). The Future of the Professions. Oxford University Press.

Reports, Tools & Resources

36. OpenAI. (2022-2024). Blog, Use Cases, and Safety Research.
37. DeepMind Ethics & Society. (2023). "Ethical Principles and Applications."
38. Stanford HAI. (2023). AI Index Report.
39. IBM. (2022). AI Governance Toolkit.
40. Partnership on AI. (2023). Frameworks for Responsible AI Deployment.
41. Mozilla Foundation. (2023). Internet Health Report: AI Edition.
42. Harvard Berkman Klein Center. (2022). Algorithmic Justice and Human Rights.

Personal Stories, Journalism, Documentaries

43. Thompson, C. (2020). "The Secret Life of Algorithms." Wired Magazine.
44. Metz, C. (2023). "The People Behind the Prompts." The New York Times.
45. PBS Frontline. (2020). In the Age of AI (Documentary).
46. The Verge. (2022). AI Weekly: Coverage on AI and Automation.
47. Wired Staff. (2023). AI Issue: The Future of Everything.
48. BBC Future. (2021). AI and the Planet: Ethics of Scale.

Core Datasets, Models, and Open Repositories

49. Hugging Face. (2020-2023). Transformers Library, Model Zoo, and Datasets.
50. Allen Institute for AI. (2023). AI2 Research Library and Semantic Scholar.

This bibliography serves not just as references—but as windows into the living, evolving conversation of our era. Each citation represents a node in the network of thought that has helped illuminate our path through the promises and perils of AI.

For deeper exploration, readers are encouraged to access open-source materials, participate in AI literacy forums, and explore the tools and courses referenced throughout the appendices.

Glossary of Key Terms

A

Algorithm

A set of step-by-step instructions for performing a task or solving a problem, often used as the foundation for software, data processing, and artificial intelligence models.

Artificial General Intelligence (AGI)

A theoretical form of AI that possesses the ability to understand, learn, and apply knowledge across a wide range of tasks at human-like levels of intelligence.

B

Bias (in AI)

Unintended and potentially harmful preferences or exclusions that emerge in AI systems, often due to imbalanced or unrepresentative training data.

Big Data

Extremely large datasets that require advanced tools and systems to store, analyze, and draw insights from—often fueling AI applications.

C

Chatbot

An AI-powered conversational interface that interacts with users via text or voice, used in customer service, education, and health care.

Computer Vision

A field of AI that enables machines to interpret and analyze visual information from the world, such as images and video.

Consciousness (in AI)

A philosophical and speculative idea concerning whether machines could ever possess self-awareness or subjective experience.

D

Data Labeling

The process of tagging data (text, images, video) with meaningful annotations to help train machine learning models.

Deep Learning

A type of machine learning based on neural networks with many layers (hence "deep"), particularly effective in image and speech recognition.

E

Ethics in AI

A discipline exploring the moral implications of AI systems—covering fairness, accountability, transparency, and human impact.

Explainability

The degree to which an AI system's decisions can be understood by humans—crucial for trust, regulation, and risk mitigation.

F

Fairness

A principle in AI development aiming to avoid discrimination or systemic disadvantage against individuals or groups.

Foundation Model

A large-scale AI model trained on massive datasets that can be adapted (fine-tuned) for many different tasks—e.g., GPT, PaLM, LLaMA.

G

Generative AI

A class of AI models capable of creating new content such as text, images, audio, or code. Examples: ChatGPT, DALL·E, Midjourney.

GPU (Graphics Processing Unit)

Specialized hardware essential for training and running complex AI models due to its ability to handle parallel processing efficiently

H

Hallucination (in AI)

A phenomenon where AI models produce information that appears plausible but is factually incorrect or fabricated.

Human-in-the-Loop (HITL)

An approach to AI where human judgment and feedback are integrated into the development or deployment of machine systems.

I

Inference

The process by which an AI model uses what it has learned to make predictions or generate outputs in real-time.

Interpretability

How easily a human can understand the logic or mechanics behind a model's decision-making process.

L

Large Language Model (LLM)

An AI model trained on vast textual datasets to understand and generate human-like language. Examples: GPT-4, Claude, Bard.

Learning Rate

A hyperparameter that controls how quickly a machine learning model adjusts during training.

M

Machine Learning (ML)

A subset of AI where systems learn patterns from data and improve their performance without being explicitly programmed.

Model Drift

When a model's accuracy degrades over time due to changes in input data or external environments.

N

Natural Language Processing (NLP)

A field of AI focused on enabling computers to understand, interpret, and respond to human language.

Neural Network

A set of algorithms inspired by the human brain's structure, used to recognize patterns and enable machine learning and deep learning.

P

Prompt Engineering

The craft of designing effective prompts or inputs to guide the behavior and output of language models and generative AI systems.

Personalization

The use of AI to tailor experiences, products, or information to individual users based on their data or preferences.

R

Reinforcement Learning

An AI training method where agents learn to make decisions through rewards and penalties in simulated environments.

Responsible AI

A framework for designing, developing, and deploying AI in ways that align with ethical values, human rights, and societal well-being.

S

Singularity

A hypothetical point when AI surpasses human intelligence, potentially triggering rapid, uncontrollable technological change.

Synthetic Data

Artificially generated data that mimics real-world information, often used to train models when real data is limited or sensitive.

T

Training Data

The information used to teach AI models how to perform tasks—its quality and representativeness greatly affect model outcomes.

Transformer

A neural network architecture that powers most state-of-the-art LLMs, enabling them to process sequences of data more effectively.

U

Unsupervised Learning

A type of machine learning where models identify patterns in data without labeled outcomes.

Universal Basic Income (UBI)

A policy concept often discussed in the context of AI-driven job displacement—offering citizens a regular, unconditional income.

X

XAI (Explainable AI)

AI systems designed to be transparent, interpretable, and accountable in their decision-making.

About the Author

Subba Rao Chaganti

He has a master's in business administration and over fifty-two years of experience in

Pharmaceutical marketing. His experience encompasses all facets of the industry, from sales and sales management to product management and overseeing overall marketing activities. He has experience in both domestic and international marketing, as well as within the Indian and multinational sectors.

He also taught a course on Advertising and Brand Management as an adjunct professor at Gitam Institute of Foreign Trade (now part of Gitam University) in Visakhapatnam for a few years and a course on Marketing as a visiting faculty member at Jawaharlal Nehru Technological University (JNTU) in Hyderabad.

He lives in Farmington, Connecticut, USA, and can be reached at: subbarao.chaganti@gmail.com.

Here is a list of his publications:

1. Pharmaceutical Marketing in India: Concepts, Cases, Strategy
2. Game Plans for Post-GATT Era: Action Agenda of the Indian Pharmaceutical Industry
3. Compete or Forfeit: Strategies for Sustainable Competitive Advantage in the Pharma Product Patents Era
4. Pharmaceutical Marketing in India for Today and Tomorrow - 25th Anniversary Edition
5. Bullseyes and Blunders: Lessons from 100 Cases in Pharma Marketing
6. Digital Pharma Marketing Playbook: Winning With the New Rules of Engagement

7. Cracking the Generics Code: Your Single-Source Success Manual for Winning in Multi-Source Product Markets
8. Reimagine Pharma Marketing: Make It Future-Proof!
9. Brand Positioning in Pharma
10. Transactional to Transformational Marketing in Pharma: The Science of Why and The Art of How
11. A to Z of Pharmaceutical Marketing: World's First and Only Encyclopedia in Two Volumes
12. The Synergy of Minds: Human+AI Orchestrating the Pharma Marketing Revolution
13. Design Thinking for Pharma
14. The Pharma Product Manager: Navigating the Digital Frontier
15. Sentiment Analysis for Pharma Marketers
16. Whispering to AI: Prompt Engineering for Pharma Brand Managers
17. Storytelling in Pharma Marketing
18. Beyond the Molecule: The Art and Science of Metaphors That Matter
19. The Voices Within: Your Body Speaks, When Your Organs Tell Their Own Stories
20. Pharma Archetypes: The Science of Meaningful Healthcare Marketing

www.ingramcontent.com/pod-product-compliance
Ingram Content Group UK Ltd.
Pitfield, Milton Keynes, MK11 3LW, UK
UKHW021346190726
13845UKWH00027B/741

9 789347 311833